John Z. DeLorean

With Ted Schwarz

DELOREAN

ZONDERVAN BOOKS · ZONDERVAN PUBLISHING HOUSE · GRAND RAPIDS, MICHIGAN

Zondervan Books is an imprint of Zondervan Publishing House
1415 Lake Drive, S.E., Grand Rapids, Michigan 49506

DELOREAN
Copyright © 1985 by John DeLorean

ISBN 0-310-37940-7

Scripture references are taken from *The Holy Bible: New
International Version* (North American Edition), copyright © 1973,
1978, 1984, by the International Bible Society. Used by permission
of Zondervan Bible Publishers.

Edited and designed by Judith E. Markham

Printed in the United States of America

85 86 87 88 89 90 / 10 9 8 7 6 5 4 3 2

To Zachary and Kathryn

CONTENTS

LIST OF ILLUSTRATIONS
(in order of appearance following page 248)

1. John DeLorean with his lawyers: Howard Weitzman, Don Re, and Mona Soo Hoo (used by permission of Cable News Network—Artist, David Rose).
2. DeLorean jury listening to the drug-arrest tapes (used by permission of Cable News Network—Artist, David Rose).
3. Benedict Tisa, prosecution witness (used by permission of Cable News Network—Artist, David Rose).
4. James Hoffman, prosecution witness (used by permission of Artist, Elizabeth Williams).
5. Gerald Scotti, defense witness (used by permission of Artist, Elizabeth Williams).
6. Assistant U.S. Attorneys Robert Perry and James Walsh, Jr. (used by permission of Artist, Elizabeth Williams).
7. John DeLorean's October 18, 1982, letter to attorney Tom Kimmerly. Reverse side of envelope shows signatures of lawyers when letter was opened on October 20, 1984.
8. Pages from John DeLorean's notes made during the testimony of James Hoffman and John Valestra. DeLorean took many pages of these "illustrated" notes each day of the trial and began each page with the date and a spiritual reminder to himself in the upper lefthand corner.
9. Sculpture by John DeLorean in protest of the Vietnam War. This piece was recently submitted for the exhibit of Twentieth-Century Sculpture at the Musée Nationale de l'Art Moderne at the Georges Pompidou Center in Paris (photographs by Roger Prigent, New York).

ACKNOWLEDGMENTS

I must express my gratitude to my co-author, Ted Schwarz; my editor, Judith Markham; and my manager, Wayne Coombs.

Ted is a truly unique combination of a tough, thorough, meticulous, investigative reporter and a warm, compassionate, spiritual being. The months we spent together were worth ten years on a psychiatrist's couch.

In the beginning, Ted knew that I was bitter, angry, and hostile. But as he and I talked through 1,200 pages of transcript, I slowly healed and developed a more balanced view, just as Ted knew I would. His comprehensive knowledge of the criminal-justice system helped us put together the true perspective on exactly what happened to me. Ted has become a dear friend, and today I frequently call him for personal advice. I think he understands me better than I understand myself.

Judith Markham, my editor, has made incredible contributions to this book. She helped me to say what I should say and to avoid those things that, while true, I should not say. I'll never forget her soul-stirring words as she, Ted, and I struggled to wrap up the book in an around-the-clock session in Grand Rapids. She said, "You're done when *I* say you're done." I love her.

Wayne Coombs is the greatest thing that has happened to me since this terrible ordeal began. He is a dear friend and adviser, a super human being, and a fabulous manager. His spiritual guidance and just knowing he's there have meant more to me than I can express. I thank the Lord for him every day.

In a government of laws, existence of the government will be imperilled if it fails to observe the law scrupulously. Our government is the potent, the omnipresent, teacher. For good or for ill, it teaches the whole people by its example. Crime is contagious. If the government becomes a law-breaker, it breeds contempt for law; it invites every man to become a law unto himself; it invites anarchy.

Supreme Court Justice Brandeis
Olmstead v. United States (1928)

October 18, 1982. It was autumn in New York. The last glow of sunset warmed the pedestrians along Fifth Avenue. As I sat at the desk in my apartment and planned my next move, I could see children playing on the swings in Central Park. Sounds of life and laughter filtered up from the street. The treetops below reflected the warmth and beauty of the changing season. All about me was life, but by tomorrow at this time I expected to be dead.

Exhausted from too many years of twenty-hour days, too many trips throughout the world in search of financing for my rapidly failing car company, I still kept going. Desperate, threatened, I had to think. *What do men do when they know they have only hours to live?*

At eight-thirty that evening I had received a call from one of my financial contacts, a man named James Hoffman.

As a result, tomorrow morning I would fly out to California to consummate the deal that would place the DeLorean Motor Company in the hands of men who were involved in organized crime. I was about to hand them the company that had been my life, my obsession, almost my third child for the past seven years, because my own desperation and ignorance had embroiled me in a situation that was so dangerous that the lives of my family and myself could be at stake if I did not. I knew too many secrets about people who valued their security above life itself.

What had happened? How had I become entangled with organized crime? How had my search for investors taken me into a world of corruption and violence? I had no answers. All I was certain of was that tomorrow I might be dead. My only comfort was that if I was killed for my foolishness, I would be the only one to suffer violence. Neither Cristina nor the children would be harmed for my mistakes.

Despite my fear and fatalism born of exhaustion, I was determined that the truth should be known. I wanted someone to understand the secret nightmare I had been living for weeks. I would write a letter to my attorney, I decided, to explain what had happened. If they killed me, the letter could be sent to the authorities, and I would have my revenge.

Yet even as I faced the loss of my company and possible death, my pride would not let me admit total defeat. I wanted to believe that I had cunningly manipulated four members of organized crime—James Hoffman, Morgan Hetrick, James Benedict, and John Vicenza—into placing $10 million in my car company. I might be destroyed, but through what I perceived as cleverness in the face of overwhelming adversity, the people of West Belfast would have their jobs, and the DeLorean Motor Company would live.

I did not realize that my letter was the ultimate proof of how sick I had become, how warped my thinking, how twisted my perceptions. I thought it was the most important document I had ever drafted.

16

"*I'm going to L.A. tomorrow to accomplish a minor miracle!*" I wrote to Tom Kimmerly, my corporate attorney. "*I will have induced organized crime to literally donate $10 million to reopen the Belfast plant—and when they figure it out they cannot do anything about it! Hoffman, Benedict, Hetrick, and Vicenza are not what they pretend to be— (don't be shocked) cocaine dealers! Too many things they have told me are literally impossible.*"

I then explained that "*without any question they are part of organized crime, and Eureka Federal Savings and Loan is a front they use for laundering money. Their cocaine charade is designed to make me feel implicated so that I won't look too hard at their source of funds.*

"*Tomorrow when they put the $10 million into Eureka and Benedict wire-transfers it to Cork-Gully, the mob will own 100 percent of DMC, Inc., a corporate shell with no assets! The Stoy-Hayward client will control the plant that the U.K. government still owns. The DMC shareholders will continue to own the American company and control every-thing. In effect, the mob will have donated $10 million to the Belfast plant and have gotten virtually nothing for it—a minority position in a government-owned factory in war-torn Belfast! Obviously they wanted to control the motor co. to use it for moving and laundering money. When they find out they own and control nothing, they will be very pissed! The reason I'm convinced they won't do anything about it is that to take any kind of action—against the company or myself—will blow their whole money-laundering operation at Eureka Federal. When they start to push I will tell them that there is a letter that is to be opened in the event of my death. They will just take a walk.*

"*If I'm wrong, and my death is from any but absolutely natural causes, take this letter to the police, otherwise destroy it. Tom, take care of my family. God bless you.*"

I folded the sheet of graph paper on which I had written the letter and inserted it in a DeLorean Holding Company envelope. After I had sealed it, I addressed it to Tom with the following instructions:

"This sealed letter is to be held in trust by you for two years, to October 18, 1984. In the event of my death within that two years, open the letter and follow the instructions. If I am alive and well on October 18, 1984, return the letter to me unopened."

I would deliver the letter to Tom's office in the morning on my way to the airport.

I left the letter on my desk and walked down the hallway to the children's bedrooms. I stood in the doorway, looking in on each of them, as I had done several times since that fateful call.

Looking down at Zachary's tousled head on the pillow, I thought of all my son had been through in his young life. I loved him so much. Would I ever see him again? Would my death seem just one more rejection to him?

And Kathryn, my laughing, joyful little girl. Would I never see her attend her first dance, graduate from school, and grow to womanhood?

Perhaps these thoughts should have come earlier. Perhaps I should have anticipated such concerns when I first began my car company. But I hadn't, and now it was too late. The life I had planned, the success I had anticipated, the future I had dreamed about would soon be over.

DETROIT

1

When I was born in Detroit, Michigan, in January of 1925, the city was already dominated by the automobile. My father, Zachary DeLorean, worked at Ford Motor Company's Highland Park plant. He was a six-foot-one, 220-pound, two-fisted union organizer at a time when auto workers' pay was limited and opportunities for advancement almost nonexistent. In those days, the factories ran full-bore until there were enough cars to satisfy the market; then all the workers were laid off, and the factories were closed until inventory could be reduced. The men took whatever part-time work they could find during the closures, but the supply of jobs never equaled the demand. Unless they had unique skills, the workers were usually competing for the same jobs. Fortunately, my father was highly skilled in carpentry, an occupation with a year-round demand, so during the layoffs, we never experienced the type of deprivation common to most of my friends' families.

We lived in a small house in a typical factory-worker neighborhood near the corner of Six Mile Road and Dequindre at 17199 Marx. From there, my dad could walk the mile or two to the Highland Park plant. Looking back, I know that both my parents must have been frustrated by their poverty and lack of opportunity, but for a long time I was insensitive to this. When you are young, you tend to be extremely idealistic, unable to forgive or justify something you see as a weakness in your parents—or in anyone else, for that matter.

My father was actually a very intelligent man, but he was a prisoner to his lack of education. There were a lot of things that he knew he was capable of, but he couldn't do them because he didn't have the training. I'm sure that much of his frustration went far back in his childhood. He was the youngest of thirteen boys born to a family in Central Europe, an area where the oldest gets everything and the youngest gets nothing. My father ran away from those conditions when he was about fourteen and came to this country. For the rest of his life, I believe, he carried a terrible frustration inside him that released itself through bouts of drinking and drunken abuse of my mother, my brothers, and me.

How my mother, Katherine, contended with and survived my father's erratic behavior is a mystery to me. In addition to being a heavy drinker, he just plain loved to fight. Every Friday night he would get in a big brawl somewhere. It was a way of life. He got his paycheck on Friday, got smashed, and beat the stuffing out of everyone in sight—or got beaten himself. The next day they were all pals again. It was his recreation!

But when this spilled out of the barroom and into our home, it was something else. During his worst bouts with the bottle, my father would explode into violence and hit my mother. On several occasions, she even took my three brothers and me to live with her parents or her sister in California.

Although I loved my mother, I never really appreciated

what she must have experienced during those periods of separation. She took any job that would provide us with food, clothing, and shelter, and she worked long hours for extra money. I didn't resent her absences, but I had no understanding of what she was enduring or how difficult her life was. If I resented anything, it was the kind of things most boys resent. Her nagging, for example. My mother was a great nagger. Of course, it was her way of showing concern and love, but I didn't always see it that way. When I was thirty-seven, she was still telling me to wear a coat or I'd catch cold. And she wouldn't say it once; she would say it eighty-five times. I also got frustrated with her propensity to worry. Even when I was finally able to set up a lifetime trust for her, a trust that provided her with her own house and new car each year so that she no longer had any financial burdens—even then, she worried. In later years, when I had dinner with her every Thursday night, she would fret because I hadn't worn a coat—and worry about the atomic bomb. These matters were equally serious to her. I suppose that since my brothers and I had grown up and relieved her of many serious concerns, the atomic bomb was the one thing she could still worry about. And she did—for the rest of her life.

When my mother died in 1969, I began to realize what a saint she was. At her funeral, the strangest collection of people appeared. Even though she had been living in the suburbs for a number of years, the man who used to sell her gasoline near the old Marx house—twenty years earlier— came to her funeral because he had so much love and respect for her. Another fellow showed up in a body cast. He was one of those wild and crazy hot-rod drivers and had broken himself up when he flipped his dragster. I didn't realize my mother even knew anyone like that. Many people from her church and other churches she had attended were there to honor her. She was an incredible lady.

Despite his drinking and our periodic separations, I also remember some good times with my father. He taught me to love working with my hands, a love that led, I believe, to my career in engineering. In fact, that may have been the only way that he, as a father, knew how to be involved with his son. I don't think he would have known how to have a loving relationship with me if he had wanted to. I don't think he ever hugged me, which may be why I hug my kids so much. But we did some things together that gave me great pleasure. For example, when he did his woodworking or repair projects, he would let me work with him on some small thing, like a toy airplane. The joy of those times stayed with me to such a degree that when I bought our New Jersey farm, I set up a small woodworking shop for my son Zachary and me to enjoy together.

I also knew that there was more to my father than barroom bluster. He was not a bully; more often than not he fought for the underdog. He was a courageous man, a labor organizer at a time when unions were hated by management. Despite his limited income, he was a man who clearly commanded the respect of his associates, and I was proud to walk beside him.

In those days, the men who worked in the automobile factories had neither rights nor benefits. Pay was low and the work was hard. The layoffs occurred with no warning and could last for several months at a time. Yet the auto industry provided most of the jobs in the area; so there were few alternatives, short of leaving Detroit, if a man disliked the system.

In addition to the right of union representation and collective bargaining, the pro-union workers like my father also demanded more stable employment. They wanted to have some kind of predictable income. In its opposition to the unions, the management never realized that year-round employment would benefit them as well by improving the efficiency of the industry. Eventually, when a guaranteed annual wage was adopted, it forced the automakers to better coordinate production and sales of their cars so that there was neither excessive overtime nor periods of total idleness. Marketing and production became closely interrelated, and the facilities were used twelve months a year instead of seven or eight. All this helped the industry grow into the multi-billion dollar giant it is today.

While many of these demands seem logical today and most of the innovations sought by the unions actually improved the financial picture of the industry, Ford management in those days, under a hard man named Harry Bennett, wanted to destroy union men like my father. In an effort to do this, Bennett hired "goons" to beat up and threaten anyone who opposed him. The goons were big, powerful men who enjoyed hurting people. A photograph showing the intrepid Walter Ruether in his blood-streaked shirt, battling Bennett's goons at the bridge at Ford's River Rouge plant, made labor history. My father's proudest achievement was that he was also bloodied in that famous clash at Miller Road Gate 4. Knowing my father, I'm sure he gave as much as he got.

Bennett's goons were ordered to invade the homes of employees and search for any "evidence" of criminality, such as a hammer stamped "Property of Ford Motor Company." Such items were supposed to be proof that an employee had been stealing and should be fired. Generally, the goons would arrive late at night, rouse the family out of bed, and proceed to tear the place apart while the family and neighbors stood around and watched. I recall hiding wide-eyed behind my seething, long-underwear-clad father who stood helpless with clenched fists as the billy-club-armed goon squad ransacked our tiny house.

Although some workers probably did take company property from the plant, much of this "evidence" seems to have been planted by Bennett's goons on honest men who had become nuisances. From Bennett's perspective, such a set-up would certainly have been justified in my father's case. But his goons never tried. They probably assumed that a strong union man must be doing something dishonest, so they wouldn't have to plant anything. Fortunately, dishonesty was never one of my father's faults. So there were no dramatic discoveries during those searches, and my father was never fired.

The only hint I ever had that my father was concerned about the violence at the plant was a discovery I made as a young teenager. At that time each Ford worker was encouraged to buy a new Ford every other year, and I believe my father had a Model A. Looking into the large pocket on the inside of the driver's door one day, I discovered a revolver. I assumed it was my father's, but I never had the nerve to ask him. Like the goons, the gun was something I learned to accept in silence.

The weapon was also evidence of my father's pioneer mentality. He used to keep his car in the old frame garage behind the house. One night he heard a noise outside and was convinced someone was trying to crank his car and steal it. So he took his deer rifle, aimed it where the thief would be standing to hand-crank his car, and fired. There was no one there. But he did hit something. The bullet went through the radiator and broke the block. He just blew the thing to pieces.

There were also hints of genius in my father. He understood machinery perhaps as well as any engineer. I still remember the time when he had an idea for a machine that would cam-grind pistons. He was unable to sketch his idea, so he could not produce the necessary blueprints, nor did he have the verbal skills to sell his plan to anyone. Instead, he built the entire machine out of wood. When he was finished, it was as large as a massive dining room table and had hundreds of moving parts. As I recall, somebody at Ford eventually used the concept. But what amazed me was that he could carve the thing by hand and make it work exactly as he had envisioned—in a material most people would have considered impossible for such a model.

Unfortunately, my father and I became totally estranged in my teenage years. I think the turning point was when I confronted him because he was abusing my mother, and he beat the stuffing out of me. Once my parents were divorced, I didn't see him for years. He ended up a lonesome old man in an alcoholic haze living alone in a little boardinghouse. I went to see him a couple of times, but he was so impaired by his drinking that he couldn't really communicate. He died about three years before my mother.

Perhaps my most emotional experience related to my father occurred after his death. At that time someone at the Ford Highland Park plant called and said I should pick up my father's toolbox that was still in the plant. When I got there, they led me to a gigantic work area. There was so much dust in the air that the bulbs were just dim glowing spots on the ceiling, and puffs of dust rose from my shoes as I walked. *What a filthy, horrible, depressing place,* I thought. *And my father spent his life here.* My dad's toolbox was chained to a large steel column near the center of the building. Although the chain and lock were very heavy, the box had been jimmied open. It was empty. I think God just wanted me to see where my dad had worked. Since then I have asked my dead father's forgiveness many times for judging him so harshly.

Although my parents were poor, I consider myself fortunate to have had the advantages I did growing up in Detroit at that time. The first advantage was a result of the Works Progress Administration (WPA). This was a program established under the Roosevelt administration whereby the government would hire artists, writers, and other professionals for various projects. One of these projects in our area was a Saturday art class, taught by professional artists, for children in low-income and impoverished neighborhoods. I took these classes for a year or two, and it was the most enjoyable experience of those early days. In fact, I have returned to my artwork as an adult and produced a number of paintings and some primitive sculpture. My friend Maur Dubin, a distinguished art dealer, has one of my pieces. It is a sculpture in protest of the Vietnam War. When he said, "It's really good, John!" I was very pleased. (Dubin recently submitted the piece for the exhibit of Twentieth-Century Sculpture at the Musée Nationale de l'Art Moderne at the Georges Pompidou Center in Paris).

The other advantage I had was Cass Technical High. Today it would be called a school for gifted children, with its music and art curriculums and its technical specializations that prepared kids for post-high-school employment in various fields. The school was so advanced that its graduates could get good jobs or be a year or two ahead of their peers if they went on to college. I signed up for the electrical curriculum for no other reason than it had more space available for students than the other programs.

Cass Tech was probably the most important educational influence in my early years. Not only were most of the teachers successful in their own fields, but they also loved to teach—the type of people you would not expect to find involved with high-school kids, let alone with high-school kids from low-income families. For example, Charles Lindbergh's mother was our chemistry teacher.

I did so well in my courses at Cass that I was offered a scholarship to Lawrence Tech, a small Detroit college. Lawrence was a good school, but my high-school education had been so thorough that I managed to get through the first two years of college with almost no studying. I had already taken advanced math courses, such as calculus, which were part of the freshman and sophomore curriculum at college. So I spent my days playing bridge and intramural basketball instead of cracking books, and I still pulled top grades. For the first time I began to think I might be just a bit smarter than the other students, and the idea intrigued me. The reality, of course, was that I had simply attended a good high school and was better prepared for college courses than they were. I got good enough at intramural basketball that I was asked to join and play for the school's top fraternity—but they wouldn't accept my good friend Ben Fox because he was Jewish, so I refused.

By this time, our country was in the midst of World War II, and in my junior year, I was drafted. The military and I never got along very well. From their viewpoint, I was probably incorrigible. From my viewpoint, I was disillusioned. I think I went through basic training more times than

28

any other soldier in history, which may make you pretty tough but doesn't do much else for you.

Back in Detroit after my honorable discharge, I found that my parents were no longer living together. This time the separation was permanent. My father was now a confirmed alcoholic, his mind and powerful body wasted from his drinking. My mother, through her wartime work in the General Electric Carboloy plant, had gained a better life for herself and my younger brothers. The factory conditions were clean and safe, and she was making a good income for that time.

I worked for a year and a half as a draftsman for the Public Lighting Commission to help get the family on a solid economic basis before I went back to college. There, I became friends with a young Nisei Japanese, Alan Tanaguchi, whose family had been thrown off their California walnut farm and sent to the Midwest along with other Japanese. Alan was one of the finest, most moral Americans I have ever met. I have never forgotten his pain at being treated as a traitor by the country of his birth. I hurt for him. It was then I first learned that even the Constitution could be perverted by misguided leaders. (Years later, another Nisei Japanese was to have a major impact on my life: Judge Robert Takasugi.)

I returned to Lawrence Tech and finished my degree. But instead of looking for a job in engineering after I graduated, I decided to find something that would help me overcome my inherent shyness. I was afraid to face people, especially strangers. I was even intimidated by the simple act of entering a store to buy a pack of gum. I knew if I was ever to get ahead in life, I had to overcome my fear. So I decided to try to sell life insurance.

Of all the jobs I have had over the years, none was more difficult or unpleasant than selling insurance. I can still recall the terror I felt when I set up those appointments. Sometimes I would sit in my car for an hour working up enough nerve to go to the door. The only thing that kept me going was the knowledge that I needed to earn money and that this was the only job I had. Eventually, I conquered my terror, and amazingly, I sold approximately $800,000 in life insurance and won a number of prizes in the eight months I worked in the business.

But insurance held no lasting interest for me, and when my uncle Earl Pribak, who was a foreman in the engineering garage at Chrysler, suggested that I go to the Chrysler Institute, I applied. There I could work part time at a variety of jobs in the plant and study part time at the Institute. By the time I finished, I would have a master's degree in automotive engineering and an opportunity for real advancement at Chrysler. The Chrysler Institute was a fine school, and because many of the instructors were working executives and top engineers, the level of applicability was impressive. No wonder Chrysler was the engineering leader of the day.

2

Chrysler was not known for its styling or sales in those days, but their engineering was outstanding. It was the ideal place for a young engineer, and I had hoped to work there after completing my degree at the Chrysler Institute. They had introduced more improvements than any other company, ranging from powerful engines that could move a car faster than their rivals to power steering, power windows, and a new engine mounting that isolated the vibration. Instead of being bolted rigidly to the chassis, this Chrysler engine rode on rubber blocks, a simple-sounding idea that actually required an extremely complex design. Many of the pioneering concepts in materials, vibration, fatigue, and basic design came from Chrysler's legendary engineers.

I was proud of my training, proud of the work I had done, and I anticipated what I might handle in the future.

Unfortunately, the head of the engineering department, James Zeder, shattered that enthusiasm on graduation day when he spoke at our commencement ceremonies. I have never forgotten his words:

"You guys have got to get over the idea that you are individuals," he said. "You are all the same to us. You're just another engineer, so don't get carried away with your graduation! It's a start, not an end."

He never acknowledged that the company was proud of what we had accomplished or even that they were looking forward to whatever contributions we might make to the company. Instead, his message was: "Fit the corporate groove, or else. . . . Forget about being an individual." At least that is the way I understood it. His attitude was both surprising and extremely upsetting to me, and I can trace the beginnings of my dislike of corporate narrow-mindedness back to this early moment in my career. And I was not the only one who felt that way. As far as Chrysler was concerned, Zeder lost half the graduating class that day.

Because of Zeder's speech, I began looking elsewhere. When I was offered a job in the research and development department of Packard Motor Car Company, I readily accepted.

The Packard automobile had once been highly prized. Now it was no longer in demand, and the company was on its way to financial ruin. Even their factory facilities were in disrepair: plaster was peeling off the walls and many of the windows were broken. Taking a job with such a firm may have seemed a foolishly naïve step for a young man trying to advance. But I neither knew nor cared anything of company finances in those days. My life was engineering. I could tell you the names of most of the better engineers in any motor company in Detroit, but I hadn't the faintest idea who ran those companies. Packard simply represented a new challenge, and they accepted me as an engineer.

My first job at Packard involved helping in the development of an automatic transmission called the Ultramatic. This was a wonderful opportunity for a new engineer because no one there understood exactly what to do. Their first transmission was a copy of a Buick Dynaflow with minor variations; now they wanted a shifting transmission. We were pioneering new territory for Packard, and this placed both the experienced personnel and those of us fresh out of school on an equal footing. Challenged by the opportunity, I literally spent day and night thinking about the various technical problems related to the transmission, the hydraulic controls, and the other facets of the unit. At one point I had a terrible time designing the complex hydraulic-control circuit for the transmission. Suddenly, inspiration came—at four in the morning! I got out of bed, went downstairs, and spent the next five hours sketching out the design. It worked perfectly and was incorporated, virtually unchanged, into the final product.

During this period a second incident occurred that would leave an indelible mark on my life. I had a deep and personal encounter with the viciousness of racial prejudice. During my childhood I lived in several different ethnic neighborhoods and had no sense of racial prejudice, though I'm certain it existed around me. So I grew into adulthood without a full awareness of the frustration, anger, and bigotry that would eventually lead to the civil-rights movement of the sixties.

My rude awakening came when I purchased a small house in Grosse Pointe Woods. Since I was proud of my first home and wanted to show it off, I invited a school friend, Charlie Fonville, to see my place one afternoon while we were studying for our night-school MBA finals. Charlie was an Olympic shot-putter from the University of Michigan and a fine student, the type of person who, if given the opportunity, would have been able to assume a responsible position in any corporation. Charlie and I walked around the house, looked over my tiny lawn with its small cherry tree, and had a pleasant time talking about subjects of mutual interest.

The next morning, a delegation of irate, mean-faced neighbors came to call. Their unspoken threats were so strong that I was on the defensive even before I fully understood what they wanted. As it turned out, they thought I was putting my house up for sale and that Charlie was a potential buyer. If I sold the home to a black man, they said, I would destroy the neighborhood. And they wanted to make it clear that, if that were the case, I would be sorry.

It is difficult to describe all the emotions I felt at that instant. For the first time in my life, I had encountered blind hatred. Handsome, brilliant, and talented, my friend had more potential than any one of the people standing in my yard—including myself. I had never discussed selling my house to him, but if I had, his presence would have upgraded, not destroyed, the neighborhood. Equally frustrating was the fact that because of this hatred, I was being told that I was not in control of my own property, that I somehow had to meet someone else's arbitrary standards of bigotry before I would be allowed to do what I pleased with what I owned.

It would be nice to be able to say that I made a glorious speech, taking a stand for brotherhood, racial equality, and the American way. Instead, I was so infuriated that I could only stammer, "Get out!" But that incident would have far-reaching implications, for it was at that point that I determined to reach out and help change that kind of attitude.

Meanwhile, things at Packard were declining rapidly. My boss, Forest McFarland, was a brilliant engineer and a good friend. He saw what was happening at Packard and took a job as director of advanced engineering for the Buick division of General Motors. Since I was considered the engineer who knew the most about what my department was doing, I was given his old job. Not yet thirty, I was heading the research department of a major company.

My delight in obtaining the new position was tempered by my growing awareness of the business aspects of the automotive world. Packard was dying, and I knew it. Thus, when I was offered a job as director of research with Thompson Products of Cleveland, a small company that is now TRW, I considered it carefully. On one hand, I wasn't sure I wanted to move to another city. On the other hand, since I didn't like large impersonal companies like Chrysler and took great pleasure in working at Packard with such world-class engineers as Forest McFarland, Herb Misch (later vice-president of engineering at Ford), and Bill Graves, perhaps I belonged in a smaller company.

My predicament became even more difficult when I received a call from Oliver K. Kelley, a man I greatly admired. Kelley was America's leading transmission engineer and assistant to the vice-president of engineering at General Motors. He asked me to join his company. I resisted at first, saying that I preferred smaller businesses because I felt the challenges there were greater. Large firms had highly specialized engineers; each worked in a limited area, becoming expert in only a small segment of the planning or technical phases. Small firms, such as Packard and Thompson Products, expected their engineers to do everything. You created your own designs and then went out in the shop to work with the men who fashioned the product. You helped install it in the car and checked it out yourself. In a sense, you had full control of your designs.

In response, Oliver Kelley used a form of psychology that has always worked with me. He suggested that I might not like GM or might not be able to make it in the "big leagues"; he agreed that maybe I was the type who needed a larger role in a small operation. "But you're barely thirty, John," he said. "I think you owe it to yourself to at least try it for a year or two and see if you can play in the major leagues. You'll have access to facilities and equipment no smaller firm can match. If you don't like it, you're still young enough to go back to a smaller company in some key position. The experience certainly can't hurt you. So why not try it for a year or two?"

Kelley's persuasiveness, combined with the incredible facilities and equipment at the GM technical center and the fact that I would not have to relocate, convinced me to give it a try.

I was offered jobs in five different divisions of General Motors and eventually decided on Pontiac. The main reason for my decision was the general manager of the division, Semon E. (Bunkie) Knudsen.

The Pontiac division was in trouble. At one time, it had produced a successful line of cars, but because they now lacked style and sophistication, they had lost their public appeal. The dealers were upset with their sales, and there were even rumors that GM might drop the line. Obviously, only major changes could save the division. Knudsen convinced me I would be part of a team that could make General Motors history by reviving a line others seemed to have written off.

Those dreams of glory were shattered when I met the man who would be my immediate supervisor, George Delaney, the chief engineer of Pontiac. I didn't know whether Delaney was good or bad at his job. I didn't know whether he was one of the causes of Pontiac's troubles or one of the people who was in the process of turning them around. All I knew was that his breast pocket was jammed with cigars and he wore high-top shoes.

I detested cigars; I had always found their aroma particularly offensive. Just looking at the chief engineer brought to mind all the unpleasant sensations I had ever associated with cigar smoke. He impressed me as a man whose concepts of engineering, no doubt developed in the thirties, could not keep pace with the present marketplace. His appearance made me want to turn around and walk out the door. And so did his first words.

"I see what you're making at Packard. That's a hell of a lot of money for a guy your age. I can't believe you're worth it. But if Knudsen wants to hire you and pay you that much . . . I guess I'll have to hire you."

I telephoned Knudsen and told him that while I was impressed with GM, after meeting Delaney, I knew I wouldn't be able to work there. Knudsen understood and told me to wait a few days, then stop back.

What he couldn't tell me was that Delaney was being

replaced by a man named Pete Estes who was transferring from the Oldsmobile division. Estes was an inspired leader who single-handedly raised the morale of Pontiac's engineering department from zero to the top in a few weeks. He eventually became manager of Pontiac, manager of Chevrolet, and finally a group executive for General Motors—the same route I would follow.

Several days later I was called to Estes' office. He took one look at my resume, the same one that Delaney had seen, and announced that he felt I should not make the same money that I had made at Packard. My previous salary had been $14,000 a year. He raised it to $16,000. With that kind of reasoning, how could I not like the man?

Later, when I reached top-level management, there would come a time I believed that many of my ideas were more progressive than those of the men who were leading the company. When they didn't agree or wouldn't listen, I just ignored them. I would take actions that, when they succeeded, were not only good for the organization but would also figuratively tweak my co-workers' noses. But that type of arrogance was not part of my thinking when I first joined GM. In fact, I never even once thought of promotion then. Although I was born with an intense sense of competition, I also had an absolute conviction that I owed all my energies to my employer. Whoever he was, he always got more than a fair day's work from me.

When I took the time to think about it, I frequently wondered why I should be so lucky. I was well paid, moving quickly, and there seemed no reason for it. I didn't think I was any more talented than any of dozens of other engineers.

This feeling of undeservedness went along with my shyness and with a certain longing I had felt for many years. It was a longing for something outside myself, for a higher power that could provide me with inner peace and contentment, with answers, with something more than my own resources could provide. God has built into all of us a deep

37

desire to know Him, and too often we let the busy bluster of our lives obscure it. My search for this fulfillment took many forms, and at one point I came to believe that we all earn whatever we get in life, that nothing good comes unless we are worthy. Yet I also knew that I was not special, that there was no reason why good things should happen to me. I had very little self-esteem. Eventually, this tension between my feelings of unworthiness and my growing arrogance would complicate my success. It manifested itself in unrealistic gambles where I frequently risked much on goals and battles of little significance.

As you will see, I have since learned the hard way that what we perceive as our reward often has nothing to do with what we have earned. We often achieve our desires, not realizing that true happiness comes only from seeking something higher. But it would be a long time before I understood this—and the learning process would demand a devastating toll. In those days, all I knew was an uneasiness about my life, a longing for understanding. But understanding what, I didn't know.

As I rose on the corporate ladder, I carried with me this longing for a deeper meaning. I attended various churches and listened for some unknown message that might ultimately provide some answers. But I seldom found comfort there because I was seeking simple answers, not a spiritual relationship or a personal commitment. As an engineer, I was looking for truths like Newton's law or the law of thermodynamics. So when the magic words of understanding did not appear, I buried myself deeper in my work and the projects I was helping to develop.

3

Each new day at Pontiac was an exciting challenge and brought a real sense of accomplishment. My work resulted in dozens of patents and led to some major changes that are reflected in the design of virtually every car on the road today. Some were minor and cosmetic; others involved the basic structural integrity of the vehicle. But each change enabled us to improve consumer satisfaction and sell more cars.

For example, automatic car washes were becoming a big thing at that time, and they all had rather crude, massive brushes that rolled over the hood, windshield, roof, and back of the car. All cars, in turn, had bulky windshield wipers that stuck out and would routinely be torn off by the car-wash brushes. This led to great frustration for car owners, until at Pontiac I created the recessed-wiper concept. Today every upper-line car, including Mercedes, uses the concealed wiper. We also developed such things as the torque box frame, a major step in improving the safety and strength of the car and one that is still a part of modern automobile construction; we pioneered such devices as the lane-change turn signal, the articulated wiper, and the elastomeric bumper.

Under Bunkie Knudsen, the Pontiac division also began putting together top performing cars and entering stock-car and drag races. As a result, we won most of the major events for the next two or three years. We redesigned our existing car bodies, added high-performance engines, and suddenly had one of the hottest things going. We were no longer the "little old ladies'" division; we had the perfect car for the growing youth market. Of course, our profits rose substantially. Knudsen taught us all well, and he gets all the credit for showing us the direction. In the beginning, most of Pontiac's management thought he was wasting resources by indulging in his own penchant for racing. He proved 'em all wrong.

At the same time, Knudsen also taught me something important about personal relationships in business. I have always been an idealist in my work; I believe that when you take responsibility for a job, you should give completely of your time and ability and never let outside pressures affect your performance. Because of my own intense drive in this direction, I was intolerant of those who thought otherwise, especially those who let personal weaknesses interfere with their effectiveness on the job.

At Pontiac we had a sales manager who was a prime example. Frank Bridge was a sweet old guy, and at one time he had been a top Buick sales manager with a good record. But in later years, probably under the pressure of Pontiac's disastrous sales, he had become a heavy drinker. Even worse, he aggravated his own problem by surrounding himself with other heavy drinkers on the job. As a result, the effectiveness of the entire sales department suffered. The criteria became how well you could hold your liquor, not how well you sold cars.

As the situation became worse, I assumed that Knudsen would replace Frank with a bright, young, dynamic go-getter whose life would be selling cars, not looking for the next drink. Instead, Bunkie kept Frank in the position, continued to work with him, and tried to help him conquer his problem, even to the point of doing a lot of the work himself when the drinking got the best of Frank.

Finally, one of the other executives (I believe it was Pete Estes) said, "Bunkie, why do you tolerate this guy? We've got everything else going, but the sales department is dragging us down."

"Pete," he replied, "Frank was the best once. I won't just toss him out. And if I can do something to help him beat this, to get back to what he was, it'll be worth it." And Frank did improve.

This lesson in compassionate yet effective personnel management became one of my guiding principles over the years, as did many other things I learned from Bunkie Knudsen. Unfortunately, I did not learn my lesson totally. Knudsen helped those who had proven records of accomplishment. I retained everyone, including people who probably should not have been hired in the first place. My not firing anyone stemmed from my reluctance to fully confront the negative, to admit defeat if the person had been important to me or the problem was originally a challenge that seemed solvable. This was why I would later drive myself to the point of destructive exhaustion to save my car company when the economic problems were approaching the insurmountable. But such awareness was for the future. During my days at GM, I was too busy learning about management, cost effectiveness, sales, and the realities of business leadership—knowledge that would prove frustratingly disillusioning.

Shortly after this period, the corporate infighting began within GM and within the auto industry in general. Bunkie Knudsen was being groomed to take over the presidency of

General Motors by the then chairman emeritus of the company, Alfred P. Sloan, Jr., the man who had almost single-handedly shaped GM into an industrial giant. When Sloan died, however, top management decided to split the job, giving Ed Cole the presidency and placing Knudsen in charge of a number of important subsidiaries, though not with the power and control he had expected. Even though Knudsen was responsible to the top management, not to the new president, he was still frustrated with this move.

Not long after the announcement about Cole and Knudsen, I happened to be having my annual physical with Dr. Barron at Henry Ford Hospital. Barron was the physician for many top executives in the automobile industry. We began sharing some of the latest gossip. I told Barron that I had heard Ford Motor Company had put out feelers to Ed Cole for a possible top job. "But," I mused, "if Ford really wants a top executive from GM, Knudsen's probably their man," and I went on to mention his frustration. Instead of taking my idle conversation casually, Dr. Barron immediately called Henry Ford II and told him about Knudsen's availability.

Henry Ford borrowed a GM car, so he would not be conspicuous, and drove to Knudsen's home and offered him the presidency of Ford. Not only did Knudsen accept, but his move to Ford created new tensions there. A man named Lee Iacocca, the genius behind such marketing successes as the Ford Mustang and one of the industry's greatest leaders, had expected to have the top job. He became as dissatisfied with that company as Knudsen had become with GM. This eventually precipitated some tough infighting, leading to Knudsen's firing by Henry Ford—and the rest is automotive history!

In 1961 Pete Estes was promoted to general manager of the division, and I took his place as Pontiac's chief engineer, the youngest man to achieve that position.

I have always enjoyed driving high-powered, exciting cars. To put a little excitement into my drive back and forth to work, I had taken a Tempest, Pontiac's compact car, dumped a triple two-barrel 389 in it, and added heavy-duty shocks, roll bars, and a Hurst shifter. The car was so much fun to drive that when I loaned it to friends I could never get it back. I priced it out and convinced Pete Estes we should put it on the market. (I had always felt the industry had it backward: The young people were the ones who wanted to drive exciting cars, but they couldn't afford them. By the time they were prosperous enough to afford exciting cars, they had become too old and conservative to enjoy them.) Pete gave me the go-ahead on the project without first seeking approval from the corporate executives who were supposed to authorize all such modifications. Pete felt they might not go along with what seemed an excellent idea.

So we offered two extremely powerful engines, a 326-cubic-inch V-eight and a 389-cubic-inch V-eight in the lightweight Tempest line, with three double-barreled carburetors for performance. We had speed, performance, and handling, and the total package was so inexpensive that young people could afford it. Then I named the creation a GTO, initials that came from a Ferrari coupe known as the Gran Turismo Omologate.

The Pontiac GTO was introduced at the end of 1963 as a 1964 model. Frank Bridge, the sales manager, bet me a dinner we wouldn't sell 5,000 cars, but we ended up selling 31,000 that year. Sixty thousand were sold the second year of production and 84,000 the third year. We had one of the hottest new cars on the market and an extremely profitable one for GM. The car became such a youth favorite that a rock group, Ronnie and the Daytonas, recorded a song called "Little GTO" that became a major hit. The favorable spillover to the whole Pontiac line was immeasurable. We were young America's car. *The* hot line.

Ironically, top management at GM was irate. (I have since learned that Ed Cole formed the opposition—it hurt him personally that Pontiac was cutting deep into Chevrolet's young domain.) The GTO had not been approved through normal corporate channels, they complained. Estes should have taken the design through the Engineering Policy Group. Fortunately, the car was so successful that the fallout was mild. (When Reggie Jackson ignores the bunt signal and hits a home run, I doubt that he gets much heat.)

In 1965 Pete Estes was promoted to the Chevrolet division, while I moved into his former position as head of Pontiac. Again I was the youngest man to be head of a division. I will never forget the day I walked into my new office in the rundown administration building (former head-quarters of the Oakland Motor Company built in the early 1900s) and was greeted by my new secretary, Hilda Brand. Hilda was sixtyish and had seen many years with the company.

"You're the fifth general manager I've worked with," she said sternly as she looked me up and down. "Don't worry. I know what to do." And she did. Hilda was always completely candid, but she was a marvelous human being and fabulous employee. I learned to lean on her and love her as a person.

I had begun my career as an engineer, but now I had to look beyond that one facet to the industry as a whole; I had to concern myself with production, marketing, and finance.

Many people talk of the advantages the Japanese have in the production of cars and attribute their success in outselling higher-priced American cars to their lower labor costs. That is only part of the answer, and I began to understand this fact even before imports were the serious challenge to our sales that they are today.

Amazingly, Japan's success depends on that most American of all motivations, the individual entrepreneur. Japanese car companies use numerous independent suppliers (one out of six Japanese males owns his own business). These suppliers know that if they don't maintain high quality at the lowest possible cost, another company will take their accounts. There is both pride in craftsmanship and a sense of responsibility for the future of the business that is lost in big companies that handle everything in-house, as our American automobile manufacturing plants do.

Pontiac was an excellent example of what has happened in America. Our plants were old and becoming obsolete. Maintenance costs were higher than they should have been, but we were so concerned with car designs that we paid little attention to the aging facilities. In fact, the first new building in many years did not become a reality until 1970. Costs were being determined by inefficient plants, top-heavy management, and expensive procedures.

I once did a study of the Japanese auto industry. The labor costs for Japanese cars came to within $600 per car of the American labor costs. For all practical purposes the cost of materials (world-wide commodities) is the same in both countries, and the difference in labor is compensated for by the cost of shipping and duty. The difference exists in the operation of American plants and American overhead.

A recent study showed that the typical American auto-industry executive will make thirty times what the average worker makes, while in Japan, the executive makes twelve times the salary of the worker. When you consider the number of executives in our top brackets, the difference in overhead for that one figure alone is staggering. Yet this was not a primary concern of anyone in the industry in the late sixties, including me. Sometimes I think our biggest problem was the insane drive for vertical integration within the industry that eliminated the tough, creative independent suppliers who brought the industry most of its innovations and its best prices. A lot of "creative" accounting was used to prove the inside supplier could compete with the outside.

The end result of the elimination of outside-supplier creativity has been a headlong plunge into innovation for innovation's sake. I consider the front-wheel drive panic a perfect example. Front-wheel drive simply gives more interior room, particularly in smaller cars for which it was created. The greatest suspension and handling engineer who ever lived, an Englishman named Maurice Olley, said, "A given tire has only so much frictional connection to the road.

You can use it for steering or traction." In other words, no front-wheel drive car will ever handle as well as a well-engineered rear-drive car. It will be interesting to see how long the world's outstanding passenger cars like Mercedes, BMW, Porsche, and Jaguar will be able to hold their principles of building the best-handling cars in face of the billions being spent in advertising by the rest of the industry to promote a less-sound but popular concept. Front-wheel drive is the technological equivalent of the tailfins of the sixties.

Another problem was marketing. While at Pontiac I began to study the consumer to see why cars were purchased. Most of the surveys at the time were too general; they did not reveal hidden consumer concerns. As a result of our own studies, we found that a low noise level in a car carried all kinds of other wonderful implications: soundness of design, quality, and value.

One of our young engineers, Hulki Aldikatchti, was assigned the job of developing the most cost-effective acoustical package with the help of the outstanding GM proving-ground sound lab. For a surprisingly modest cost, which was carefully applied, Hulki developed sound-reducing approaches that enabled us to produce sound levels lower than those found inside a Rolls Royce, the ultimate standard of luxury and manufacturing excellence in the eyes of the motoring world. We then prepared advertising that showed the Pontiac prominently displayed in front of a soft-focus shot of another car, obviously a Rolls Royce. We never mentioned the Rolls by name, but we did say that the Pontiac was quieter than the "world's most luxurious car."

The internal reaction to our innovative campaign added one more coal to my growing fire of frustration with upper management. The Cadillac Division was irate; they felt the advertisement stepped on their toes as the luxury-car division. When they took their complaint to the Fourteenth Floor (where GM's top executives have their offices), we were forced to pull the ads. The joke was that Cadillac didn't have the sense to see a winner and at least adopt the concept for themselves. Eventually, of course, Lincoln brought out a campaign that compared their car with a Rolls, and then Ford came out with its own adaptation of the approach: "Quiet is the sound of a well-made car." Both campaigns were extremely successful.

Another example of the kind of problem I encountered at GM was when I decided we needed a new tire design for the Pontiacs. We wanted the entire car to be unusual enough to appeal to the youth market, a plan that had already proven a sales success with the GTO. The result was a tire known as the "Tiger's Paw," a creation of the United States Tire Company, now Uniroyal. The tire had a thin red line between the tread and the rim, a slight design modification that changed the appearance of what was basically a utilitarian item.

U.S. Tire was so pleased with the reaction to the tire that they established a nationwide campaign using a tiger as part of the sales pitch. Then I decided to adjust our advertising for Pontiac to match what the tire company was doing (today it's called being "synergistic"). The ad agency hired Barbara Feldon, the attractive comedienne and actress who became famous as Agent 99 on the popular television series "Get Smart." Our tongue-in-cheek ad featured her on a tiger-skin rug, growling out the virtues of Pontiac.

The dealers loved the campaign, and Pontiacs around the country began sporting give-away tiger tails as proof of the promotion's success. But just as sales began to rise, General Motors' Chairman, Jim Roche, insisted we stop. He didn't like the animal campaign; it was too aggressive. Roche was a true gentleman, and I'm sure there was a valid case to be made for his view. But we never got to present our side of the argument—that it worked!

In spite of these internal frustrations, Pontiac became an extremely profitable division under my leadership, a fact that resulted in my being promoted to head the Chevrolet division in 1969. By this time, however, I was gaining a reputation as a corporate maverick, not only for attacking the system from within but also for my lifestyle.

4

I have been married three times, but I have had only one mistress—my work. While in many ways I am proud of this drive and devotion, I also recognize that it has contributed to personal failure in my relationships with others. This was particularly evident in my first two marriages. For me, each marriage was a deep and firm commitment I thought would last forever. Yet my life was always engineering. I could devote endless hours to my job, totally consumed by what I was doing, but I could never devote myself to another person. As a result, I never had a truly deep personal relationship with my wives. In fact, I never let anyone become the type of close friend and confidant I now know we all need.

My first wife was Elizabeth Higgins, whom I met when I was still a student engineer at Chrysler. I was close to thirty;

all my friends were married; and I think the fact that I found Liz sexually attractive and fun to be with convinced me that marriage was right for me, too. Whatever the reasons, one night I went to bed, and the next morning all my friends had received wedding invitations.

Once married, I plunged right back into the work I loved. We bought a small colonial house in Grosse Pointe Woods where my biggest concern was the crab grass. Liz took care of our home and worked full-time with the telephone company. If I thought about it at all, my major concern as a husband was that she be available when I wanted her, and that she relieve me of what I felt were minor pressures related to our home. It was a selfish existence on my part and a lonely one for Liz, even when my salary increased to the point that she could quit her job and enjoy a relatively leisurely lifestyle in a beautiful home, socializing with the wives of other rising executives. She deserved more. The insane drive that kept me at the factory seven days a week late into the night was grossly unfair to her. The ultimate failure of our marriage was entirely my fault.

By the time Liz and I divorced, my economic circumstances had permitted me to move to Bloomfield Hills. Bloomfield Hills is a northwest suburb of Detroit where the key to admission is a big salary, generally from the auto industry. The Bloomfield Hills Country Club could be considered the Polo Lounge of the automotive world. The old money in Detroit, like the Buhls and the Fords, lived further east along the river in Grosse Pointe and belonged to the Grosse Pointe Country Club. Bloomfield Hills was the place most automotive executives lived.

A few of the "Bloomfield wives" had careers of their own or were active in charity work, but most spent their days shopping, lunching, and gossiping. News of promotions, firings, and other career shifts usually dominated, since these affected the family money. The second subject of interest was who was dating whom, who was marrying, and who was having an affair. As a rising young executive, my personal life was as good a subject as any for the lunch crowd at the country club, especially after Liz, a lunching regular, and I divorced in 1969, and I was seen with other women.

I was never a particularly social creature in the sense of enjoying rounds of cocktail parties and the other staples of the social circuit. I am no good at small talk and don't care for alcohol, but I do enjoy the company of attractive women. For reasons I am only beginning to understand now, I never chose women who challenged me. Women who impressed me as intelligent, able, and deserving of respect for their personal accomplishments made me extremely uncomfortable. In fact, they terrified me. I know now that I was personally insecure. And the result was that I dated women who were beautiful, sensual, and did not seem personally threatening. Any other kind of woman was only a casual dinner date, not someone I expected to see again after the evening was over.

One of the women who entered my life at that time was Kelly Harmon, the daughter of Tom Harmon, the famous University of Michigan football figure. Kelly was twenty, a fashion model, and one of the most beautiful women I had ever seen. Her sister had married singer Rick Nelson, the son of Ozzie and Harriet Nelson of early television fame.

Kelly and I had no business becoming seriously involved. Not only was she more than twenty years younger than I was, but we had nothing in common. To this day I can't remember one meaningful conversation we had. I should probably have simply had an enjoyable affair with her and then moved on to more mature relationships.

Not me. I confused primal drive and flattery with love and honor. So Kelly and I married, had a few months of wedded bliss, and then realized we had made a mistake.

That John DeLorean had married a twenty-year-old model was ideal gossip for the Bloomfield Hills "ladies who lunch." Kelly eventually became part of some of these rituals, and she was accepted both as a new source of gossip and because she was married to a rising young executive who was taking over Chevrolet. It was better to be nice, regardless of what the women might truly have thought of

51

Kelly and me, than to risk her displeasure and discover too late that one of their husband's futures might be dependent upon me. Corporate politics was always in the minds of most auto-industry executives and their wives.

But in spite of what was said, the age difference could not have been a major shock in Bloomfield Hills. Many executives in the automobile industry routinely married younger women. Ed Cole's second wife, Dollie, was more than twenty years his junior. When Pete Estes' first wife died unexpectedly, Pete almost immediately married his secretary, an extremely attractive and much younger woman. With each of these marriages there was the initial undercurrent of scandal and rumor, followed by the immediate acceptance of the new wife because of her husband's power in the industry. Bloomfield Hills tongues may have been sharp, but they were also pragmatic.

It was about this time that I began to see that, in many ways, the automobile industry was a business of style and fashion. Yet all of us executives were about as unfashionable as you could imagine. Most of us were overweight, extremely old-fashioned in dress, and intolerant of those who deviated from our "example." How could we manage or promote style if we didn't know what it was? This also carried a serious physical corollary: We made the company our lives—and those who retired usually died within a year or two of their retirement. I did not like what I was seeing.

My first concern became my own appearance. I had quit smoking and had ballooned in weight to approximately 235 pounds. (Today I weigh 168.) My pants were at least four inches above my ankles, something that happens when you buy a suit and then gain weight. My sport coats were probably at least double the size of the ones I wear now. I decided if I was going to sell style to the world, I had better get some myself. So I cut back on what I ate and began an exercise program. Also, at my barber's suggestion, I started coloring my hair to eliminate the grey, an appeal to personal vanity and possibly an attempt to dispel the disparity in age between myself and Kelly.

These changes were all duly noted and commented on in the Bloomfield Hills community. But oddly, the most controversial action was my cosmetic surgery.

I had had corrective jaw surgery as a youngster. By coincidence, during this period when I was determined to improve my health, style, and appearance, a piece of that jawbone became impacted. The doctor removed the bone impact and reconstructed the area—but rather badly, as it turned out. My face swelled into an unsightly and grotesque balloon. Sensitive about my appearance, I took a month's vacation to recover. By the time I looked reasonably presentable, the doctor wanted to redo the surgery to correct the scarring and disfigurement. This time I refused, preferring to leave the ugly scar tissue rather than risk repeating the trauma I endured after the first surgery. No one questioned my appearance; they just assumed it was part of "the new John DeLorean." To this day much has been written about this subject, but I don't recall anyone ever asking me directly.

Toward the end of my marriage with Kelly, something happened that would change my personal life forever. One day, while I was playing tennis with a doctor friend, Buzz Ely, he happened to mention a young patient of one of his partners. She was a college student and had become pregnant as the result of an affair with one of her professors. They were concerned for the girl because of the agony she seemed to be having in deciding what to do with her baby. She didn't feel she had the resources to support the infant when it was born, yet she also loved the growing life too much to consider an abortion.

As my friend described this young woman's problem, something deep within my soul responded. Despite my outstanding achievements in my vocation—I was now heading GM's largest division, Chevrolet—my personal life was a shambles with one failed marriage and another rapidly disintegrating. I longed for "something more" in my life, something not based on money or power within General Motors. Part of it was a spiritual longing, and I continued going from church to church, often in the inner city of Detroit, where I sensed greater peace and love than I saw among the congregations of the wealthy. That spiritual search would remain an ongoing part of my future. Another part of my longing, however, was the desire to love and nurture a child and to earn the love of a child. Liz had been unable to have children as a result of surgery after an ectopic pregnancy, and Kelly had miscarried her only pregnancy.

That day, as Buzz talked, I knew that I wanted to adopt that girl's unborn child. I was ready to commit my heart to another human being. I knew that by becoming a parent I could satisfy at least that one aspect of my longing for something more. It was perhaps the most important decision of my life.

My son Zachary was born while Kelly and I were still married, but we both realized that this was my commitment. Our marriage was crumbling, and Kelly was spending more and more time with her parents in California. So I became Zachary's father knowing that I would probably raise him as a single parent, and the adoption became final after the divorce was completed.

I immediately made plans for my life to revolve around Zachary's care. I hired a wonderful red-haired Irish nurse, Nancy, and took the two of them everywhere I traveled. If I had to fly somewhere to give a speech, Zachary and his nurse went with me. I had no intention of letting my son take second place to my work.

I am almost embarrassed to admit that I did not learn what it meant to truly love another person until I was in my late forties when Zachary first taught me what selfless caring is and how essential it is to existence. I did not know it then, but in loving Zachary I was taking my first step toward learning to love God.

Throughout my life I had engaged in many high-thrill turn-ons—like driving 120 miles an hour in a thick fog or creeping along a narrow ledge twenty stories up from one hotel window to the next for a practical joke. Until I had my son, I never really worried about dying. To me life was the ultimate gambling stake. Suddenly I had to survive—for Zachary.

5

While Zachary was changing my personal life dramatically, my position as head of the Chevrolet division was making my business life increasingly complex and exciting. It thrust me into the very heart of the joys and frustrations of corporate management. It also thrust me into the headlines.

Chevrolet was in a disastrous slide, and its executives, who had already had two former Pontiac managers who did not help them, greeted me with virtual disdain. They had decided Pontiac was so small compared with Chevrolet that no Pontiac manager could understand their problems.

Chevrolet was having trouble in the marketplace: trouble with customers, dealers, and of course, profitability. Resale value looms large in demonstrating the success or failure of an automobile line. Traditionally Chevrolet had been the resale leader in the low-priced segment of the industry; this factor figured heavily in Chevy's ability to outsell Ford. But over the previous six years Chevrolet's resale value had slipped below Ford's. As the new vice-president, one of my urgent concerns was to find out why and to correct it if I could.

All car companies constantly monitor their competition. At GM we dismantled every Ford and Chrysler product to understand exactly how they were made, where we needed to improve, where they were more cost effective than we were, and where we were better. We ran 50,000-mile durability tests on their cars, much as we did on our own. But our measurement of the marketplace and the actual reasons for Chevrolet's precipitous decline were grossly inadequate and not useful.

First of all, I did my homework. I interviewed every large Chevrolet dealer in small group luncheons. In a company like Chevrolet, less than 20 percent of the dealers sell 80 percent of the cars, so these were the men I talked to. They told me what I needed to know. I also interviewed virtually every member of second- and third-level management in the division. These were the people who knew much more about what was going on than the executives.

As soon as I had the facts, I decided to swim against the tide of accountants and adopt the viewpoint of the potential buyers. I worked with our engineering and design experts not only to improve the mechanical quality, but also to increase the interior quality.

One example of the changes we made was the Chevrolet Blazer, a four-wheel-drive vehicle whose direct competition was the AMC Jeep. The Blazer was actually a more sophisticated vehicle that could be used as a family station wagon or taken off road—a concept that gave it wide appeal. It also had the potential for handling better than other vehicles in intense rain and snow. Yet we were selling just a few thousand a year, and customer satisfaction was nonexistent.

The most serious customer complaint with the Blazer was that it was not water tight. To better understand the problem, I went to our St. Louis truck plant where the Blazer was manufactured and ordered the plant manager to get in a Blazer with me and drive through the water leak test (a test in which water is sprayed heavily and thoroughly over the vehicle). By the time we stepped out, we were both soaked. My suit was sopping wet, my hair hung limp, and water was dripping off the end of my nose.

The manager, Cliff Vaughn, complained, "It's a bad design, John. We're doing the best we can with it."

We made the necessary design changes; quality control became a primary concern; the Blazer was developed into an excellent product; and sales eventually rose more than 1000 percent. In fact, we were so successful that today most of the industry, including the Japanese, offer four-wheel-drive vehicles of similar design.

Another problem we faced was with the dealers themselves. Many felt they were being mistreated by Chevrolet, and frequently they were. In turn, customer complaints about dealers were also high. I found that many dealers did not understand why customers complain in the first place. In most instances, the problem is quite minor, and the customer is not out of line in what he or she is asking. But when that customer is not treated with respect, suddenly every minor rattle and slight flaw in workmanship becomes a major problem. Soon the owner is attacking the entire car line, turning away other potential customers, and creating serious problems.

For many years the management at GM encouraged home-office people to socialize with the dealers when it was appropriate: play golf with them; have a drink with them; take them to dinner. After all, they were our *only* customers. But it was also true that while the dealers enjoyed the friendship of GM executives, and at times might even have been flattered by it, their primary concern was whether they were making money selling GM cars. Most dealers start out with every cent they can beg or borrow invested in their dealership. It is not just a salary to them; it is everything they have in the world. Management support toward keeping them in business makes for harmonious relations, not the wining and dining.

When I took over Pontiac, I phoned five different dealers each day to get a firsthand grasp of what was going on in the field. They were shocked to hear from me but delighted with the personal contact from the division manager. These calls seldom lasted more than five minutes and brought substantial results without wasting their time or mine. Obviously, when a dealer told me about a problem, I had better get it corrected. I also was increasing dealer loyalty at a time when many foreign car companies were moving into the American market, seeking good dealers with proven records. Since this technique had proved successful at Pontiac, I now used it at Chevrolet.

Another of my increasingly urgent concerns was with the hiring practices at Chevrolet. In fact, I was concerned with the hiring practices throughout General Motors, for I had first become aware of and involved in solving the problem when I was at Pontiac. But I saw my position at Chevrolet as giving me an even greater opportunity to bring about change in the corporate system.

At the top and on most of the way up, General Motors was essentially a white, Anglo-Saxon, Protestant corporation. There were no Jewish executives; there were no blacks in management. (Many years before, in the DuPont days, there had been a Jewish financial executive, a man named Meyer Prentis, and he was often cited as an example of GM's lack of prejudice.) Minorities had no opportunity to rise in the business. This had been especially obvious at Pontiac because the plant was located in a predominantly black neighborhood. These men and women could make the cars on the assembly line, buy the cars from white dealers, but they could not become part of management.

While at Pontiac, I had asked why there were no blacks in management. I was told, "Show me a qualified black, and we'll hire him. Color isn't the problem. We just can't find qualified black people." Being "qualified" meant, among other things, that the person had to have a college education and business training. The fact was that most bright young blacks who lived in Pontiac, Michigan, could not afford college. It was a Catch-22.

At Chevrolet the same racial barrier existed. At first I believed that if I could bring a qualified person into the organization, the management would help him rise to the top, which was why I was so pleased when I met Hayes Jones.

Hayes was an Olympic medalist who, when I met him at the opening of the New York GM building, headed the Parks and Recreation Department for the City of New York. Born and raised in Pontiac, Michigan, this handsome, extremely intelligent, and extraordinarily capable man had a record no one could question. He was more than "qualified." Had he been white, everyone in GM would have wanted to recruit him.

I invited Hayes to Detroit for the position of zone manager at a salary close to what he was receiving in New York. I knew he would be excellent in this position as soon as he was given intensive training in the automotive business, training that was routine for anyone brought in from the outside. But the moment the top Chevrolet sales brass discovered I wanted to have a black man contact dealers in conjunction with our sales effort, they were irate. They exerted so much pressure on Hayes that he told me he simply couldn't consider working for GM.

"I'm not wanted here, John," he finally said to me. "I'd survive while you're here. But the minute you get promoted, they'll force me out!"

Hayes eventually took a position with one of the major airlines. Although he was a great loss to GM, no one took it seriously because of the color of his skin. This experience proved to me that minorities were not going to be given opportunities for advancement, regardless of the corporation's official line—or America's for that matter. Even today this is a problem. Take, for example, Tom Bradley, the mayor of Los Angeles. I have never met the man, but after watching his success with the 1984 Summer Olympics and other

61

projects, I have concluded that he is one of the greatest manpower bargains in America. If he were white, corporate headhunters would be camping at his doorstep. I can only hope that in politics he can achieve his full potential.

There were a few changes in attitude during this period at GM, but none of them had anything to do with getting minorities into management. For example, there was a growing willingness to let minority-owned businesses act as subcontractors, and a few blacks were given car dealerships in predominantly black areas. As head of Pontiac, I personally put the first black dealer in Watts, California: Adam McFadden, a truly wonderful man.

After much reflection, I hit upon a plan that I thought would satisfy the need for training while using an existing facility, the General Motors Institute. The Institute had been started by Alfred P. Sloan during a period when college education was not responsively directed to men seeking work in a corporation like GM. Most colleges stressed classical fundamentals. The Institute took students sponsored by the various GM divisions, gave them free tuition and high pay as they studied three months, and then employed them for three months in the plants. They learned the essentials of becoming valuable employees at GM and earned a relatively good living while they did it. Eventually, however, the Institute became a rather nepotistic arm, since most of the students were related to corporate executives or their friends.

By the late sixties, however, many schools around the country, including the University of Michigan and the University of Detroit, had similar work-study programs (three months of study alternating with three months of work). Since the original purpose of the GM Institute could be accomplished by other institutions, I proposed that we adapt to meet the needs of the day and that Chevrolet could start by sponsoring only minority group members at the Institute, giving them a real chance to become a part of GM's management, and correcting the existing racial imbalance.

Management was horrified (much to my delight, I now

confess). Many lower-level discussions were held. Ultimately, I was called to the board chairman's office to discuss my stubborn refusal to alter my proposal. There were several executives there, including the president, and most of them were GM Institute graduates.

"You're wrong," they said. "You're showing prejudice against whites." I couldn't believe these guys were arguing about reverse discrimination at a time when they had done nothing for others.

Finally, I implied that word of my proposal and their refusal would probably leak out since they had made so much of it. This shocked them and caused them to take note of the potential publicity value of at least some changes in policy. We finally agreed upon a compromise: they would admit only minority group members for half of each new class. Ironically, when the U.S. government began cracking down on industries with a history of ignoring minority rights, General Motors cited its program as being in the vanguard of change for having admitted so many minority group members.

In all honesty, my actions in those days were of mixed value. On one hand, I truly believed in minority education and was willing to alienate management and sacrifice my own career potential to implement it. On the other, I saw myself as anti-establishment and delighted in "snapping the braces" of the top men in the name of what was obviously a good cause. It was fun to step on their toes and watch them squirm. The GM Institute fight was an example of a man accomplishing good ends for the wrong reasons. I was subtly corrupting my values by thinking that the good results justified my extremely bad attitude. My sin was as bad as theirs.

There was one program, however, in which I became involved simply because I believed in it. This was an organization that provided short- and long-term stability, discipline, and love to children in trouble. It was operated as a camp on a 300-acre farm just outside Pontiac. There were several large old houses on the farm, and each housed a family consisting of the parents, two or three natural children, and a changing group of twelve children. Since the total number of children being cared for at any given time was fairly large, the operation was always in need of special support.

Most of the children were from the inner city, and many were emotionally disturbed or otherwise troubled. The only alternative for many of them would have been an orphanage that probably would have fostered anger and violence, creating adults who would be a menace to society. The farm helped restore these young people to emotional health and enabled them to have a more productive and hopeful future.

Although my involvement with the camp was superficial, it was well-meaning and sincere. I provided gifts of support and occasionally spent time with the kids, talking, counseling, and playing with them. I needed to reach out to others, and this was a safe way of doing it.

6

By the time I had been at General Motors for two years, I was earning more money than I had ever anticipated while still in school. Eventually, with my salary and bonuses, I had the financial freedom to indulge myself in almost any way I wanted. The trouble was that I had no serious interests other than my work. Occasionally I bought an expensive sports car for the sheer love of a quality machine. (I remember taking Pontiac dealer Frank Audette for a 180-mph ride on an unfinished stretch of freeway in a Maserati. He turned ashen white and could hardly get out of the car when I took him back to his dealership.) I could afford costly vacations, though I usually had little interest in taking time off for more than a short period of skiing or a long weekend at the Christmas holidays. Accumulating material things for their own sake never interested me.

But I did want to take advantage of my increasing wealth, as well as protect it. For that reason I became involved with investment counselors, who soon advised me to invest in sophisticated stock offerings. These investments probably helped the individual companies, certainly helped the broker, but eventually proved of little value to me. The same was true of oil and gas exploration projects in which I became involved. I invested in limited partnerships that "could not fail" because they would theoretically pay extensive dividends or would result in tax write-offs, either of which would be of value. Unfortunately, my investments almost never worked in the manner my advisers said they would. (In retrospect, I would have been as far ahead to pay my taxes and keep the balance; and as in most tax shelters, the country would have been better off.)

Early in my career, however, I began to invest in real estate. Perhaps it was the longing of a city boy for the romantic appeal of country life. Perhaps it was the influence of my old-country parents who believed in owning land. Perhaps it was because farm life represented a quiet order, a well-defined pattern devoid of the aggressiveness, greed, and struggles for power I encountered in my daily life. Whatever the reason, I started my real-estate purchases by buying a farm in Michigan. Later I gave this farm, along with our home, to Liz when we divorced.

My next venture was in Idaho. This farm was owned by an unusual couple, the Reeses. Mrs. Reese was from an extremely wealthy Eastern family. She had first seen the Idaho mountains and farmland while on a student tour during her college years. She fell in love with her tour guide, a strapping outdoorsman who knew and loved the beautiful, magnificent country. Together they bought acreage on which they raised purebred cattle for over forty years.

When I met them, they had decided to sell their farm because they were too old to run it. Mr. Reese had had a stroke and could no longer work the large herd. They decided to keep forty-five acres and their house on the river bend and sell the rest to me—approximately 2,800 acres. I also bought a small potato farm across from their property, eventually accumulating about 4,000 acres. Everything was on a long-term land contract at 6-percent interest, typical of that period of farm and real-estate history.

Eventually, I acquired a farm manager who was paid approximately $20,000 a year to run the place, in addition to receiving food and meat from the farm, a Chevy Suburban, and other needs. He had an excellent living arrangement, and I had someone to run the farm. The return on operations was marginal, but the difference between the income and my expenses made it affordable. Later the ranch not only earned enough to pay the bills, but also gave me a place to escape from the pressures of Detroit. I could take my vacations there, ride the range, go up into the hills, and camp out in the clean air. It was a wonderful experience for a city kid raised on a twenty-five-foot lot.

I didn't know then that the farm would come back to haunt me. When I eventually founded my own company and needed to focus my whole attention on that, I was approached by a man who wanted to lease the farm and to pay me exactly what my mortgage costs had become, with an option to buy. His attorney drew up the lease, and I signed exactly what he sent me. He also bought my cattle, machinery, and other equipment with notes secured by the cattle and equipment. Unfortunately, the man, who I now believe to be much more of a real-estate speculator than a rancher, not only never paid me, but immediately sold both my cattle and my equipment. Then he convinced the bank that he still owned all that cattle and equipment, borrowing $600,000 on his nonexistent collateral. He eventually defaulted on this bank loan too. I believe he took the bank and me for over $1.4 million.

The case was tied up in court for three years. The judge finally ordered the man off the land and returned it to me, yet he was never forced to face the issue of nonpayment because he pleaded poverty. I simply dropped the matter and sold the farm after the court returned it to me. As a matter of fact, I used the payment for this farm as the down payment for the farm I now own in New Jersey.

But these problems are relatively recent. Those early days with the farm were extremely pleasurable. As with most farms in America, the profits were small, but the increase in the value of the land allowed me to borrow more and more against it. (This can eventually catch up with you, of course, as America's farmers know well. Many have overborrowed to buy equipment and more land, usually with the encouragement of financial institutions. As a result, today many farms are being repossessed. This is a tragedy for America—we need those farmers, and they need their land.)

I began using whatever money I could accumulate to buy other real estate, ranging from the farm in New Jersey to an apartment in Manhattan. Whenever I wanted something new, I found that I could either make a trade or sell an older parcel that had increased in value, investing the money into what would otherwise have been an unaffordable property. My personal wealth increased without my having to risk great sums of money. Virtually all the money I have is a result of investing in that manner. If I have any investment advice for young people, it is to buy good quality properties, starting with a home, at the market price. (Bargains are usually not!). The sometimes agonizing discipline of making those monthly payments puts a forced saving into your economic life that will eventually accumulate into a substantial net worth.

I came as close as possible to leading the life of a recluse while working as a GM executive. I have never enjoyed lavish parties. I also hated the phoniness of suppliers who were your "friends" only as long as you could do them some good.

Liz and Kelly had delighted in indulging themselves on my income and were far more comfortable than I with the various affairs we had to attend. But I stayed home as much as possible.

Between marriages my social life was slightly more active. I frequently had dates with beautiful women, and the press delighted in categorizing me as a glamorous playboy, a characterization that, on one hand, made me the envy of some of the married men I knew but, on the other hand, seemed humorous to my former wives. Actually, I would have been delighted to have led the scandalous bachelorhood the media created for me. In fact, it was not until my third marriage that my social life became fairly active. But that marriage also started me on an emotional roller coaster I am still riding.

7

I was flipping through a copy of *Vogue* magazine during a flight to a business appointment when I first saw Cristina Ferrare. She was the featured model on a five-page spread. I thought she was cute and attractive, with the kind of appealing face that jumps off the page at you. I had no idea who she was, but I did something I had never done before: I tore the pages out of the magazine and tucked them in my briefcase. I felt a bit sheepish, like a teenager with a crush on a movie star.

One Saturday, many months later, her name came up in the men's grill at the Bel Air Country Club. Ten of us were sitting around chatting when my friend Roger Penske said, "A friend of mine who runs a model agency is getting me a date with Cristina Ferrare."

My divorce lawyer, Ed Hookstratten, was one of the

71

group, and when he saw I was interested in her name, he took me aside and said, "I know Cristina well. She and my wife are good friends. If you'd like to meet her, she's modeling a dress at the opening of Gucci's new fall line tonight."

In addition to being a model, Cristina Ferrare was, I learned, one of the Hollywood starlets whose lives revolved around the wealthy and famous. She was one of a group of attractive young women who were determined to make it in the film industry but who had either limited or unproven talent. Because they were attractive, however, they were in demand. They would accompany rich celebrities around town and, in some instances, around the world.

Cristina was with Fletcher Jones when I first met her in September of 1972 at Gucci's. She was Jones's current companion, although their relationship was a convenience rather than a love affair. Jones was the quintessential playboy—handsome, rich, and charming. He had dated nearly every beautiful starlet in town. Actually, he was in love with another woman, but their romance was a stormy one. Whenever they would fight and Jones found himself in need of an attractive companion for dinner, a party, or some other event, he would call Cristina. The relationship gave her a good time and an opportunity to meet influential people in the entertainment world who might be of value in furthering her ambitions.

In November of 1972 Jones was killed in a plane crash. Sometime after his death, I called Cristina for a date and took her to lunch at the Daisy on Rodeo Drive in Beverly Hills. We got along quite well, and I found her as appealing in person as I had on the pages of *Vogue*. Since I had plans to go skiing at Vail over Christmas, as I usually did, I asked Cristina to accompany me, though I had to break a previous arrangement with another woman to do so. I had no qualms about it; I wanted Cristina for Christmas.

Vail offers any type of living arrangement you want. I happened to be going to a large condominium owned by Roger Penske and his friend Bill Smith. Roger and his girl friend were there, along with his two sons by a previous marriage. With me were one year old Zachary and his nanny. I arrived the day after GM shut down for Christmas. When Cristina arrived four or five days later, our host gave us separate bedrooms in a balcony area that we had to ourselves.

After my separation from Kelly, I had come to believe that Hollywood starlets were extremely insecure. To put it mildly, Hollywood is a highly competitive world with hundreds of attractive, talented women competing for a limited number of parts. Because physical appeal was such a valuable commodity to them, they seemed to need constant reassurance that they were attractive and desirable.

Once aware of this, I surmised that the easiest way to gain intimate attention from such a woman was to ignore her. Ignoring a starlet fed on her basic insecurity and forced her to make the first move. This was the technique I used with Cristina, and it worked.

I would love to say that Cristina and I had a storybook romance: the merging of two hearts and minds into one idyllic interlude of total commitment and deep interpersonal involvement. The reality, I suspect, was that both of us enjoyed the initial physical attraction, which eventually developed into a comfortable relationship. Cristina, who had been accustomed to traveling with wealthy men, now became my companion. In February 1973 she flew to Detroit and moved into my home.

My days were filled with my challenging business life, and my nights were filled with the pleasure of the company of a beautiful and desirable woman. In retrospect, our relationship at that time had little to do with love and nothing to do with commitment.

There have been many falsehoods written about our time together, the most outrageous being that I used David E. Davis, a man I never socialized with, to act as a "beard," a man who appeared to be dating Cristina so that no one would know I was her lover. The allegation was nonsense. Cristina and I lived together quite openly, a fact that did not escape the gossips of Bloomfield Hills. We were constantly together in restaurants and at social gatherings; we had friends visit at the house; and generally, we were completely open about our relationship.

I was enjoying everything I wanted from life—a rather self-centered way to view the world, but there seemed no reason for me to change anything. Cristina, however, made certain that my complacency did not last. I came home from work one day to discover her waiting downstairs, her luggage packed. She stood there smiling smugly and said, "We've been together long enough for you to know everything about me. We are either going to get married, or I'm going on my way."

The answer was obvious. I had become accustomed to having Cristina around. It was convenient to have a lover waiting for me when I arrived home—and a lover who was a fabulous Italian cook! Moreover, I liked the thought of being a true family, with Cristina becoming a mother to my son. Marriage would provide me with the instant warm, loving family arrangement I had always wanted. Above all it was easy. All I had to do was say yes.

Sex and convenience are not the best foundation for a long-lasting relationship, but I did not see it then. In fact, I wasn't really building a relationship at all. I loved Cristina physically and found her desirable as a woman. I knew that she was intensely ambitious and that, while she liked modeling, she was absolutely desperate to be a television or movie star. I knew that she enjoyed having wealthy men spend money on her. But I wanted to believe that she was in love with both me and my son.

I did realize, however, that since Cristina was more than twenty years younger than I, there could come a time when I would be old, infirm, and unable to be an active companion while she would still be young and vigorous. Our relationship might not withstand such circumstances, and I told her so.

"Cristina, the Lord has created millions of attractive, beautiful people. If you ever want to leave me for someone else, I'll understand. I only want you to be honest—leave me and go do your thing—I don't want a dishonest relationship. And I'll do the same for you."

She agreed but also stressed that that would not happen. She told me, "I'll never leave you. I love you."

John Noonan, my lawyer in Detroit, convinced me that we should put together a prenuptial agreement to protect our own assets. Before meeting Cristina, I had property in San Diego, Michigan, and Idaho that was rapidly appreciating, substantial savings, and other things of worth. She, in turn, was a successful model with a future that could include stardom. She had the potential for making large sums of money if her talent and ability equaled her ambitions. We drew up an agreement saying that neither of us would have the right to the current or accrued wealth of the other should we ever part. In other words, the only gains either of us could make from the relationship were personal, not financial.

Cristina took the agreement to her lawyer who told her not to sign it, and not to marry me if I insisted she sign it. She was very upset but chose to sign because, she said, she wanted to marry me and because we were both committed to a lifetime together. Ours would be a marriage of love, not greed.

Naturally, the Bloomfield Hills gossips had a field day when Cristina and I announced our intention to marry. No one was thrilled. Cristina was too young, they said; she was a starlet, a model, and simply did not fit the Detroit scene. Even the wife of GM's president, Dollie Cole, discouraged me from marrying her. "Wait a year or two, John. All of your critics will retire by then," she said.

But once we were married, pragmatism again took control. Cristina was allowed to become part of the local society, accepted by the corporate wives.

Marriage to Cristina proved to be filled with surprises. She had a quick temper—something she had managed to

75

control all those months we were living together. Once I was so shocked by how quickly she could flare up during an argument that I asked her, "How did you ever manage to control your temper before we were married?"

"It wasn't easy," she said. "It almost killed me."

My home arrangements also triggered an uneasiness in her. Nancy, the nanny who was caring for Zachary, had become accustomed to being the head of the household. She had been a substitute mother for Zachary, had watched him take his first steps, had listened to his efforts to speak his first words. She and Zachary accompanied me wherever I went. She planned meals, coordinated the running of the house, and generally controlled my domestic life. I never imagined that Cristina would see Nancy as a threat. Cristina was a gourmet cook and delighted in being in the kitchen, and she also wanted to establish herself as Zachary's mother. There was great conflict between the two women and, eventually, Cristina gave Nancy her notice.

With Cristina firmly in charge of our home, our love for each other seemed to deepen and grow. We decided to have a child, but for some time we were unable to conceive. Even as we made this decision, though, I wondered what my feelings would be if Cristina and I were to have a second child. Would I love one more than the other? Would I favor Zachary, or would I think that the new life was somehow more precious than my son?

When Cristina finally did become pregnant, I was thrilled but worried. I did not know then that a father does not love one child more than the other. He does not place them in competition, trying to see which is cuter, which is smarter, or which is the more pleasurable.

Kathryn was born when Zachary was six, and never have I favored either child. I love my daughter as deeply as I love my son. I never compare them—only cherish their uniqueness. Zachary and Kathryn are the best of both Cristina and myself. And they are the finest legacy I have.

8

There is only one sin in Detroit. Pride, envy, lust, greed, gluttony, and the other human failings the rest of the world knows as the seven deadly sins are not of serious concern. In fact, most of them are practiced rather routinely in the business and social lives of auto-industry executives and their wives. But there is one sin in Detroit, or perhaps more accurately in Bloomfield Hills. The commandment reads: Thou Shalt Not Leave General Motors, Ford, or Chrysler.

My decision to sin, Detroit style, was prompted by several troublesome pressures: my growing awareness of and even participation in engineering and marketing practices that made me uncomfortable; my disgust with corporate infighting; my extreme dislike of political games; my views on minority rights; and my desire for individual responsibility and decision making.

While I felt forced out by circumstances, I was in good company. In fact, the four men I, and most others, consider the auto industry's best were all fired at some time in their careers: Lee Iacocca, whose accomplishments dwarf all others; Hal Sperlich; Bunkie Knudsen; and Bernard Hanon, one of the most brilliant minds in the industry.

Others, such as Ed Cole and Pete Estes, stayed in their jobs despite the fact that at times they brought forth products that were not worth promoting. I finally decided I could not continue to live with corporate distortion to keep advancing. I was not enough of a "company man" to consider spending the next twenty years at the top of GM.

My repugnance and distaste for selling and marketing a product I did not believe in had reached its peak at Chevrolet with the Vega, an absolutely disastrous car designed by Pete Estes, my predecessor at Chevrolet, and Ed Cole, GM's president and "chief engineer."

The Vega was a disaster from the word go. For the first time in my memory, GM announced a new car years in advance of its market introduction. Chairman Jim Roche had announced the new Vega's price, weight, and production date at the dedication of the new GM building in New York. We missed them all—the price by hundreds of dollars, the weight by hundreds of pounds, and the market introduction by a full model year.

When the project was first sold to corporate management by Ed Cole, I was still at Pontiac, and it was to be a joint Chevrolet-Pontiac car like the Camaro and Firebird. In the early styling sessions I ran afoul of Ed Cole at every juncture. We were on different wavelengths. I wanted to build a really fine small car, a mini-BMW, not just a super-cheap car. In the technical meetings with the engineering staff I rebelled against his "novelty" approach. Ed had fallen in love with a new process developed by Reynolds Aluminum to cast aluminum engine blocks without the traditional cast-iron sleeves by using a special wear-resistant high-silicon alloy. It was new and untested and imposed severe design limitations that could not be solved in the time available. But Ed Cole was a master corporate politician. Suddenly, Pontiac was dropped from the Vega program so that I was no longer permitted to attend design meetings.

I was relieved. It was inconceivable to me that the Vega could succeed. My relief was short-lived. Chevrolet was in serious trouble. Its market penetration had dropped from 32 to 24 percent—with each point worth $100 million in profits in those days. The dealers were in rebellion.

On the basis of Pontiac's performance during my stewardship, I was promoted to general manager of Chevrolet, and Estes was moved aside. "He won't bother you," were hatchet man Roger Kyes' words. Kyes had forced so many executives into medical retirements that the big joke among the GM financial staff was: "When Kyes tells you you're sick, you're sick!"

In any event, in early 1969 I became responsible for the Vega. At that time I think it still had its code name "898." The first prototype was sent to the GM proving grounds for durability testing. After only eight miles on the Belgian blocks it broke in two. At the same time, the Chevrolet engineers descended on me to change the cylinder head—it looked like a 1917 farm-tractor engine—and everyone was willing to commit to an impossible time schedule to redo the engine.

Worse than that, the Lordstown plant was being automated to a degree unheard of in the industry to produce this poorly engineered ugly duckling. But it soon became clear that no provision had been made for the inevitable breakdowns of the automatic equipment. There was no provision for "float" of bodies or components between stations. As a result, every machine that broke down on the line shut down the entire plant. What a fiasco! (One of the Canadian plants later built Vegas by the old-fashioned hand methods, and they beat Lordstown's costs.)

When it came time to market this horrible little car, Tom Staudt, our marketing genius, convinced us, via intensive consumer analysis, that we should put a little chrome and larger tires on the car and sell it a bit upscale. The engineering policy group liked his ideas and approved the plan. Six months later as we approached production, the same group of people wearing the hats of a different committee threw out the plan and stripped the car to the bone.

We were devastated. Morale was zero. All of our marketing and advertising plans were out the window. Plus, we had just gone through an agonizing defeat in naming the car.

As a result of market-testing hundreds of names, our people had decided on a clear winner: "Gemini." At that time the moon rockets were called Gemini so the name was in the news every day. It had familiarity; it had G and M in it in a pleasant way. Ed Cole, however, convinced the corporate management that Chevrolet was usurping the initials GM and that we shouldn't be allowed to use the name. He lobbied to call the car "Vega."

In a heated exchange I said, "Cole, it sounds like a venereal disease!"

Ed was always a gracious winner, though. And he should have been—he won every confrontation we ever had.

The entire Vega disaster reinforced all my frustrations with the system. I didn't have the political savvy to get the right things done; I didn't belong to anyone's clique. I was the perennial outsider, a radically different man from such survivors of the GM jungle as Ed Cole.

Ed may have had his share of disasters but he understood corporate politics. He was a brilliant corporate strategist. During the well-publicized struggle between him and Bunkie Knudsen over the GM presidency, I saw one Cole strategy I'll never forget.

Cole contacted an old pal of his in Knudsen's department and dug up some obscure bit of information—as I recall, it related to the number of proving-ground drivers working on Saturday. Later, in an administration committee meeting, Cole cleverly brought up the general subject, then embarrassed Knudsen by demonstrating he knew more about Knudsen's business then he did. A cheap stunt, but it worked. I wanted to get up and explain that to Knudsen's credit he didn't concern himself with minutiae—that was why he was such a great overall strategist—but I didn't. I guess I was a little short of guts that day.

Once I understood the ploy, I saw it coming when hatchet man Kyes tried it on me. When he turned the obscure information question on me one day, I said, "If I wasted my time delving into that kind of minutiae, this division would be right back into the same kind of trouble it was when I came in." Kyes turned beet red and shut up.

I don't mean to imply that I didn't like Ed Cole. He was one of the most charming, personable, and exciting men I have ever met. Certainly the most charming, personable, and exciting man at GM. As a result he could sell any program. And he did: the Corvair, the Turboguide, the Quadrajet, the rotary engine. Every one a disastrous failure that cost GM billions of dollars. But Ed Cole, bless his heart, could overpower all of them. I recall when he was selling the rotary-engine project that cost GM $500 million. One of the top engineers who spoke to the engineering policy group—I believe it was Daryl Caris, an old pro—said if every car had a rotary engine and someone invented the reciprocating engine, it would replace all of the rotaries (Wankels) in ten years. It didn't matter. Cole sold his program. (It was cancelled virtually the day he retired, which was surprising because GM had already spent $500 million for the development work including $40 million for the licensing fees. To own the paid-up license, they would only have had to invest $10 million more—something they would not do. As a result they lost the license and all the money they had put into development.)

There were other paradoxes within General Motors besides the longevity of questionable leadership. Those of us in management were encouraged to take the opportunity to address college and university students about business, the marketplace, and the free-enterprise system. In general, such speeches were written or approved by the company. This was not a formal policy, but we all knew it was

81

expected. Since I didn't want to be a company spokesperson or apologist, I delivered my own speeches without company approval. At times this meant that I was at odds both with GM and the industry.

I felt justified in doing this, however, because the speeches produced by the Public Relations Department under Anthony DeLorenzo were often so poorly thought out as to be a detriment to the corporation. For a business that was supposed to be conscious of its image, some of the mistakes were inexcusable. Take, for example, the speech written for presentation by Chairman James Roche to automotive executives from all over the world. This occurred at the Society of Automotive Engineers (SAE) annual meeting in Detroit, an event planned around the theme the "International SAE."

When we got to the gigantic Cobo Hall banquet room, there were more than a hundred people on the dais. These were men who were the presidents or chairmen (or both) of every automotive company in the world. The American executives were greatly outnumbered by the men from Germany, Japan, England, France, Italy, and elsewhere. The public-relations department knew that this was an international event and was aware of the prestige that was associated with having the GM chairman, Jim Roche, speak to them. All of us assumed that in the spirit of friendship and cooperation, the speech would lay aside competitive differences. Since Roche undoubtedly expected the speech to fit the gathering, he did not take the time to read it ahead of time. This proved to be a major mistake.

A hush fell over the room as Jim Roche stepped to the podium, looked out on the many different faces from all over the world, smiled, and began his speech. To his horror, the words that came from his mouth were possibly the most humiliating of his career. Thanks to the GM public-relations department, he started to expound the theme "We must drive these foreign S.O.B.'s back into the ocean."

As Roche realized what he was reading, his voice got softer and softer, and the silence and humiliation became intolerable. It was a horrible insult to all of the prestigious men who had come thousands of miles to attend.

I was not cynical about the need to protect the company's image, but I differed with corporate policy in a way that eventually got me into trouble. I would not stop talking freely about whatever I felt was right or wrong about management style within the company. Sometimes this was a part of my casual conversation with fellow employees. Other times it involved such important matters as minority rights. Since it was a era when white, Anglo-Saxon Protestants from the right prep schools and colleges were considered executive material, and others, regardless of ability, were not, my decision to become involved with minority rights was an extreme embarrassment to the company.

The civil-rights movement was extremely strong during this period, and I was an ardent admirer of Dr. Martin Luther King, Jr., the man who was leading a series of nonviolent demonstrations to achieve equal rights. His goal was freedom and equality for all, regardless of race, creed, color, or economic status. His message was so basic, so undeniably correct, that I felt very strongly about him and his work. I believed then, and I believe now, that Dr. King was the greatest American of this century—he was our Gandhi. Even today, when I see the film of Dr. King delivering his famous "I have a dream" speech at the Washington Monument, my heart stops. His picture is the only non-family portrait in my library.

General Motors was still paying lip service to the minority issue, while avoiding any meaningful action in the corporation. Promotion of minorities was nonexistent, as were minority incentive or training programs. Thus, my views on minority rights were not appreciated by the management. They were further upset when I was overheard in an argument at the Bloomfield Hills Country Club.

On Saturdays I would usually work until noon and then go the club for lunch and golf. Bloomfield Hills was close to the office, had the best food in Detroit, and the golf course was nearly always deserted. They discouraged women from playing, and most of the members were elderly, so there was seldom a soul on the course. On that day I was meeting John Bugas, a vice-president at Ford. John was a nice human being, but he was totally dedicated to FBI chief J. Edgar Hoover. As a former FBI regional director, Bugas felt Hoover could do no wrong.

While we were waiting for two other guys to join us, he told me that he had just returned from Washington, D.C., and a meeting with "The Director" (that's what he always called Hoover). "The Director was telling me that he refused to shake Dr. King's hand and that Martin Luther King is stealing money from the SCLU. Not only that, but he's a sexual pervert." And then it came out that Hoover had asked Bugas to contact the Ford foundation to ask them to terminate funding to Martin Luther King, which Bugas had done.

I was outraged. I blew up. "Hoover's attacks on Dr. King are inexcusable," I said. "Instead of respecting this man's humanitarian goals and accomplishments, Hoover is trying to smear him with false stories and outrageous comments." I had even heard that Hoover had arranged to have the King of Sweden approached in an effort to keep Dr. King from being awarded the Nobel Peace Prize and that he tried to prevent the Pope from giving audience to Dr. King—actions that fortunately failed. Such disreputable efforts by the head of what should have been the nation's most respected law-enforcement agency left me absolutely livid.

Bugas was furious at what I said. Blinded by his worship of Hoover, he said I had no right to speak about him that way. His anger was intense, and we became estranged over the whole thing. The incident got quite a bit of publicity. Everything that happened at Bloomfield got publicity.

I never met Dr. King. I never talked to him. But I have been one of his greatest fans. I have read every book written about him, listened to every speech ever recorded. He was an incredible human being, the hope for our nation. Yet because some people didn't like what he was saying and doing, they wanted to malign this great man. I knew nothing of his personal life, but if you destroyed every American leader who "strayed," there wouldn't be many left in Washington or in the nation's board rooms.

Needless to say, the scene in the country club, my efforts to add minority group members to the General Motors Institute student body, and my civil-rights concerns did not sit well with top management.

Then one day I received a call from the office of Senator Ted Kennedy, asking me to meet with him and some other executives at his home to discuss civil-rights and equal-opportunity issues as they related to business. It was an excellent opportunity for GM. Or so I thought. I told my boss, Ed Rollert, that I wanted to go.

Rollert knew I felt strongly about it. He encouraged me and even suggested that I take a company plane to save time. Instead, I scheduled myself on a commercial flight that would enable me to work all day at the office and still get to Kennedy's home at the appointed time.

General Motors maintained a fleet of aircraft to shuttle executives around the country. Sometimes a private plane is cost effective and increases productivity, and this was occasionally true with GM. But usually the planes were nothing more than expensive monuments to the egos of the top executives. The flights could just as easily have been made on commercial airlines for a fraction of the cost. The expense of flying a plane is the same no matter how many passengers are on board. When you can divide the cost among many people, you can travel for relatively low fares. When a single executive is in that same plane, the cost per passenger mile obviously becomes extraordinarily high.

I routinely tried to arrange my schedule so that I could be practical and still take public transportation. If I had to get somewhere not effectively reached by commercial routes, I used our private planes, figuring I was saving the company considerable money.

Shortly before the day of the meeting with Kennedy, Rollert suddenly began hinting that it might be best if I didn't go. I told him I thought it was too late to withdraw. He didn't press me further, but again suggested that I take one of our company planes from Willow Run airport. Since I had won the major issue of being allowed to go without further interference, I agreed.

When I got to Willow Run for the flight, I was told that there was a mechanical problem with the plane and that there would be a delay. I waited while a check was made, then was told that the plane would have to be taken out of service. It was not safe to fly and could not be repaired for several hours at best.

By this time, it was too late to make one of the commercial flights, and I knew this scenario was more than coincidental. Even as we talked, I could see three or four other available General Motors planes of similar size. Naturally, I had to cancel, using the problem with the plane as an excuse. Yet I knew it was no mistake. GM didn't want me involved in civil-rights, and where they could exercise some control to stop me, they would.

Months later I did attend one of those sessions at Ted Kennedy's house. I found Kennedy to be intelligent, interesting, and genuinely concerned about the problems of the people he represented, especially the disadvantaged. He has a great heart.

Despite some of the brouhaha surrounding my personal views, Tom Murphy came to me one day in September of 1972 and told me the corporation was extremely pleased by my outstanding performance at Pontiac and in turning Chevrolet around. "We want you to head all our North American car and truck operations," he said.

At first I declined; I wanted to stay in line operations. Tom and I had a running two-week dispute. Finally, he prevailed, and I became group executive for the Car and Truck Group and moved to the Fourteenth Floor of the General Motors World Headquarters in Detroit, the youngest GM executive ever to hold such a prestigious position. Now I was responsible for five American car divisions

(Buick, Cadillac, Chevrolet, Oldsmobile, and Pontiac), the GMC Truck and Coach Division, and all Canadian truck and car operations—approximately 80 to 85 percent of all General Motors profitability. The last four or five men who had held that position had become presidents of General Motors.

On the Fourteenth Floor, the phoniness of the entire system suddenly became more apparent. I had always been uncomfortable with the sales approach used by American car manufacturers and had told my associates, "I can't keep selling the 'vastly improved' new model when I know it's a lie." Why should someone purchase a new car every thirty-six months just because a few different twists and bends in the metal altered its appearance slightly? Why should someone feel embarrassed to own an older car when the newer one exhibited no innovations that mattered? If a family was going to turn in their car on a new one, they should do so because there were improvements that mattered or because the old car was worn out. Provide better brakes, superior handling, better suspension, higher performance, better mileage, or increased safety features—*there* was reason to buy a new car. Change only the physical design, and you create a product with false value. The American auto industry had perfected waste and extravagance to a fine art.

When I reached the Fourteenth Floor, the pinnacle of executive power at GM, I was suddenly in charge of all those divisions that had been selling in ways with which I was not comfortable. Now I was no longer a lower-level critic; I was part of the decision-making process that could change or perpetuate the problems I had seen. Yet I soon discovered the severe limitations of my new position. In many ways I was in a powerful spot without power. I had to be part of the team—or else.

On the Fourteenth Floor you enjoyed what top management enjoyed. For example, take such a simple matter as personalizing an office. When I was head of Chevrolet, if I wanted to upgrade the carpeting a bit, change the furniture, decorate the walls, or otherwise make the office an enjoyable work environment that was uniquely mine, I could. The expense was relatively minor, and GM never argued about the costs for executive perks.

But on the Fourteenth Floor, personalizing my office was not acceptable. All offices were decorated the same way, in an extremely somber style, and meant to stay that way because the president, the board of directors, and the other men at the top did not value such personalization and were not about to let anyone else have what they did not value.

On the other hand, I could ride in an expensive corporate jet, have the finest liquor and food wherever I traveled, and could be met by a retinue of executives and public-relations people if I wished. On the road, I could be treated like a king, with my hotel suite quite literally stocked with all the luxuries of life if that was what I desired.

Another frustration was that once I reached the Fourteenth Floor, I was no longer the quarterback of the well-oiled Chevrolet team where my performance was measured only by the daily reports of market penetration and my division's profits. I had set new volume and profit records at Chevrolet that had not been matched (and still haven't). There I was invulnerable. But now my future depended on my charm and personality—and in both departments I was in deep trouble. While I was still a young engineer, Pete Estes had tried to induce me to take the Dale Carnegie course, "How to Win Friends and Influence People." I refused, feeling I couldn't be a phony. As one bad joke goes, "Uncouth? Who says I ain't got no couth?" In retrospect, of course, I know Estes was just trying to help me. He realized that my lack of diplomacy would ultimately hurt my career.

Through the years, I had certainly been aware of the major problems at GM, such as the Corvair debacle, the swing axle on the Tempest, and others not so obvious or serious for the buyer. I was familiar with them all. I simply accepted many of them, denouncing them privately but remaining silent in public. I limited my crusades to those I felt strongly about and felt I could change: dangerous motor mounts, inadequate braces, the break-apart cruciform frame, sharp projections on fenders and hoods.

Like most of the men and women who worked for GM, I did my job, uneasy about some decisions and taking great delight in others. No matter how radical my personal life might have seemed to management, the reality was that I was only one-tenth a rebel in a group where consensus ruled. I was part of the team, although I seldom thought of myself that way. But on the Fourteenth Floor I discovered the realities of corporate management to be both shocking and personally repellant.

For example, in 1971 we had a strike at the Norwood, Ohio, assembly plant that left hundreds of Camaros on the line in the middle of production. This was a period of tightening pollution and safety standards, and compliance was federally mandated for all 1972 cars. The government would not allow cars manufactured after September 1, 1971, to be sold without meeting the new 1972 standards. When the strike was over, the on-line cars were completed to 1971 standards but after the law had gone into effect. They could not be sold without modifications, and it was too costly to modify them.

There were only three honorable options available. We could rebuild the cars to 1972 standards regardless of the expense; we could scrap the cars and absorb the loss; or we could give them to trade and high schools offering training in car repair and maintenance so that the students could take them apart as a mechanic's training experience.

Those were the honorable alternatives. But the Fourteenth Floor had other ideas. Richard Terrell, my boss, chose to ship them out of the United States and sell them in Canada where safety and smog restrictions were not so severe. In effect, we were saying that the Canadians deserved less safety and air quality than we did. It was an insult to the people of Canada, our closest international neighbor and a continual good customer. It also was a simple way to protect our investment.

The Canadian scheme did not work. There was a leak to the Canadian public by some public-spirited citizen in the plant, and the publicity was extremely unfavorable. In the

89

end we did give the cars to auto mechanics classes in various high schools and took the tax write-offs, but in trying to dump the cars in Canada, we badly hurt our corporate image.

It was also typical of top management to avoid taking any action at all on matters of importance. Every major decision required a report within sixty to ninety days, followed by a study on the report. By the time someone got around to forcing the issue, there was a good chance that it was too late: the problem had been handled by the division concerned, in defiance of policy; or we had lost whatever value might have been gained by a faster decision; or we had been beaten to the idea by a competitor and had to play "catch-up."

Within a month on the Fourteenth Floor I was fed up with the corporate infighting. I realized I would never be happy in the headquarters environment. I wasn't a "team player." My lifestyle did not match that of the other executives, and that was offensive to them. While I was trying to decide what to do, I had several long talks with Ed Cole, who was nearing the end of his GM career. Because of the power of the corporate financial staff, Ed had been slowly but surely relegated to a purely technical role in GM, a "chief engineer president."

Ed said to me, "You and I have fought a lot, John, but I think I'm the only one here who understands you. No one will ever top the sales and profit records you set at Pontiac and Chevrolet. But you should get out of here, or you'll wind up like me—with your fangs pulled. I'll help you find a dealership, and you get out of here. Go be chairman of a growing company. If I was your age, I'd do it today."

The one problem with leaving GM was the way bonuses were paid. Each new position had given me substantial increases in earnings through bonuses. These bonuses, however, were paid over a five-year period, 20 percent a year. If I wanted to leave early, I either had to forfeit the bonus or resign to take a dealership that would allow me to earn out that bonus while no longer working in GM management. Historically, a Cadillac dealership was a license to make a lot of money; the dealers generally became millionaires. When I was informed that a Cadillac dealership in Lighthouse Point, Florida, would be mine if I wanted it, I suddenly had a way out.

On April 2, 1973, at age forty-eight, I placed my resignation before General Motors Chairman of the Board, Richard C. Gerstenberg.

Instead of leaving General Motors and becoming a car dealer, I made the transition by becoming the head of the National Alliance of Businessmen (NAB), an organization GM supported to the level of paying my salary but no bonus while I worked for that group. This would allow time for my dealership to be built, and it was a nice move on the part of GM.

The National Alliance of Businessmen was a Washington, D.C.–based organization founded by Lyndon Johnson and Henry Ford to provide employment opportunities to Americans in need. As president of the group, my job was to convince business leaders to hire and train disadvantaged workers, needy young people, and ex-offenders. I had dozens of meetings in every major American city with the chairman or president of most of America's major corporations. (I think they saw me because I was a curiosity.) I asked them to go back and ask their personnel managers about minority and disadvantaged employment. That was all it took. When the boss got interested in an area, the job got done.

Unfortunately, my personal life was not as happy as my professional one. Cristina hated Washington and the intellectual society and social life there, where power politics determines who is invited where. She returned to Detroit with Zachary, and I ended up commuting on weekends, a situation I found tiring and frustrating. Still, that year proved a valuable one for my personal growth.

After I had completed my work with the NAB, I was approached by Patrick Wright, formerly a *Business Week* reporter, who asked if I would consider doing a book on my experiences at General Motors. After I had dictated my recollections, he would edit the tapes into a book. I had no idea if the book would be successful, but I agreed to do it, and Wright and I signed a contract stating that we would make an even split of the profits.

The relationship seemed a good one, though I had a feeling that Wright had some bias against General Motors, which occasionally crept into the tone of his editing. Perhaps 5 percent of the book seemed to reflect this bias, a fact that I asked to have changed. In fact, I rewrote those sections several times, attempting to show that, no matter what my negative feelings, everything I knew about automotive engineering, business management, and the entire corporate world came from GM. Even my lifestyle, which was one of great luxury, came from the tremendous income I had received from GM. I wanted such facts to be made clear in the book so that people would understand the good with the bad.

Wright published the book, *On a Clear Day You Can See General Motors,* but the tone still wasn't quite what I had hoped. When Wright appeared on radio and television talk shows, he frequently mentioned our split and the fact that he was keeping half the money for me. He said it was just waiting for me to ask for it. But when I requested my share, he told me to drop dead. My understanding is that the money earned from the project eventually amounted to $1,650,000 in addition to the money he saved when I had to defend myself against a libel suit brought about because he had misquoted me in part of the book. Even worse, though the book was written in the first person and he worked from my tapes, he copyrighted the project in his own name.

I thought about suing Wright for my share of the money, but as I have already mentioned, I have tended to avoid confrontations. I simply walk away from a bad situation, recognizing that I must never again deal with that person.

Finally it was over. Although I had severed my connection with a company I had served for eighteen years, I was well-to-do, married to an attractive and vital woman, and young enough to pursue any business venture I desired. Many firms wanted to hire me as chairman or president or member of the board. Others wanted me as a consultant. I could have lived an easy, leisurely, high-paid life. Instead, I made another choice. I decided to design and build my own car, to fulfill a dream I had been harboring for many years.

DREAMS

9

I had started as an engineer at General Motors. But the higher I rose on the corporate ladder, the further I was from the engineering I loved. Creative engineering was important to me and I felt a great void without it. It made me understand why Ed Cole never quit dabbling in engineering.

When I first entered the industry, there were people who could design an entire engine—indeed, an entire automobile. By the time I left GM, the industry was filled with specialists. One engineer might be limited to a fuel system, another to connecting rods and pistons. The days when one person could handle everything on a design project were coming to an end. Only the small entrepreneurs were still creating engines, designing cars, and generally doing the type of individual craftsmanship I loved and admired. Only in the small specialist companies could a person creatively stretch and grow, and I wanted to be part of such an enterprise. I wanted to create, build, and sell a car of my own design.

I had always had fantasies about what I would do if I could start my own company to design and build my ideal personal car. Over the years I had sketched ideas on paper, then discarded them. I had dreamed of innovations that would improve performance and handling, others that would affect safety, and still others that would create public demand for the vehicle. Yet I never had the time, the money, or the opportunity to do anything other than dream. Suddenly there was nothing stopping me from becoming a glorified backyard tinkerer.

There is no way the individual entrepreneur can ever compete with the major car companies of the world. General Motors, Ford, Chrysler, Toyota, Nissan, Honda, Volkswagen, and the other international giants have an established range of products, encompassing everything from subcompacts to luxury vehicles. Attempting to create a line, establish a dealer network, advertise effectively, and survive for several years until the public became aware of and accepted the product could take billions of dollars, a multinational organization custom designed to your needs, and could include a risk so great that no one in their right mind would consider it. On the other hand, there was one type of car that could be created as part of what would be little more than a backyard industry, and it could be sold through existing dealers of other lines. This was the two-passenger sports car, the type of car routinely created by designers seeking to sell to only the tiniest fraction of a very large market. And this was the type of car I had always wanted to build.

My original idea was to design a car that would be fun to drive, safe to operate, and long lasting. The owner would sell it because he was tired of it, not because it had rusted away. A rust-free car is not as impossible as some people think. The American automobile industry has long been accused of what was once called "planned obsolescence." This means that each car is designed to be replaced in a few years with a newer model. In areas where salt is used to remove ice from the roads in winter, cars almost rust away before your eyes. Road salt costs American car owners billions each year. Rust spots on an otherwise usable car drastically lower the resale value and make "junkers" of cars that could have been serviceable for many years. Such deterioration can also be dangerous. I remember a time when I was young and a gang of us were going somewhere in somebody's "old clunker." I was sitting in the back seat with two other boys. Suddenly, we hit a bump, and the entire rusted-out rear floor fell out of the car. We were lucky we weren't seriously injured or killed.

The idea of a lifetime car is not dramatically new. The Rolls Royce is an example of a car that can serve its owner for many years. It is not at all unusual to see a well-maintained 1936 Rolls Royce still in service today. The body looks almost as new as when it was first purchased, and the resale value of the car has risen to three or four times what the original owner paid, due to inflation. The Rolls is a car that can be used daily and not just sit in a temperature-controlled garage as a collector's item. It remains a working car, just as it was intended to be when it was first constructed. But even with the Rolls, it is the affluent owner's loving maintenance that preserves the car, not the materials themselves.

Given the correct materials, I was certain that I could create a moderately priced, long-lasting car. One such material was brushed stainless steel; it is both durable and beautiful.

In addition to durability, I was concerned with safety. Air bags were largely being resisted by the American automobile industry, which had reluctantly adopted shoulder harnesses. The advantage of air bags is that they gently arrest the forward movement of the occupants in a crash, even when the passengers are not wearing restraints. They are not overly expensive to add, can be used for both driver and passengers, and have proven to be the most effective safety device available for front-end crashes. I was pleased to see Mercedes offer air bags in their 1984 models; it is typical of their courage and leadership.

Oddly enough, General Motors had first demonstrated the air bag thirty years ago, long before anyone else in the auto industry thought of it. When I was made Director of Advanced Engineering for Pontiac back in 1956, I was invited to GM's research division, along with all the other engineers, where we were shown various products the division had been developing. One of those products was the air bag. A brilliant young engineer named Bill King showed us a film of a crash test in which a dummy was protected by the air bag. In fact, the high-speed filming revealed that it was the perfect safety device, and there was talk of including the air bags in the seats of all airplanes to eliminate or reduce injuries during crash landings. But every time I tried to get the company to let me do development work on the air bag at Pontiac or farm it out to the University of Michigan, they were against it. Years later when I requested the files on the test results to make a point with Tom Murphy, I found those records had been destroyed.

A third area of importance to me was door design. Sports cars are notoriously difficult to enter, especially for someone like me—I am six-foot-four and have long legs. Usually the doors are low, the leg room limited, and you find that you enter by bumping your head, then drive by wrapping your knees around the steering wheel. Conventional doors also require fairly ample room to be opened. So if you have to park twelve inches from the car next to you at the mall and you have a conventional door approximately eight inches thick, you will have four inches of space to maneuver yourself from the car—an impossible squeeze!

The answer to the problem was a design that had been used by Mercedes Benz in the past on the legendary 300 SL sports coupe: a gull-wing design whose operation and appearance give the undeniable impression of a futuristic aircraft. This type of door lifts upward in a very short sideward space. You can completely open the door in approximately twelve inches of side room, and have then a full opening through which to enter the car. The gull-wing door also provides the option of parking in less space than would otherwise be possible, and is even more efficient in a home garage. Its disadvantage is that it is very expensive since it must be counterbalanced against gravity.

A final concept that interested me was a new type of plastic that could be made into elastomeric panels that would be strong, safe, and cost efficient. These panels would be lightweight, could absorb great shock in an accident, and would be easily replaceable when necessary. They could also ultimately be produced so inexpensively that it was conceivable to design a car that would be dent-proof, be at least as crash-safe as steel, and be so simply constructed that the panels could be replaced by the owner. By changing all the panels of the car, the owner could even change its color.

It is fair to say that many people were involved in the design of the DeLorean Motor Car. But it all began with sketches I had made through the years and my early focus on leg and comfort room for tall drivers, a stainless steel body, gull-wing doors, and mid-engine placement. These features and the incredible Giorgetto Giugiaro's styling eventually were incorporated into the final car by Colin Chapman, in my opinion the best automotive engineer the industry has produced.

All these plans and ideas kept racing through my mind as I left GM. Was it possible to build my dream car? I talked with friends at GM about what I had in mind, and a few of them warned me I would never succeed. "You have too many enemies here, John," one said, repeating the same tune I heard from several others. "There are more men here who would be happy to try to ruin you than who would help you succeed."

"Why should they bother?" I asked. "No matter how successful we were, we'd never be more than a gnat on GM's not inconsiderable posterior."

"That won't matter to them. They will not want to see you build a successful business of any kind—but cars are their bailiwick. They'd do anything they could to ruin you.

101

Not at the start. That would be too obvious. But a year or two down the line. They've got some big screws to turn when they want to."

I did not take these warnings seriously. Of course, I knew it was possible. I was the boy who had stood behind my clench-fisted father in our house on Marx Street and watched Harry Bennett's goon squads search for an excuse to fire my father. I had seen GM attempt to destroy consumer-advocate Ralph Nader because he dared to criticize the Corvair, even though the engineers within GM had been warning that the design was dangerous well before the Corvair was put into production. GM retained retired FBI agents in a misguided effort to prove that Nader was gay— the ultimate indictment in the eyes of GM management and Hoover's FBI. (Little did I know that GM would soon generate a false report that I was having homosexual relations with one of our best GM dealers, or that history would strongly suggest that Hoover himself was homosexual.) Yet I did not take the warnings seriously. I knew I would not be stealing their thunder, and I was certain that no one would care about John DeLorean after I left the company. Apparently I was wrong, though I had no foreboding at the time.

While I had never worried about money before, I was now aware that I needed to do something to improve my finances before I began "playing" with my own car design. As a result, when I finished my NAB assignment, a year after leaving GM, I became a consultant for Ryder, Allstate Insurance, Renault, W. R. Grace, Piper Aircraft, and other firms. In my first two years as a consultant, between my various activities I was able to earn a total of $5 million.

As a consultant, I was able to make significant contributions to several major companies. For example, when I became a consultant for Ryder, I realized many of their truck leases included fixed fuel costs. When the price of gasoline and diesel fuel skyrocketed, Ryder had to absorb the difference. In addition, there were no escalation clauses for differences in interest rates, and when rates rose, Ryder again was absorbing the loss. It was easy to see that all you had to do was survive until existing leases expired and then write new ones that were either "dry" (without fuel) or with escalating clauses for fuel and interest rates. I knew that the future stock options I could get would be worth millions.

To make matters even worse, loan covenants required Ryder to maintain certain financial ratios, something the company was unable to do. To raise cash, I helped sell some side businesses in which Ryder had invested in more lavish times. For example, they had purchased a small oil refinery in Louisiana in the belief that refining their own crude oil would cut their costs. What they had failed to realize was that the cost and source of crude was the problem—not refining it. At the eleventh hour I was able to sell the refinery to the Hunts who owned substantial oil production nearby. For them the refinery made good sense. For Ryder it was a disaster.

I managed to save the company and, while doing so, to recognize that I had no interest in doing this type of work for the rest of my life. At one point I seriously considered either staying in consulting or taking a job as head of a major business such as Ryder. There is excitement and challenge in entering a company whose profits are going downhill and helping to turn them around. Certainly Lee Iacocca and Stan Seigleoff will go down in history as the great managers of the eighties as a result of their turnarounds of Chrysler and Wickes. Instead, I decided to build my own car.

As I began to seriously plan the DeLorean Motor Car, the magnitude of the undertaking meant that I had to hire others to do much of the work. I wanted to have the top people in the industry on my side; I wanted to hire the best. Unfortunately, when you have limited money, no established business, and no predictable future in an industry as unpredictable as the automobile field, you enter the employment game at a disadvantage. Top men of proven competence were earning as much as $1 million a year in salary and bonuses with the major automobile companies, and their bonuses were tied in with their staying a certain number of years. Many had clauses forcing them to forfeit their bonuses if they went to work for another car company. They had too much to lose to want to come to work for me.

The answer, for me, was to hire men I knew to be competent but who had not risen high enough to be seduced by the corporation. What I failed to realize was that, in some cases, these men had not been promoted faster or higher because they had severe problems that affected their ability to perform on the job. For example, I hired an articulate, extremely competent design engineer who had been dismissed by General Motors styling. I had seen some of his work while he was with the company and thought it was excellent. I didn't know why he was let go, but assumed that he had probably had a confrontation with someone on the Fourteenth Floor. In reality, the man was mentally unstable, a brilliant worker when he was in control, and seriously depressed at other times. Eventually, his wife found him sitting in his car in the garage, the doors and windows closed, the car exhaust slowly asphyxiating him. His suicide attempt depressed all of us. Despite the tremendous mental deterioration caused by the carbon monoxide, I kept him on the payroll and tried to help him, but his presence was a mistake. Later he was to make unfair and uncomplimentary remarks about me.

One man was an alcoholic who had a good financial mind before noon but drank his lunch and was worthless the rest of the day. He later had a nervous breakdown when he saw how far behind our bills were. Again, we kept him on the payroll. Another man, a top executive in our North American operations, effectively cheated the company out of fairly sizable sums of money.

This is not to say that I blame the staff I hired for the problems that eventually plagued my company. On the contrary, we had some excellent people who had never before been given the opportunity to show their skills, and they performed honestly and brilliantly. Had I been able to obtain more capital at the start, and had I had the courage to terminate the employment of those people who were not doing their jobs, I would have created fewer problems for myself.

Despite personnel limitations, the company slowly began to grow. The first step was the establishment of my consulting company, the John Z. DeLorean Corporation (JZDC), in January of 1974. A little over a year later, in April 1975, we set up a subsidiary, Composite Technology Corporation (CTC). This was a business whose sole function was to develop applications for new construction materials, most specifically the Elastic Reservoir Molding process that I had licensed from Royal Dutch Shell in the Netherlands, Dow Chemical, and Freeman Chemical. This was a process for making precise composites by sandwiching foam between sheets of fiberglass, one of the new construction techniques I was considering for my car. (Today, W. R. Grace, who bought this product out of DMC's bankruptcy, is making over $50 million a year and expects this to multiply very rapidly. Its success proves we were right; we just didn't survive long enough to fully develop and test the process.)

In October of 1975 I established the DeLorean Motor Company (DMC), followed by the DeLorean Manufacturing Company, which was responsible for the production of my new cars. Other companies were established as well, a situation that may seem somewhat confusing. Actually, what I was doing was standard business practice and was meant to protect the investors as fully as possible.

When a corporation is created in the United States, it must state its purpose for existing. All its legal responsibilities and obligations will be determined by that corporate statement of purpose. For example, suppose I established a corporation whose business was to design cars, build cars, sell cars, make tires, and invent products for use in automobiles. Now suppose that the research section was extremely successful in creating new products, which were worth $1 million this year and, predictably, $100 million in five years. But then the portion of the corporation that was building cars discovered that no one wanted their products. All the dealers refused them, and they had a loss of $7 million. In addition, the tire division made a mistake in the rubber formula and the first 400,000 tires they built fell apart after being driven only 1,000 miles despite a money-back guarantee paying for each tire if it did not last at least 40,000 miles. Again there would be a loss of millions of dollars.

With a single corporation handling many different projects, all losses are combined, weighed against the profits of whatever division is successful, and the bottom line proves the fate of the business. In the example I just provided, the losses would be so great that the entire company would be bankrupt, despite the fact that the research division was showing such spectacular potential. Thus, a company might fail simply because it was trying to serve too many different purposes.

By comparison, many businesses form what are known as umbrella corporations. They start with one corporation that is essentially an empty holding company, usually consisting of just two or three people. This is the "umbrella" for other corporations created to handle individual functions.

I wanted a corporation involved with research and development so that any products with broader applications than just my car could be sold wherever such a sale would be appropriate. If the car failed I might still have a separate, though related corporation that could make money for the investors. At the same time, if the research and development company was not successful, it could not hinder the sales in the car activity. Each business was unique, with its own functions, yet meant to be used in tandem, much like the pieces of a jigsaw puzzle. There was nothing sinister about such business decisions; many major corporations are subdivided in much the same manner.

A decision that eventually proved controversial was the matter of our renting rather luxurious office space at 280 Park Avenue in New York for our U.S. headquarters. Many people thought this seemed an extremely high-rent district. But no one realized that at the time we made our arrangements for the space, which included half of the forty-third floor, we paid $17 per foot; this was among the cheapest real estate in midtown Manhattan, and we got the almost new furnishings for less than 20 percent of their replacement cost. I wanted it because it gave us a prominent identification in the Banker's Trust Building and was a good "storefront" from which to sell our company. In addition, the quality of the interior fittings as well as the purity of the overall design of the space were in complete accord with the direction I hoped my new company would follow.

The space we rented was a portion of a massive location once rented by the Xerox Corporation. The company had an extremely long lease that had been negotiated during a period when real-estate prices were depressed in Manhattan. At the time Xerox signed the lease, the vacancy rate in offices was high, and entire buildings were unoccupied. Charges were extremely low to get renters to fill the buildings.

Under their existing lease, if Xerox moved out and sublet any portion of the space, they could charge either what they had been paying or the current rate, assuming that the current rate was higher. But if Xerox sublet for a higher rent than they had been paying, the difference would revert to the landlord. Xerox saw no sense in raising the rent for a sublet tenant simply to benefit the landlord, particularly if it would prove prohibitive and make it impossible to sublet the space that was costing them money if it were empty. With minimal initial outlay, DMC was able to use, for its own public relations, the hundreds of thousands of dollars Xerox had lavished on the space.

So we were able to rent luxury space at a highly desirable address for a cost per square foot that was identical to what we would have had to pay in a low-rent district. Unfortunately, our critics never bothered to check the full story before accusing us of squandering investment money on opulent surroundings—not the worst lie told about us. Which brings us to another problem I was facing.

It was essential to be careful about our cash flow during

the development of the company. I had to be responsible to both the investors and the real needs of the business, but I also had to maintain an image of success. We had initiated a project that everyone said could never succeed. We needed to look successful if we were to attract the investment we needed. I was told a story once about Aristotle Onassis before he made it big. When he had only $2 in his pocket he would stand at the bar in the 21 Club and nurse one drink for hours. He looked fit and tanned, but no one knew his tan came from a sun lamp in his tiny room. He looked successful and became successful as a result.

Much has been said, pro and con, about the matter of image making. It has been the subject of numerous books, including J. B. Priestly's marvelous satire *The Image Men* on the business of "the selection, creation, and projection of suitable and helpful images." I have already alluded to the fact that I have been both victim and player in this game. But the reality of American business life is that everyone wants to be part of a winning company. If you want a perfect illustration of this, you only have to watch Wall Street. I knew that I had to convince the people I needed that they would be working with a winner—someone who could make them money.

Of course, part of my image of success could be built on my recent history with General Motors. The corporate offices in Manhattan were another part of the image. If visitors did not know about the low rent I was paying (and I never mentioned the fortunate arrangement that made the location affordable), they would assume that only an extremely successful company could be headquartered there. Everyone who came was impressed, and those whose help I sought, both dealers and investors, were comfortable with the location.

The actual start of DMC involved a small nucleus of people who worked with me on establishing a prototype vehicle. At one point we were working with Allstate Insurance Company on a cost-effectiveness study of air bags, which we eventually presented to the Department of Transportation. I warned Allstate that the minute GM found I was doing an air-bag study they would terminate my unearned bonus, some $600,000. Allstate finally agreed to sponsor $600,000 of development work on our first prototype as a safety car, the same amount I would lose if my bonus was cancelled. True to my expectations, GM immediately cancelled my unearned bonus. They hated air bags—and maybe me.

We set about to design a vehicle with better crash protection for the occupants; economical operation, maintenance, and repair; advanced anti-theft features; superior braking; and less risk of damage from low-speed problems such as occur when one car backs into another in a parking lot. We hoped that all this would lower insurance-company costs and benefit both the company and the consumer.

What I did not realize was that when you create something new, that creation eventually keeps developing beyond your expectations. At first I thought I would invest a couple of hundred thousand dollars and see what developed. Then the car began to take on a life of its own. Parts had to be purchased, and the car adapted to the best of what was available. For example, if I wanted to tool a unique front suspension ball joint, the cost would be absolutely prohibitive. In a company like General Motors this would not be a major matter of concern because they could amortize the expense over millions of units. And even with the existing equipment, there are constant modifications to adapt the body design to what is available. But when you are making your own, you realize that you can only adapt existing equipment to what you are creating or the cost becomes astronomical. In truth, many companies started this way. Early Porsches used VW components; Volvo and SAAB used other companies' engines and components extensively until they became large enough to develop their own.

For the initial design work, I turned to one of the finest designers in the world, Giorgetto Giugiaro of Ital Design in

109

Turin, Italy. Giugiaro's creations are well known to all car enthusiasts. He is a master of style and engineering and is responsible for creating such exotic designs as Alfa Romeo's Guilia Sprint GT and Alfeta GT, the Isuzu Impulse, Maserati's Ghibli and Bora, the Fiat Dino Coupe, and Volkswagen's Dasher, Scirocco, and Rabbit. He has more cars in production than any other five designers in the world. I consider Giugiaro and Tony Lupine of Porsche to be the greatest automobile designers in the world.

I presented Giugiaro with a set of statistics. My car had to meet all United States safety standards; it had to be capable of mass production versus limited hand tooling; it had to have a drag coefficient of around 0.33 for performance; it was to have a one-piece, elastomeric bumper fit flush with the body yet able to compress eight inches in the event of an accident; it was to be designed to resist minor dents and scrapes for the entire body; and there would be gull-wing doors and numerous other features. I also wanted to maintain specific internal measurements to insure adequate leg and head room for an extremely tall driver.

While Giugiaro was working on the design, Bill Collins, our design engineer, hired Michael Pocobello, a former Chevrolet engineer who had founded Triad, a private engineering firm that was experimenting with a drive train and other features that might be incorporated in our car. To do this, Bill bought a used Fiat X1/9 and modified it in ways the former owner would have been shocked to see. The four-cylinder engine was removed and replaced by a Ford V-six. A special drive train was connected to a five-speed Borg Warner gear box, and other modifications were made. The car provided extremely high performance, but we discovered the modifications were not appropriate. There was too much strain on the gear synchronizers, and the transfer case eventually blew apart. But we did sort out a lot of ideas with this car.

All this experimenting cost money, of course; the knowledge had a price tag, and a steep one. Each week drained away thousands of dollars, but the car was taking shape. I was too absorbed with its development to ever take stock of the business of building the car. Had I just stopped at some point and analyzed how much money was coming into the company, how much was being spent, and whether there might be a point when restructuring was sensible, I would have had fewer problems.

I also quickly learned that my expertise in business management came from working within an existing company with all the financial management and controls in place. I knew absolutely nothing about obtaining venture capital. To me, all money had to come from individual investors as it was needed. I did not realize that my methods were not maximizing our potential.

Most of the $5 million I had brought in through consulting and other activities had been spent by the time we finished our second prototype. At that point we were able to put together a limited partnership to help pay for the ongoing development work, and I was able to raise $3.5 million. Had I known more about investment banking, I would have completed the entire financial package at that time.

One of our fund-raising ideas involved a program that was fairly new to the tax laws. It was the creation of a Research and Development (R & D) partnership. This limited partnership allowed investors to take a tax deduction during the period when the money was being used for research and development and also allowed them to benefit if everything worked. They could receive stock or some type of royalty arrangement, depending upon what was practical. Thirty-five wealthy partners placed $100,000 each into the R & D concept. If the company were successful, they would be traded preferred stock for their interest on a tax-free exchange basis. If everything had gone as hoped and the public offering of DeLorean Motor stock had been completed, the initial partners in the R & D concept would have netted $600,000 or $700,000 in capital gains for their initial investment. It was an idea designed to ensure that the earliest risk takers were rewarded for their help. A number of these

111

limited partners contributed all or part of their interest to charitable institutions while our company was still viable. They did well with their investments, showing a substantial tax profit.

With these investors helping to finance the preliminary research, I began my search for the balance of the funds required.

Although my first love was cars, my business became raising money. No matter how impossible my car project became, I did not stop and analyze if there was going to be a point where it was no longer cost effective to continue. I always thought, with a little more money, a little more time, everything would work out.

10

"Why in the world did you build your plant in Northern Ireland of all places? You must be insane!" I can't count the number of times I heard that question or a variation of it. We originally wanted to build within the continental United States. We were contacted by and hired an expert on government grants and loans who told us that if we would locate in certain economically depressed areas, we could obtain government-backed loans totalling $40 million. This would involve a loan guarantee of $20 million from the Economic Development Administration (EDA), available in their designated areas, and additional loan guarantees of up to $20 million from the Farmer's Home Administration (FHA) in the areas they designated. Fortunately, there were certain areas that were designated by both agencies, permitting a total of $40 million. This then became our base rate in considering all other possibilities.

Most governments, at every level, have programs designed to attract new businesses. They recognize that bringing industry to certain areas makes good sense, because the increase in employment can add to the tax base, improve prosperity, and improve the community over the long term.

Among many others, we spoke to First Boston, the investment bankers, about funding. They sent to us a man named Montilla who represented the Securities Corporation of Puerto Rico, a firm in which First Boston was a part owner. He said Puerto Rico was interested in my company because jobs were few and poverty was extensive. By the same token, Puerto Rico was a designated area of both the FHA and the EDA, so that the whole $40 million maximum was potentially available.

The Securities Corporation of Puerto Rico then approached us with what seemed to be a fine financial package: For the first ten years, corporate income is not taxed in Puerto Rico. The tax savings would be enough to compensate for any loan costs if the company were lucky enough to grow at the anticipated rate. This option made Puerto Rico look very attractive, so we asked the Securities Corporation to begin putting together more concrete arrangements, and we began a careful study of the pros and cons.

There were certainly negative considerations. For one thing, the people of Puerto Rico had no existing automotive skills to offer us; there was no history of automotive or mechanical manufacturing in the area. In fact, there was no tradition of building anything. There were some minor assembly operations, but nothing like we were planning to do. What the area offered was a marvelous climate and a labor force willing to work for modest wages because the alternative was no wages. We knew from the start that the best deals were likely to come from areas where we would have to train all the assembly-line personnel and supervisors. Yet we also believed that, with training, we could have an effective work force of men and women who really wanted to work. So we were not too concerned that heavy manufacturing was not native to the area.

There was one major advantage: because Puerto Rico was part of the United States, we could qualify for the loans we needed from the U.S. government as well as from Puerto Rico. And there was no import duty.

My excitement over the Puerto Rican connection increased when we learned that they would give us a hundred acres of land on the northwest corner of the island that had been part of Ramey Air Force Base during World War II. At the time, the federal government had appropriated the land and removed the farmers who owned it. After the war, the land was given to the government of Puerto Rico by the Federal Aviation Agency (FAA).

But suddenly we were informed that there was a problem. The FAA had not had a clear title to the land. Many small farmers still had claims on the land. Because there was no clear title, the Puerto Rican Government Development Bank would not lend money (some $11 million) or be the mortgage holder on our plant and equipment. We asked the governor of Puerto Rico to use the right of eminent domain to clear the title, but he was concerned that he might be criticized for hurting the small farmers by this action. It was a dilemma we were not able to solve.

Next, we found that the interest on the loans the U.S. government guaranteed would be too high. We would be paying approximately 3 percent more than the market at that time. Later we learned that there was a hidden kickback in the form of a $1.1 million "finder's fee" for the Securities Corporation from the note buyers, General Electric Credit. This was an alarming development.

Then we discovered that to do business in Puerto Rico, we had to work through a system of "special payments." First, we had to pay a local engineer to approve the plans we were already having prepared by a highly reputable Detroit firm, which was familiar with automobile manufacturing needs. The payment would be 1 percent of the cost of constructing a $40 million plant, or $400,000. The engineer had no background in automobile manufacturing and was not capable of evaluating the plans. Next we were informed that

115

the notary public we had to use would receive 1 percent of the face value of the agreement. This meant that another $400,000 would go out for meaningless involvement by local people.

I told the governor, "This is ridiculous. My secretary is a notary. She charges a dollar to notarize a document—and if you smile, it's free!"

Obviously, the money we would be generating in jobs, payroll, and the like was not going to keep everyone happy. It was a shocking situation and a financially impractical one.

Our total inability to break the land-title logjam, coupled with these pyramiding "special payments," drove us away from Puerto Rico. We began to look elsewhere, a fact that became public knowledge when Detroit's fine mayor, Coleman Young, asked us to consider the Detroit riverfront. Unfortunately, because of the way federal loan applications had been established, it was not possible within the federal bureaucracy to quickly shift the arrangements from Puerto Rico to some other part of the United States.

While we were negotiating with Mayor Young's people, a representative from the Republic of Ireland Development Agency (IDA) heard about our situation on his car radio. He stopped the car at the nearest phone booth and called our office to asked if we would be interested in locating in his country. I think he first spoke to Bill Collins, our engineer. Bill didn't quite take him seriously but, in case he was for real, invited him to our offices.

In New York we met with IDA director Seamus Cashman, the finest, most professional industrial-development executive we had ever met. He said, "Unlike Puerto Rico, we speak English in Ireland. We have similar tax incentives, and a work force with automotive skills." He soon developed a proposal, and we flew to Dublin to see about closing a deal.

The IDA proposed that we consider the abandoned Ferenka Cable Plant in Limerick, about 250,000 square feet. We hired Booz, Allen and Hamilton to review the potential of the area and other engineers to look over the plant. The plant would require extensive modification and a new roof, certainly surmountable problems. But as Booz, Allen and Hamilton discovered, the labor force was another matter. Apparently, the Ferenka plant manager had been an impossible tyrant, and the plant had closed because of poor labor relations, culminating in the plant manager being kidnapped for an extended period. Our consultants were concerned whether the relationship with labor could ever be patched up. At the same time, Arthur Andersen, our auditors in Dublin, got into an argument with the government over interest rates. Things were deteriorating rapidly.

About that time, John Plaxton, our investment banker and a Wood Gundy representative, got a call from the Northern Ireland Development Agency (NIDA). Basically, NIDA said they would beat by a mile any deal the Republic offered. Plaxton met with the NIDA representatives and called me. "They'll give us anything we want," he told me with great excitement.

By then it was clear we were not going to make any deal in the Republic, so I said, "Let's go meet 'em."

Plaxton's boss, Edmund King, president of Wood Gundy in New York, became very upset. "We don't even open mail from Belfast," he said. "We send it out to have it X-rayed for letter bombs first. You can't go there. It's too dangerous."

"It's there or nowhere," I said. "We can't survive long enough to try to set up another arrangement. We're deeply in debt and totally out of money."

I did not realize that these few fateful words would soon involve me in a six-hundred-year-old-war that would make me as sure a casualty as martyr Bobby Sands.

So we went to Belfast—I, with a show of confidence; and the rest of my people thinking it was probably better to be dead economically in the U.S. than just plain dead in Belfast.

11

It is difficult to describe the mixed emotions I experienced on my first visit to Northern Ireland and West Belfast.

The first thing you notice is the security. It is easier to reach the president of the United States than it is to get through a hotel lobby in Belfast. The Europa Hotel, where we stayed during the negotiations, had been bombed twenty-eight times. Every person who checked in went through a metal detector and a full body search, and all luggage was unpacked and searched down to the last sock.

In a land torn by civil and social strife, with some of the people fighting for independence from England and others engaged in hostilities between the Catholics and the Protestants, terrorism is rampant. Everyone is suspected of carrying a weapon, bomb, or incendiary device. Everywhere there are highway and sidewalk checkpoints, military half-tracks and bulletproof Land Rovers, metal detectors, barbed-wire barriers, and dogs trained to detect explosives. Obviously, when there is a bomb threat in Belfast, you believe it.

Next, you notice the children. The Irish children are easily the most beautiful to be found anywhere in the world. They are often redheaded, with freckles adorning their faces like islands dotting a smooth sea. They laugh easily, approach strangers shyly, yet have an openness and peace that seems to have survived even the most brutal events that so many of them have witnessed. Their resiliency and courage are the hope of the future for Ireland.

And finally, there are the workers. The people I met in Northern Ireland were hard working, loving, and skilled. Their love of life—even a difficult life—was a thing of great wonder and inspiration to me.

In *A Moon for the Misbegotten*, Eugene O'Neill eloquently expressed the courage of the Irish in the face of overwhelming hardship. As one of his characters, an Irish immigrant farmer, says: "If cows could eat [the rocks] this place would make a grand dairy farm. You ought to pay me, instead, for occupying this rockpile, miscalled a farm. But I have fine reports to give you of a promising harvest. The milkweed and thistles is in thriving condition, and I never saw the poison ivy so bounteous and beautiful."

All my life I have tried to help the oppressed and disadvantaged, but nowhere have I seen a human-rights situation more tragic than the treatment of the Catholics in Northern Ireland. The Catholics are denied jobs, education for their children, and in many instances basic human dignity. I am a totally nonviolent person. I have never hurt anyone physically, nor could I. Yet I can certainly understand these stalwart people as they struggle for independence, and I honestly don't see how their bid for freedom, their fight for human rights, is any different from our American forefathers who kicked the tea into Boston Harbor.

My staff people and I set about trying to learn more about the work history of West Belfast. Everywhere we looked, we saw burned-out and bombed-out stores and boarded-up businesses. We saw hunger, fear, and a generation with little to expect except "the dole," the welfare system that allows families to survive.

At the same time, we learned that these were a fiercely proud people with a history of great manufacturing skills. They were shipbuilders and master craftsmen who had been forced from the jobs they loved and did so well because of the lack of demand for their services, brought on by the Japanese and Korean shipyards' very low prices. They knew nothing of cars, but they understood the pride that comes from aspiring to master your craft. Given the opportunity, they were people who could not only do the work we desired, but could also bring with them a heritage of craftsmanship that would ultimately make for a superior product.

In hindsight, I can say that going to Northern Ireland was a mistake, though not because of the people. For them, we represented hope. Hope for a renewed chance at self-respect through meaningful work with a future. Hope for a payroll, without regard for religious or political affiliations, that could help clothe and feed their children and create a demand for other businesses. The people of Belfast wanted us to succeed and worked hard toward that end. If it had not been for the people we found there, we would have had far greater problems than we did.

In searching for a location for our manufacturing plant, we explored several possible sites. The best was down in the shipyards. There was a lot of vacant space there, and the location would make the inbound shipment of components and outbound shipment of cars a relatively simple matter. Unfortunately, the Labor government wouldn't hear of it. They wanted us in war-torn West Belfast—nowhere else.

Eventually, we settled on a location that was physically less than perfect but, we were told, ideal for the community. It was a cow pasture in Dunmurry, where, when I first saw the land, cows were still grazing. But it was part of the support arrangement the government provided us, making it a take-it-or-leave-it situation. It was located exactly between Protestant and Catholic sections so that it was, in effect, neutral territory for everyone. Catholic and Protestant workers could walk to work there.

But while the local administrators wanted us, no one else was pleased with the prospect of our succeeding. We represented a threat and an embarrassment to too many people. Most obvious, of course, was the British Conservative party. To them, Northern Ireland meant people in a constant state of revolt against the Crown. An independent company like ours, bringing jobs and prosperity to Northern Ireland, could make the people feel even more independent and further question the need for British rule.

Our company had been supported by the Labor Party. If we succeeded, the Conservatives would have one less political issue. Our failure would help the Conservatives, a fact which made us vulnerable to individuals struggling to obtain power, even at the cost of the Irish people.

Also, we hired in a manner that insured an even distribution of both Catholics and Protestants throughout all levels of labor and management, an action which proved that the people could work together and leave their intense differences outside. This displeased the extremists, but showed there might be hope for a united people, if only in the work place.

We were also too small to make the type of deals that could have brought us what amounts to protection through selective business arrangements. I see most of this with hindsight, of course. At the time, I was just anxious to get any deal done to begin manufacturing. Besides, there were plenty of immediate problems that took my time and concern.

The most critical of these was that Northern Ireland was perceived as being dangerous. We could not hire any construction-engineering firms to work in Northern Ireland except the French, who sent people everywhere. But when we wanted to retain plant and construction engineers connected with the SERI Division of Renault, the French government company, to help with the construction of the plant, few would come. Those who did received a terrorist bonus of 50 percent.

The British mainlanders felt genuinely threatened in West Belfast. Consequently, the vendors we needed to supply our components would not even visit Belfast. We had to set up a purchasing operation in Coventry, England, rather than in West Belfast, where it would have been infinitely more practical and economical.

As problems like these multiplied, I was suddenly faced with a harsh reality: my costs were going to be ridiculous. I was constantly playing politician, engineer, supervisor, motivator, and money man. The project was far beyond the capability of one man, yet to whom could I shift authority? Almost all of my top people were company men; they were skilled specialists within an organization, but they were not entrepreneurs. Since it was my project, the work fell on me. Although I did not want to admit it at the time, it was more than one person should have tried to handle. Certainly, *this* one person.

Despite all this, we built the DeLorean Motor Car Company in record time. Our Dunmurry plant site was a soggy area, and we had to reroute two streams before we could build. Renault handled the basic factory layout design, but two local men, Brodie and Hawthorne, served as architects. We also used local construction firms, Farrans, and McLaughlin and Harvey.

The ground-breaking ceremony was scheduled for October 2, 1978, amid circumstances a more objective person would have said were extraordinarily dangerous. At the time, a number of Irish Republican Army people were being held in the dreaded Cell Block H in the massive Maze prison. These men were political prisoners being held by the British because of their extremism and militancy. They were men beloved by the IRA, and their followers were determined to force the British to treat them as political prisoners and to follow the rules of humane imprisonment of Amnesty International. Toward that end, they held protests any time British government officials gathered for any sort of ceremony, and ours was no exception. Our ceremony attracted a group waving protest banners and shouting a constant barrage of obscenities and epithets such as "killers" and "murderers."

We had been led to believe that Prince Charles would attend, but he did not—I would assume because of the hostile situation. But we did have such dignitaries as Don Concannon, Northern Ireland's Minister of Industry, and the Lord Mayor of Belfast. As the demonstrators angrily shouted their slogans, Don Concannon constantly reassured me that the venom was directed toward him, not me or my company. "This is just another chance to attack me," he said.

Cristina was there as well. At the time, she was filming a segment of the television series "Vegas" in Las Vegas, but I had asked her to fly over for the ceremony. I had been raising money, constantly telling people that a plant could be successful in Northern Ireland, explaining how essentially safe the area would be for everyone. I felt I had to have my wife along or the statements I had been making would be meaningless. Our presence together was "proof" that I was convinced of the safety of the area. So Cristina flew from Las Vegas to London, where I met her, and together we journeyed to Northern Ireland.

Once there, however, I became concerned for her safety during the demonstrations. But Don Concannon kept insisting there was nothing for us to worry about. "It's me they hate, not you!" Everything would go smoothly when we were on our own.

12

Our first cars came off the assembly line in March of 1981. I had expected them to be bad; I couldn't imagine them being that terrible! Seventy or eighty unfinished models finally had to be taken over to the property fence and parked; nothing else could be done with them. These were the cars our suppliers and our people learned on, our training cars.

The basic car that emerged from all our work was a combination of equipment from a number of different designers. We used the P-R-V-6 engine, and for opening and closing the gull-wing doors, we used a Grumman "cryso-twist" torsion bar. The heater–air-conditioning unit was produced by the Harrison Division of my alma mater, General Motors. Colin Chapman of Lotus, one of the most outstanding racing and automotive engineers in the world, was the inventor of a unique fiberglass technology; we felt he could be most helpful in certain specialized areas. In the end, the chassis engineering we adopted was to have been the next model of the Lotus Esprit. It was the only way to meet our time schedule.

We worked with the men and women on the assembly line, the engineering staff, and the suppliers to correct our problems as rapidly as possible. For example, we used an inertia switch with the fuel-injection system that was meant to turn off the pump if the car rolled over in a crash. Without the switch, the pump would keep working, pumping gasoline and increasing the risk of fire. While the switch was designed to shut off the pump when the car was inverted, some of the first ones were faulty and could be triggered by the hard slamming of the car door.

In addition, we found that we had to add guide blocks to the doors to ensure that they would close properly. Otherwise they would sometimes fit perfectly and other times would be slightly off and impossible to close tightly or would sometimes stick closed—always embarrassing. There were many other minor problems of design, quality, and fit.

But it is important to stress how typical all these problems were. No all-new car is built without them. Actually, we had fewer difficulties than Jaguar did when they introduced their latest model, and Jaguar has been in business for years. The Cadillac 4-6-8 engine, designed to save fuel by varying the number of working cylinders under different driving conditions, was frequently in for repairs after it first came out. I believe GM is now up to its twelfth safety campaign on the X-car, after a reported billion-dollar engineering job. In fact, it is doubtful whether a car has ever been introduced with mechanical innovations without problems. The public always finds ways to use a product that the designer cannot anticipate. And there is always the simple reality of human error. When we create something for mass production, the production process and the number of cars resulting from it just increase the chances for error. Once those errors have been discovered, corrections can be relatively simple. But first the discoveries must be made.

To insure that the customers received quality cars, we elected to repair all cars to perfection before they were shipped to the dealers. Eventually, we knew we would correct all problems before the cars left the plant, but for now, the plant had all it could possibly handle with a brand-new "green" work force in a country that had never built a car before. So we decided to establish two correction facilities in the United States, one on the east coast and one on the west coast near the ports of entry. This would allow us to make corrections before the dealers received the cars.

By the end of May 1981 we were ready to begin shipping cars, though we still had to correct problems at our facilities on both American coasts. We had been in training and pilot operation since November of 1980 without making any money. We had nothing but overhead for those first six months as we learned to build cars; but by the end of 1981, with only six months of stumbling production, we had earned approximately $25 million. We had a solid backlog of orders that would have guaranteed us between $45 million and $50 million for 1982, according to both our accountants and the government's consultants.

Our first year's profit was $6.5 million after covering the first six months' losses, the only profit made by any automobile company in Britain that year. Our sales figures already matched those of Mercedes Benz in their fifth year in the American market. Jaguar, maker of one of the most popular sports cars, had taken seventeen years to sell as many cars in the United States as we sold between July and December of that first year. Even better, the corporate stock was to be publicly offered by a major investment banker. I had almost fulfilled my dream of creating my own successful car company.

Tired and worn from years of frustrating work but glowing with our success, we decided to hold a Christmas dinner celebration at the 21 Club in New York after our final board meeting of 1981. This gathering of the top management and directors was one of the happiest moments of my life, a day when my personal pride could be indulged to my heart's content.

One by one, the men I had hired to help me make my dream a reality stood and offered toasts in my honor. C. R. Brown, our sales manager, was the most complimentary of all. We had built our plant in record time, just thirty months, on a cow pasture in one of the least desirable areas in the world for any business. As a result, other businesses that had been closed had either reopened or new businesses had taken their place. Children who had gone to bed with only minimum nourishment now had parents who could afford to indulge them a bit. Families were able to afford new clothing, to repair their homes, and to enjoy luxuries they had thought beyond their reach. I had helped, in a small way, to change a society, and we would all soon be making large sums of money as a result.

And so, that night in the 21 Club I accepted the accolades, attempting to maintain a superficial humility I did not feel as I reveled in the glory of the moment. Beside me was my wife, Cristina, a woman as glamorous as my triumphs, whose face adorned the pages of the world's leading fashion magazines, and whose sensual appeal I felt made me the envy of almost every man I met. We shared a family I adored, two children in whom I delighted. I was rich. I was famous. I had everything a man could desire.

What I did not know was that my determination to succeed would soon bring me face to face with men who shared my obsession for personal power and control, men who wanted to destroy me, at any cost, for their own glory. Nor did I realize that when I eventually looked into the face of the enemy, I would see my own reflection. For I, too, had to triumph at almost any cost.

None of this did I realize that night. I was basking in the light of my own glory. It was a wonderful feeling, and I delighted in every moment of it.

13

In many ways I have lived in a shell, hiding my deepest feelings behind a natural shyness and reticence. At General Motors, I respected many of my fellow engineers and stood in awe of the great innovators who had made the company grow. Yet overall I was not at ease with my co-workers. I felt myself a maverick, constantly at odds either inwardly or outwardly with some aspects of the corporate structure. I knew that GM had given me opportunities seldom offered to anyone. I knew that I owed the honing and polishing of my engineering skills to them, and that all of my management skills had been learned or developed through my experience within the company. And for all these benefits, I had been paid an annual salary that was more than many people make during an entire career. I owed GM everything. Yet I never felt that I fit in, that I really belonged. I suppressed my deepest feelings, buried myself in the work, and sometimes took pride in my own accomplishments.

In my personal life at that time, and later after I left, there were only two people who had been able to break completely through my emotional shell: my children, Zachary and Kathryn. They had taught me to reach out. And I loved them as selflessly and completely as a father can. I delighted in them and was genuinely concerned about their happiness. They were the most important people in my life.

On another level, however, my personal life was less than satisfactory. My relationship with Cristina, which had seemed to promise the fulfillment of so many things missing in my life, often lacked the intensity of emotion I know now should be an integral part of marriage. Much of this was a result of my own failure, brought on by stress in our relationship and weaknesses I saw in Cristina, weaknesses that periodically would haunt me.

Cristina wanted desperately to be an actress. She had achieved fame and some fortune as a top-flight fashion model, but that was not enough. She wanted to be a movie star. Although she was ambitious in the sense that she wanted something, she was not willing to work at it or for it; she believed that success was only a telephone call away. So she worked at taking advantage of her exceptional looks rather than studying acting or developing expertise in the business of entertainment.

This became evident when her agent told her that the reason she wasn't getting parts in films was because she wasn't living in Hollywood. If she lived out there, he said, the producers would be more likely to call her. This information excited her, and she immediately flew to California to live with her parents and await that magic telephone call. On a number of occasions she did this and was gone for weeks, sometimes months. She would leave the children and me in an instant if it might mean a part in a movie, though I tried to convince her she was only five hours from LA by air anyway and could always fly out for an interview.

At the same time, I felt Cristina was naïve about the

business. She had opportunities to do television commercials, one of the most lucrative fields for a model and one that would keep her face before the camera. But she had no interest in doing commercials. The fact that many major stars boosted their careers through television commercials did not persuade her. She always felt my advice on her career was uninformed; I wasn't in "show business."

I was not pleased with some of the decisions Cristina made in trying to advance her career. For example, she accepted a part in a low-budget film called *Bloody Mary,* a picture whose script stressed nudity over plot. It was the type of film often called "soft pornography," though it was edited enough eventually to be shown on late-night television. It was the type of film that can cause everyone involved to be considered jokes in the industry, and I knew that such a role could hurt her career. Yet when I expressed my feelings, she said it was because I did not want her to have a career. She never understood that I *did* want her to have a career, but not a tawdry one; I wanted her to have a career of stature and dignity.

It is hard to express my own sense of values during this time. All of our friends and acquaintances thought we had the perfect marriage. I was certainly not the martyred, long-suffering husband hoping for a perfect wife. The fact that I tried to avoid confronting the full implications of what Cristina seemed to be telling me from time to time was a reflection of my own weakness. I know now that I should have done more. I should have tried to understand whether my fantasy of our life together could be made a reality or whether I was living with a woman who did not share my values at all. I should have talked with Cristina more honestly, perhaps even sought counsel for both of us.

Instead, I continued to love Cristina as completely as I was capable of loving, suppressing my growing feelings of betrayal and my doubts and fears about our marriage. I avoided facing the reality that, despite the happy moments, the *Good Housekeeping*–type family photos, and the Christmas card portraits, our marriage was often far from perfect.

I was wrapped up in myself and my business; Cristina was wrapped up in herself and her modeling career and her acting ambition. I guess it was only with our children that we truly met emotionally. Then, with the founding of my car company, another "person" entered my life. I said earlier that the car took on a life of its own. That was also true in another sense, for the car came to demand as much from me emotionally as any member of my family.

By the time our factory was completed, I felt like a new parent, and the company was my "baby." And with each passing day, it became more obvious that my child was in trouble. The success we had celebrated at the 21 Club meant that our future was secure in terms of product acceptance, necessary orders, and public interest. But rumors had been circulating about the British government, General Motors, and our position in Ireland. As obstacle after obstacle was thrown in our way, we began to realize that the rumors might be based on fact.

When you realize your child is seriously ill and could die without treatment that you know you can't afford, you reach a point where you begin seeking any kind of help available. In the extreme, you even pray from the depths of your soul for divine intervention, at the same time knowing you will do anything necessary to raise the help in other ways.

14

I'll call her Sonja. She had a storefront business just off Fifty-fifth Street in Manhattan. Her sign read "Palm Reader and Adviser," and she claimed to be able to read the past, present, and future. She was just one of many such people who rent space throughout New York, but she was clever and manipulative enough to afford an unusually expensive location. Cristina had discovered her in 1977.

I don't know why Cristina first entered Sonja's place. I suspect it was because she was depressed over her inability to become pregnant. We loved Zachary dearly, but both Cristina and I wanted another child, and for some time had been trying everything possible for her to become pregnant. She had become increasingly depressed about it.

Cristina never fully explained what she and Sonja discussed on that first visit, but because of what she did tell me, I suspect they talked about Cristina's desire to have a baby. She told me about one of the "signs" Sonja conjured.

Supposedly, the woman went to the water tap and filled a Mason jar with ordinary water, then set it under her chair. Both women ignored the jar during the session. Then when they had finished, Sonja reached down and revealed that the water had turned to blood. It was "proof" that Cristina would become pregnant. Cristina came to me for the $10,000 Sonja wanted to "help" her get pregnant. She said the money was to be used in some mysterious way I was never told about. I humored her and gave her the money, in cash. Cristina soon became pregnant and repeatedly gave all of the credit to Sonja.

As hostile as I was to Sonja, though at this point I had not met her, I was intrigued by the coincidence of Cristina's pregnancy in such close proximity to her visit. I didn't really believe that whatever powers Sonja had were the cause of the pregnancy. It was just a coincidence. But an interesting one.

Because of all my problems with the new company, Cristina constantly urged me to see Sonja—to let her help me. I finally agreed to meet the woman, and Cristina took me there for the first time during her pregnancy. I had expected some old gypsy crone with a crystal ball. What I found was a warm, loving woman in her late thirties or early forties, an extremely intelligent woman who could make you feel as though you could share your personal problems with her. There was a slight hint of a New York accent in her voice, indicating that she had probably come to the city in her childhood.

Sonja's place of business was not impressive. There was a lower-floor waiting area with a beaded curtain and various religious items. Above this, in a sort of loft or balcony, was the area where she met with clients, also decorated in a manner that stressed religion—small icons, pictures of Jesus, crosses, and the inevitable smell of incense.

Sonja told me, "God works through me. I do not benefit in any way personally from this. I am just a channel. My life is devoted to serving others."

During our initial encounter, she was able to draw me into conversations about my life, my ambitions, and my business. Instead of the storefront fraud I had expected, I encountered an intelligent woman who understood business and the problems that arise when a company is struggling. She was one of the most astute people with whom I had ever discussed my company, and that alone made me feel comfortable. What impressed me even more, though, were her spiritual characteristics.

I think my relationship with God during my "Sonja days" was much like my feelings toward my advancement at General Motors. I could not accept the idea of good things happening to me without some sort of "worthiness" on my part, some reason for it outside of me. While part of me felt capable and somewhat deserving of all the advancements and opportunities that had come my way, another part was uncomfortable with my success because it seemed to have happened so easily. I recently saw an announcement for two books touting something called "the impostor phenomenon." The authors claim that a large number of successful people suffer from self-doubts, feeling they do not deserve the success that comes to them. I, too, experienced self-doubt, but I believe it goes much deeper; I believe it is part of the spiritual needs we all have as human beings created in the image of a greater being—something I did not recognize at the time.

When I thought at all about how God works in someone's life, I felt that somehow I had to earn rewards by being more spiritual than I had been. As a result, when I was in Manhattan, I went to St. Patrick's Cathedral every day; I listened to the service and lighted a candle to St. John. I did not try to become a part of the congregation. I did not interact with the other parishioners, except for an occasional greeting as I hurried out to continue my business. I was performing the rituals I felt God required to make me somehow worthy of the good things that had happened and the good I wanted to happen in the future.

So when I met Sonja, I saw someone I considered to be

truly spiritual. She seemed serious about God, as evidenced by her conversation and the artifacts with which she surrounded herself. A growing need within me for a spiritual alliance with a force beyond myself was becoming evident, and my first feeble steps to satisfy this new hunger seemed to bring me a brief reassurance.

Sonja stressed that she had no personal powers whatever; everything she was able to do came as a gift from God. She would never have great wealth. She would never be able to use her powers for personal gain. She was merely a conduit, a helpful servant who was given gifts of value only as she interacted with others. She also stressed that she worked through a prayer group at her church. She would "see" things, "sense" things, and she could let spiritual messages flow through her lips to help me, then take my problems to her church's prayer group so that many people would lift their voices to the Lord to ensure success. The few actions she suggested I take, such as lighting a candle, affirmed the rituals I was already doing.

But despite my impression of Sonja's sincerity and spirituality, I did not consider getting involved with her. If anything, I simply felt less uncomfortable with Cristina's contact with her. My own involvement with Sonja and her occult mesmerization would begin much more subtly.

15

My critics have stressed that what truly destroyed the
DeLorean Motor Company was that I increased the production schedule for the cars to an unrealistic rate of 14,700 cars
per year. What they do not realize, or choose to overlook, is
that our production increases were far less than our orders
and that our plant and organization could not have survived
at 7,000 cars a year. We had designed the company, the
tooling, the facilities, and the organization to "leap" into
business at about one-third of Corvette's production and
sales rate of 45,000 cars a year. The generous financing of
NIDA had made this possible, but the onerous debt service
made it mandatory. By the time we began production, our
marketing people had eighteen months' worth of firm dealer
orders at our highest production rate. I still have a November
1981 letter from our North American division president,

C. R. Brown, suggesting that we raise production because we had the sales and orders; on its basis, we did. All of us—Don Lander (our president), Joe Daly (our finance vice-president), and I—questioned Brown and the sales department. Brown insisted that we expand to meet the orders and that the expansion was financially sensible because of the orders.

What no one has said, but what I can say now in retrospect, is that we should never have gone into production at all! When it became clear that the new Conservative British government was not going to honor the contract we had signed with the previous Labor government, I should have closed the company.

This does not mean that I think the company failed because it could not succeed. It did succeed. When we were put into receivership by the British, we were sold out for the next two years' production. Our difficulty was working capital, an area where all of us knew that when government funding guarantees were not met we were in trouble. If we could not find an alternate source, we were dead. The same idea, the same manufacturing location, and the same car, all put together with adequate working capital, would have made the automotive success story of the eighties. So the reasons why I should not have gone ahead had nothing to do with the viability of the business. But I am getting ahead of my story. . . .

The reality is that the DeLorean Motor Company never had enough operating funds. We only existed because everything was working as planned. The first unforeseen problem could kill us. Unfortunately, the unforeseen did happen.

First, there was a problem with General Motors.

GM manufactures the Corvette, the only true American sports car with a long history of success. It was first created in the early fifties and has been built almost continuously ever since. There were Corvette owners' clubs, rallies, and even television shows using the Corvette as an integral part of the series. (Remember the old "Route 66" series?) Yet when I began my company, the Corvette was in the process of being redesigned. It was out of production for a short time, and when the new design was complete, the "New Corvette" was introduced with great fanfare.

If we had a competitor, it was the Corvette, for I did see Corvette buyers as one potential market for my car. Based on the British-pound and American-dollar currency ratio at the time we began the company, the cost of the two vehicles would be approximately $18,000, setting them head to head in terms of price. However, when the unexpected happened and the pound changed drastically in the foreign exchange rate, 40 percent, we were forced to up the price we would have to charge the American buyer the same 40 percent. Almost overnight, my $18,000 car became a $25,000 car. There are many ways to cut corners in the automobile industry, but altering international exchange rates is not one of them.

Price competition was not the only problem I was facing with GM. I wanted the DeLorean to be sold through existing dealerships whose product line did not contain a competing car but whose customers could afford such a sports car. This meant dealerships such as Cadillac. I knew some of the owners of these dealerships from my days at General Motors, and most of them knew of me. Since the congressional upheaval of the late fifties, dealer agreements did not contain any sort of exclusivity clause in their contracts. By this I mean that a Cadillac dealer did not have to sell only Cadillacs. If he desired, he could add a Mercedes Benz or even a Rolls Royce to his line. He could also add a DeLorean, and it was toward this end that I began to approach such people.

Many of the dealers were enthusiastic. They knew the DeLorean buyer would either be different from the Cadillac buyer or would have the money and interest to buy both cars. My line would not hurt Cadillac sales, and it could bring a different type of buyer through their doors. There was nothing but profit to be made from the connection.

What I did not realize was that some of the people at General Motors were so anxious to ensure my failure that they would do almost anything to keep me from succeeding, including making subtle threats against those GM dealers who, by contract, should have been free to offer any item they desired.

Typical of the problem was a major Cadillac dealer in one of the big money cities of Texas. This dealer had known of me from my days at GM, liked the DeLorean car, and was under no legal restriction that could prevent him from offering automobiles other than Cadillac. He agreed to handle my car.

Then one day he called me. "John, I'm not going to be able to handle your car. I'm sorry."

When I questioned him, I learned that the regional sales people handling Cadillac for GM had told him that if he took on my cars, he would have some serious problems with the factory. Naturally, my cars were not worth that type of aggravation to him.

It appears that General Motors also put political pressure on the British government. Many months after the fact, my lawyers and I were able to obtain a copy of a State Department transmittal by Kingman Brewster, who was at the time the Ambassador to the Court of St. James. The document implied that an American company, unnamed in the heavily censored material supplied under the Freedom of Information Act, was quite upset with the various financings my company was receiving from the British government. They felt that I would have an unfair sales advantage over the U.S. competitor. Since there was only one American company producing a car in any way competitive with the DeLorean, I have to assume that the complaint came from General Motors. I also have to assume that the report was improper because much of the message was deliberately deleted from the telegram before the copy was sent to me. In any event, as a result of this message to Brewster and the threat it contained, we were slapped with a $371-per-car "royalty" to the government, more than any company has ever paid in the history of the British motor industry. We didn't know it, but we were dead before we stuck the first shovel in the ground.

The idea that there could be some international manipulation related to my company was not a surprise. Many of the facts are still unknown, but what is known creates a highly suspicious situation. First, my company could have been perceived as a threat in Northern Ireland. The people of West Belfast were seeking independence from Great Britain. My company, essentially independent other than through the loans and financial assistance, was able to give the people greater pride in themselves and hope for the future. In a way, we were a symbol of what a private business could achieve in Northern Ireland without being totally controlled by the British. This could have been viewed as a first step in proving to the people of Belfast that they could be self-sufficient, which would make further problems for the Thatcher government.

This is not to say that the area was without tension from all sides. The violence was frequently irrational and often cruelly vicious from both the British and the IRA, though the IRA's cause, *not* their methods, was meant to help the people in a very bad situation.

For example, one of the saddest tragedies with which I was familiar occurred when a British soldier dared to fall in love with an Irish girl. They courted, were married, then, just as they were leaving the church, a reputed IRA assassin shot the soldier in the head as a lesson to both the British soldiers and the Irish women.

As horrible as the murder of the soldier were some of the British actions. At one point two little boys were throwing rocks at an armored vehicle. As the rocks bounced off the heavy steel, some soldiers, perhaps frightened by the tensions, fired at the boys and killed them.

Such blatant tragedies and seemingly irrational violence enabled the British to create situations I now think were meant to unnerve me. For example, many times during this period I was warned through MI-6 (British Intelligence) that my life was in danger. They told me to stay in London and only visit Belfast for the day. When I did stay in Belfast, they posted twenty-four-hour guards around me and made me

travel in a caravan. I now believe their threats were a hoax
designed to keep me off balance and away from the Belfast
operation.

I also knew that GM officials had for years maintained
that they would never consider investing more money
anywhere in England, much less in Northern Ireland,
because they had never made money with plants in England
and similar countries with histories of intense labor strife.
Certainly, they had no interest in West Belfast where they
would face unpredictable shutdowns. Yet as I was forced out
of business, GM opened facilities in Northern Ireland that,
ironically, employed approximately the same number of
people as my company was employing at that time.

Was there complicity between the British government
and GM to force us out? I do not have proof, but the
possibility seems great because of the amazing "coinci-
dences" that should not have existed. Eventually, we will
get the hundreds of State Department documents under the
Freedom of Information Act that should tell us all. Based
upon the vigor with which the government opposed the
disclosure of the documents under "sovereign to sovereign"
privilege, it may take years.

According to sources within the creditors' committee
established by the British—the head of it, John Putt, for
one—there was growing hostility to my success and strong
feeling that since the company was financed by the British, it
should be owned by the British. Had my company continued, I would eventually have profited handsomely from my
shares of stock. According to my sources, the idea that an
American should profit from a West Belfast venture under-
written in part by the British government was extremely
upsetting. They wanted to force me out so that a British
company could take over DMC. Both John Putt and his
father said this. They also told us that Sir Kenneth Cork, the
British government receiver, deliberately aborted our Bank
of America financing. Again "circumstances" seem to bear
that out.

The games played to hurt us were subtle and foolish. For example, part of our cash flow was dependent upon a form of loan guarantee called export guarantee financing (ECGD), which would provide us with cash for each completed car before its sale. This type of financing, based on collateral of the finished product, is the safest financing a lending institution or government agency can provide. Because the product is "real" and has a market, it can be sold to meet the obligation of the debtor should the debtor default. The British government did not deliver as it promised contractually, and our cash flow could not stand the loss of the loan financing that was ours by contract.

I was horrified. We had the finest plant, excellent tooling, a well-trained and rapidly improving work force, and an outstanding product that was being enthusiastically received. In our master agreement with the British, we were to receive 90 percent of the dealer net price of our cars as ECGD as the cars went to the dock. This amounted to about $18,000 per car but was fully secured by the cars themselves. When the cars got to America and the dealer paid for them, the government would get their money back plus interest and would give us the balance. Every other exporter in Britain gets ECGD, whether they manufacture cars, turbines, or toothbrushes. The government kept telling us we were going to get it—but never honored the contract. If we had known we were not to receive it, instead of expanding our production we would have shrunk it down and slowly built our working capital up over the years. If we had done this, however, we would not have attained promised employment targets and would have lost our company anyway. They had us coming and going.

As a result, we were left in a very unstable situation. We were buying components on 60-day terms, engines on 180 days, trying to get the cars built, shipped to the U.S., and paid for soon enough to buy more components from the suppliers. I knew, as did our brilliant finance manager, Joe Daly, that the first interruption would spell disaster. This interruption came in two steps.

First, a shipping strike between the mainland and Belfast shut off supplies of some vital parts.

Second, the American auto industry experienced the worst slump in forty years. Industry sales rates dropped from 8 million to under 5 million a year. It all happened so quickly that domestic suppliers couldn't slow down quickly enough, and their dealers were swamped with too many cars. The dealers' lines of credit were exhausted.

The DeLorean Motor Company was hurt far more than most by the automobile-industry recession; we were the world's newest car company and were totally devoid of working capital. Since 75 percent of our dealers were GM and Ford dealers, cutting off dealer financing meant they couldn't pay for the cars they had ordered from us, many of which were already on ships or for which components had been ordered.

With ECGD financing we could have survived the month or so we needed to make alternative arrangements. We didn't. The U.K. government put us in receivership over my violent objection.

The receivership came about in February of 1982, the result of our inability to pay $800,000 in interest due the British government. Ironically, the cash-flow problem that left us indebted to the British actually stemmed from that same government's deliberate failure to pay its debts to our company.

Several months earlier, Bobby Sands, an imprisoned member of the Irish Republican Army, had staged a protest against the British government's inhumane treatment of prisoners in the dreaded H Block. Sands refused to eat, the only passive protest he could realistically lead in jail. At first, his fast was ignored; it was assumed he would eventually become hungry enough and break down. But Sands had far greater determination than anyone realized. Days became weeks, and soon he was wasting away, his body consuming itself in a desperate effort to stay alive.

144

The British government was inflexible when it came to meeting Sands' demands: that the IRA prisoners be treated as political prisoners, not criminals. "A dying terrorist is still a terrorist," was the government's attitude; it would not alter its stand. If Sands refused to eat, there was nothing they could do. He had chosen his fate. The British stance drew fire from around the world as they were criticized for human-rights violations by many organizations, including Amnesty International. Amnesty had previously protested the British treatment of Catholics in Northern Ireland, the lack of due process in the British legal procedures there, and the inhumane treatment of prisoners in Maze Prison and most particularly in Cell Block H.

So the dying Sands became a rallying point in Northern Ireland. Anyone who hated British rule, whether or not they had approved of Sands' actions in life, saw him as a symbol of the fight for freedom from England. And when he died on May 5, 1981, the people took to the streets.

Sands' body was placed on display during his wake, and the horribly emaciated body of the martyr stirred deep feeling among the residents. The Royal Ulster Constabulary, in an effort to stop the spread of demonstrations, bottled up the Catholic Twinbrook Housing Estate, adjacent to our plant, where Bobby Sands' mother lived. They surrounded the Catholic development with soldiers, bulletproof Land Rovers, and half-tracks. No one was permitted to enter or leave.

The reaction among our workers and the people of West Belfast was extremely interesting. Obviously, our plant had to be shut down, being at the epicenter of the "troubles," and an unusual number of guards was posted. Yet we were never a deliberate target. Perhaps this was because we were from America, and many Americans were known sympathizers with the Irish. Or perhaps it was because we had provided jobs without regard to politics, except for making certain we had equality of Catholics and Protestants at all levels of responsibility. Whatever figured in the minds of our employees, our plant was not deliberately attacked during the rioting.

Unfortunately, when the bottled-up youths in the Twin-brook Housing Estate began throwing fire bombs, any property in the vicinity was likely to be struck. They lobbed 143 Molotov cocktails over our fence, just to let off steam. But regardless of intent, a fire bomb damages or destroys everything in its wake. This was the case with one of our office buildings—the one close enough to the fence to be hit. The blaze destroyed all manner of valuable business equipment in addition to most of our records. It was weeks before personnel and engineering records, inventory and production control sheets and similar items could be reconstructed. Some were lost forever. Naturally, this shut us down and meant substantial financial losses, both in the physical damage and the consequential loss of production and profits.

The British government had provided all Northern Ireland industries with special criminal damage insurance for exactly this kind of loss resulting from the hostile and unstable political situation. According to the government's criminal damage auditors, Peat, Marwick and Company, our company was owed $21 million in damages. Had even a much lower figure been arrived at and applied as a company credit to offset the interest payment due ($800,000), we would not have been placed in receivership. The fact that the government ignored this minor internal paper-work juggling, which was suggested to them numerous times, even by the people who were monitoring in the Department of Commerce, seemed further evidence to me that they had no intention of letting us survive, despite all the money that had already been spent to help us get started. It made no sense, but nothing made sense to me any more.

We also had a stock offering that would have allowed us to go public at a time when such stock would have brought millions of dollars to the new company. During the third quarter of 1981 there was a "window of opportunity," and our offering had been planned for this period. Over $6 billion in new stock issues had been sold to that time in 1981, but there were deliberate government delays until it was too late to take advantage of the circumstances. The

British government demanded more stock than they were entitled to by the contract they had signed, and they attempted to renegotiate a number of other areas of the master agreement. It was pure blackmail. This was the offering that would have saved our company and made me wealthy, if only on paper.

It is important to note one fact here, a fact of which the British government was aware: under "blue sky" laws of the state of Texas, a state where the stock was being offered, I would not have been able to sell my stock for several years because certain conditions that we had agreed to before we could sign dealers in Texas first had to be met. These laws required that the company had to earn 5 percent on equity two years in a row and were designed to keep me from selling out, becoming rich, then turning my back on the company. I was forced to escrow my stock to the state until the profit conditions were met. My "wealth," therefore, would remain wealth in name only; it would not provide me with any access to cash for at least two and a half years and only then if DMC was extremely successful.

In England, receivership is a business activity without stigma. Sometimes it is a way for the company to reorganize; sometimes it is a way for the government to take over the operation of the firm. Whatever the circumstances, there is no problem. Rolls Royce, a major manufacturer of aircraft engines and the company that produces what is considered the most luxurious car in the world, had been through receivership and was never hurt.

In the United States, placing a company in receivership is similar to forcing it into bankruptcy. In effect, the company is managed while being liquidated. Receivership ensures that creditors are treated fairly and that a business is operated as well as possible during its final days. Whatever the business, whatever its early promise, generally it no longer has a future. This is especially true in consumer durables; in expendables it makes little difference. As a result, when people hear that a business is going into receivership, most are unwilling to buy the company's product, especially if it is one that will require long-term maintenance, replacement parts, and service, such as a car.

But the British are not accustomed to American business practices. Sir Kenneth Cork, the British government receiver, argued that receivership would be good for us; we could "hive off" the debt and have a better company. He was very persuasive and convinced many of our DMCL board members. But my understanding of the buying public was better than his. The mere act of putting DMCL in receivership virtually destroyed our chance of survival.

The value of our cars in inventory dropped $20 million the day we were put in receivership. They might sell, but for thousands of dollars less than if people could be assured of long-term servicing. In my heart I knew there was no way back, but I determined to fight to the end. I was the captain of the Titanic—trying to bail her out by hand.

Months earlier, when the company was first in trouble, I had met with the Minister of Industry, the head of the Department of Commerce, and the other officials, with what amounted to my resignation. I knew that they were working against me by not honoring our agreements. At that time I did not understand the reasons for their hostility and subtle, destructive actions, but I had been told and truly believed that if I was eliminated, the company might be allowed to continue—with all agreements honored. So I presented them with what was to be the hardest decision of my business life, a decision even harder than the one to leave GM.

"Take my company," I told them. If there was some psychological problem with having an American head this business, I would remove myself entirely and give them my stock for absolutely nothing. I would stay on as a corporate employee if they wished; but if that was not possible, if they insisted I simply remove myself entirely in exchange for the corporation to continue under total British ownership and control, then so be it. The DeLorean Motor Car would be theirs.

"I'll walk away from the business if you'll just keep it alive." I knew that if it were integrated into the British Leyland, which the government already owned, the company would affect many economies and be even more profitable.

To my shock and dismay, the British refused. In effect, the government said they would rather throw away their investment of more than $100 million than see the DeLorean company succeed.

Now my worst fears had come true. We were in receivership.

16

In the midst of all these external pressures, we had also developed internal problems. Some of these centered around our public relations manager, William Haddad.

I had originally hired Bill Haddad because of what I believed were his personal and political connections. He had told me that he was close to the Kennedy family, a family loved by the Irish and thus a beneficial connection in Northern Ireland. In fact, I remember Bill telling me, "I was the only person with Jackie while she cleaned Jack's effects out of the Oval Office. . . . Ted Kennedy calls me every day of his life for advice and counsel. I can get the Kennedys to actively support your project, guaranteeing no 'troubles' for our operation."

For reasons unknown to me, however, Haddad took some actions that apparently had much to do with the destruction of the company. These actions were documented by the British government from testimony, including that of Marian Gibson, an executive secretary and administrative assistant for the DeLorean Motor Company.

Other British government documents show that Haddad used a DMC check to purchase an investigative report prepared for GM when I was still there and my views on civil rights were not very popular, a report that purported to show (à la the false attack on Ralph Nader) that I was a closet homosexual. Haddad sent the report to the British government.

Haddad also constructed a memo in which he spoke of problems I was creating, attempting to make both me and the company look bad. This memo, which has figured largely in accusations against me, was supposedly typed by Haddad's secretary on December 26, a date when the office was closed and his secretary on vacation. According to Parliamentary documents, Haddad admitted to Scotland Yard that the memo was a fake that was never sent to me.

Marian Gibson later admitted that she went to the British government and press with false information concerning the company, information she believed to be accurate at the time because of statements made to her by Bill Haddad. The most damaging was the story Haddad fed her that I was paying off the IRA, an allegation repeated in Parliament during the time I was writing this book. That alone would account for the British terminating DMC!

In addition to this internal undermining, we had some employees who betrayed our trust in other detrimental ways. For example, the financial actions of one of the high-level executives involved with our stateside operation created great problems for us. This man was extremely important in handling the importation and distribution of DeLorean cars in the United States, but apparently he felt his efforts were unappreciated and that he was not given enough credit for the work he did. Eventually, the Auditor's Committee received documentation of his misappropriation of funds, and I was forced to dismiss him. As I write this, legal steps are being taken as a result of the documentation. Some time after his dismissal, however, the man and another employee still with the company were caught charging hundreds of dollars' worth of long-distance calls to DMC.

With all these problems, I knew that the one action I could take was to continue my efforts to raise essential capital. I began to spend every waking moment seeking investors. I would talk with anyone who claimed to have money or access to cash. Sometimes these were among the biggest names in the business world. Other times they were people of whom I had never heard. I talked with people who had oil money, people who had become rich in entertainment, and people who had inherited wealth. I also talked with liars, con artists, and even mentally ill men and women who truly believed that what they were saying about their resources was true, even though they were penniless.

I quickly learned that appearances meant nothing. A man arriving in a chauffeur-driven limousine might have no money at all, while a man in torn jeans and driving a battered Volkswagen "bug," which he had purchased twenty years before as a secondhand car, might prove that he had a net worth of $100 million.

The result of all this was intense emotional strain. I could not afford to ignore anyone. There were constant meetings with almost every imaginable type of person. I would travel anywhere at a moment's notice if a potential investor called. My long-distance telephone bill was enormous, and I was always hoping that the next person I met would come through with the money.

With each passing hour, my situation became more desperate. I was haunted by specters of concern and ambition: the people of West Belfast; those men at GM who had laughed at my dream; and my car, the culmination of a dream that promised so much. . . . If only there was time.

Yet despite the pressure, I never dared show my true feelings. Outwardly I had to be the calm, cool, sophisticated businessman who had a very worthwhile investment opportunity to present. "It's just that with our cash flow, an investment of forty or fifty million dollars would solve our problem." Cash flow! Our cash-flow problem was caused by our success; the more cars we built, the more money we needed for components and inventory. It was simple and explainable, but I just couldn't get it done.

Each day it became harder to voice that false optimism. Each morning I looked in the mirror and saw a man hours closer to ruin. My face was tired and drawn. But John Z. DeLorean, CEO of his own company, the man in charge, the celebrity, Mr. Cool, the glamorous husband of the beautiful Cristina, could never let on that he was close to ruin himself—financially, physically, and emotionally.

I was out of control, a situation that, for me, was a sin as great as the "sin" other people credited to me when I left General Motors. If I couldn't rely on *my* skills, *my* incredible good luck, the special touch that had propelled *me* through General Motors faster than any man in recent corporate history, then where could I turn? I *had* to be in control. I had to be constantly "up" for others so that I could generate enthusiasm in them and, as a result, fresh money I was desperate to have. I . . . I . . . I . . .

Deep inside, I knew I needed something more. My arrogance and pride were killing me.

It was in those desperate hours that I decided I needed a little assistance from a higher power—just until I could get on my feet. I still had to be the one in charge of my life, but I could use a little boost from "the man upstairs." Just a turbocharge boost from God so I could continue being in control. And that's when I turned to Sonja in earnest. She suddenly became the only person in the world to whom I could tell the truth about our company's situation.

17

When I look back at that period of my life, I find it frightening that I became involved in what I did. People speak of the "wiles of the devil," a phrase straight from the Bible by the way, or as one of the contemporary translations puts it, "the devil's schemes" (Ephesians 6:11). Many may think such ideas superstitious or archaic, but I have seen these wiles. I know they exist, and they are beautifully disguised to woo the unsuspecting. They came to me in the form of "a trusted friend and adviser."

I will never question the fact that Sonja had certain gifts I do not understand. And I don't mean her ability to turn water to "blood" as she did for Cristina. Such "mystical signs" can be recreated with magic-shop items available for purchase in any large city. What Sonja had was an occult sensitivity or power. She could tell you specific things about your life that it would have been impossible for her to know aside from some special sense. For example, when we got into trouble in the Republic of Ireland, she told Cristina that another (Northern Ireland) would come through immediately.

When I was numb from exhaustion, she became my turbo charger, my power boost. Through her, I believed, I could directly reach some divine power source.

But I did not realize that Sonja was a master manipulator. She did not pursue me as a client at first. She acted as a friend, an adviser who understood the business problems I was having. She understood the cash-flow crisis, the implication of the British not honoring our contract, and the other intimate details of my company's problems. She was also trustworthy. I could tell her my problems, and they would go no further. I could reveal my doubts, my fears, and my anguish over what was happening, and it would never reach an employee who might become demoralized.

At first she was just "a friend who wanted to help." For example, she knew an Iranian who was extremely wealthy and who might be willing to invest. She was also advising him on his affairs so she knew that if she told him to invest in DMC he very probably would. When I checked out the man, I found that he actually had many millions of dollars. Sonja had possibly found our savior.

The Iranian did not invest, but the fact that he was a genuine prospect, looking for investment areas and with enough capital to do as he pleased, increased my respect and trust for Sonja. She was being altruistic. All she wanted was for me to succeed. She wanted my life to run smoothly. She wanted nothing for herself, just the regular rate for her time; she would not personally benefit. She was only a vehicle for God's work. She stressed this continually, talking of the gift God had provided.

Gradually, however, I began to rely upon Sonja as though she were a trusted insider. If I had a question about hiring someone, I would ask Sonja. If I had an important business decision to make, I would ask Sonja. And when her judgment proved correct, my faith in her personal and spiritual counsel deepened.

What I did not realize was that I was being sucked into the occult. I was using a spiritualist to guide my every move, deluding myself into thinking that she was special, perhaps my own gift from God to help me through this trouble. When I began paying her ever-growing sums of money, I believed I was only donating to her church. She had to reward the people who were praying for me. That only made sense, especially since she never altered my religious activities. She encouraged me to continue lighting candles. She encouraged me to make my daily visits to St. Patrick's Cathedral. But I was being slowly led into hell by my belief in a woman whom I was convinced had such a strong spirituality that she could make everything work out as it should.

At first my life seemed to be going better, and Sonja reinforced my misguided belief. She reassured me that I was only going through a period of trial from which I would emerge in charge of my life and my business. She played on my pride and my foolishness. Everything seemed so sensible, so logical, so seductively simple.

DISASTER

18

I didn't know it, of course, but I was on a collision course with other forces being set in motion. My future was being planned on quite another plane by the Drug Enforcement Administration. With the information we now have, I can place this in perspective. To do this, however, I must set the scene and introduce the men whose machinations would change my life.

Many different types of people are involved with drug trafficking. Some are criminals who find cocaine, heroin, marijuana, and other drugs to be quite profitable. Others are law-enforcement officers who understand both the criminal marketplace and the actions of their legitimate counterparts on local and federal police forces. Still others are men who simply live for excitement. Many of them were in the Vietnam war, often working for the Central Intelligence Agency in one capacity or another. These men developed skills in transporting goods through unusual channels, learned ways to make large sums of money, and have often reached a point where they enjoy living life "on the edge." Narcotics trafficking brings them both great excitement and large sums of money. Whatever their background, many of these Americans have joined with South Americans and others to take advantage of the ever-growing demand for illegal substances. A number of books purport to offer substantial proof that the CIA itself was the largest heroin dealer in the world using Air America, their in-house airline, and Air Asia, to bring drugs out of the Orient. These profits were used for clandestine activity for which Congress would not approve funding.

Cocaine, the substance that became central in my arrest, is one of the most subtle of the drugs. It provides pleasure at first, then becomes totally addictive. But for the men and women at the top of the drug trade, the realities of cocaine matter little. One kilogram (2.2 pounds) of this white powder can net more profit for the importer than some executives earn in a year. A yearly income of $50 million is considered relatively low for the average importer. Incomes of $200 million are not unusual. And always the importers see their work as normal business deals; they care no more about the devastation their products cause than do the sellers of alcoholic beverages who destroy five times as many lives each year—legally.

The men and women who fight drug trafficking distinguish several hierarchies within the trade. The lowest level is the street junkie, the user who can be arrested for just possessing the illegal substance. Then come the small dealers, the pushers who sell to anyone who will buy, from school children to co-workers in industries ranging from assembly lines to executive suites. Pushers are often users themselves, selling to support their own habits. The next level of dealer handles larger quantities, often two or three kilos at a time. Usually such a person knows enough about the drugs being sold not to use them on a regular basis, if at all. And above them are the major dealers and importers whose personal incomes can exceed the gross receipts of many large corporations.

Narcotics has become a major industry. It is estimated that many lawyers, often labeled "dope lawyers," spend their lives (and make a great deal of money) defending narcotics violators. A multitude of police, FBI and DEA agents, and prosecutors make their living from fighting dope. (Secretly I doubt that any of these people want the business to change, even though it clogs up the courts.) Our antiquated laws and the great financial incentives for both sides of the business help to make the U.S. the only developed country with major narcotics problems and widespread use. (Our laws need drastic revision; those proposed in the late seventies by the *Consumer Reports* study on the subject seem most logical to me.)

For the Drug Enforcement Administration (DEA) agents and other officials working in narcotics, arrests at these different levels help make their careers and earn them promotions. Many city police departments have their narcotics squads work on what amounts to a quota system. An unofficial point score is assigned for each level of individual breaking the narcotics laws. The users are the easiest people to arrest and, when arrested in the right quantity, help the law-enforcement officers meet the expected quotas. Of course, more points are given for arresting criminals at the higher levels, but such arrests take much more time and effort.

The federal agents of the DEA, however, do not concern themselves with the lower-level sellers. Their job is to spend the time necessary to bring in the big convictions—to get the men and women at the top. To do this, they will use any method they think might work. One of these methods is the sting.

In running a major sting operation, the federal officers of the DEA or FBI frequently use paid informers. One such professional informant was a man named James Hoffman. (At least, this was his name when I met him. Later I learned that he was born Timothy deJong, and I understand that today his name is Tim Hughes.)

James Hoffman was to law enforcement what Sonja was to true spiritual understanding. While I was placing my hope and faith in Sonja's advice, the DEA was turning to a false prophet, a man who would do anything for money.

19

While I was working my way through the GM corporate structure, James Hoffman was working his way through the intricacies of a business just as large, just as complex, and far more dangerous. He was becoming both a narcotics runner and an informant for the federal government.

Apparently, Hoffman had been involved with dishonest activities all of his adult life. When investigating his background, we found that at one time he allegedly ran a Bible-selling scam. He would obtain a name from the obituary column, then go to the house of the deceased. He would ask for the person he knew was dead and express great shock upon being told that the person for whom he was asking was no longer alive. He would explain that he was delivering the Bible that had been "ordered" by the person, usually convincing the family to buy it for an unusually high price. If you remember the movie *Paper Moon*, this is the scam that actor Ryan O'Neal played to perfection. For James Hoffman, it was real life.

At some point, however, Hoffman must have discovered that narcotics were more profitable than Holy Writ. He became involved in transporting and selling drugs on a high enough level that when the narcotics agents eventually caught him, he faced a very long prison term. Instead of going to jail, however, he became what is known in the drug trade as a "turned informant."

Turned informants provide information leading to or aiding in narcotics convictions. These are men and women who have been caught in criminal activities but are given a chance to work with the law in exchange for a reduced sentence, a forgoing of prosecution, or some other benefit. This person has been "turned" into someone who is helping law enforcement. Although they are one of the most important sources of information for the Drug Enforcement Administration, turned informants are by no stretch of the imagination honest citizens. Usually, they are held in disdain by criminals and officials alike, and are treated as if they were "the scum of the earth."

The typical informant will turn against friends and business acquaintances if it will protect him from the consequences of his own criminal acts. He is a "snitch," a "squealer," a "stool pigeon." Although informants may be needed to build major cases, they are not respected by most federal agents. It is a symbiotic contempt-hate relationship in almost all instances.

James Hoffman was one of the most despised of these despised people. His only real success as an informant resulted in the conviction of his two best friends to save himself. The other major case he was involved in, the Faez Boukaram case, which concerned the indictment of allegedly the largest hashish smuggler in the world, resulted in acquittal because of Hoffman's total lack of credibility.

Also, Hoffman had seriously embarrassed the government in a Florida case when he came out of a house totally surrounded and under intense surveillance and said he had seen two supermarket bags full of cocaine. Agents immediately broke in and found nothing. It is probable Hoffman sold out to the dealers in the house and put them on alert.

Despite this, Hoffman made large sums of money for his actions on behalf of the government. He was paid over $160,000 (undocumented reports indicate as much as $300,000) in a very short period, essentially tax free. How much more he earned from strictly criminal activities unrelated to his work on behalf of the DEA is not known. We did uncover some of his illegal activity when we found a secret post-office box he and another man maintained under various aliases (more about this later). Whatever the circumstances, James Hoffman was extremely well paid.

Enter William Morgan Hetrick. According to Hoffman, Hetrick was one of the major transporters (flyers) of narcotics into the United States. Reported to be making $1.5 million per trip for smuggling 300 kilos of cocaine into the U.S. from Colombia, Hetrick had successfully escaped prosecution for years. He did not involve himself with obtaining, processing, or selling the drugs. He was simply a great pilot and was extremely well paid for his skill in eluding law-enforcement officers and transporting large quantities of cocaine without loss or discovery.

Hoffman knew Morgan Hetrick and his sons, and he convinced the DEA agents that he could lure Hetrick into a scheme so that they could make a case against him. The agents didn't learn until later that Hoffman had stolen money from Hetrick and that Hoffman had admitted he perjured himself in the suit Hetrick brought to get the money back. With Hoffman, there was no honor among thieves. (On one videotape Hetrick said, "Hoffman would —— his own mother for twenty-five cents!" Hetrick disliked Hoffman, partly because of Hoffman's poor personal hygiene and partly because he knew Hoffman was totally amoral. The other informant in my life, William Haddad, also seemed to have very poor personal hygiene. Do all informants smell bad?)

The biggest problem drug dealers have is what to do with their money. Narcotics is a cash business, and the cash involved can often be hundreds of thousands of dollars. In an effort to identify such large-scale cash movement, federal laws require banks and other financial institutions to report the names of people depositing more than $10,000 at a time. Since a man such as Hetrick could easily have hundreds of thousands in cash at any given time, he needed a place for his money. He had already invested in numerous ventures, including a land-development deal worth approximately $20 million.

There are several ways drug dealers solve this problem. One approach is to become involved in legitimate businesses where large sums of cash are routinely handled. Then the drug money is "laundered" through such companies. For example, a drug dealer places large sums of money in a chain of restaurants. The money is reported as though it were obtained from regular customers; often the records are faked to indicate food purchases equal in volume to the amount that would have been used had there been as many customers as the day's receipts indicate. Corporate taxes have to be paid on the money deposited in this way, of course, but though less than the original cash, the money is now available for the criminals' "legitimate" use.

A second approach to laundering is to find a banker who is willing to violate the law. Arrangements are made to accept the money being brought by the narcotics dealer without reporting the volume to the government. If only the banker himself handles the cash, it is doubtful that even the auditors will catch the criminal activity.

James Hoffman convinced the DEA agents that he could set up William Morgan Hetrick with the latter, the money-laundering scam.

In May of 1982 Hoffman arranged to help Hetrick launder his money through the Eureka Federal Savings and Loan Company in San Carlos, California, with the help of a supposedly crooked bank president, James Benedict. What Hetrick did not realize, of course, was that James Benedict was actually undercover FBI special agent Benedict Tisa, who was acting with the cooperation of the real chairman of the savings and loan company, Kenneth Kidwell, who had made the bank available for such undercover operations in the past.

20

By June of 1982 the case against Morgan Hetrick was becoming solid. This was a man who was an admitted pilot for loads of cocaine, a fact that was recorded at the Eureka Federal Savings and Loan by undercover FBI agent Benedict Tisa. While Hetrick had officially retired from this business, he had discussed his past and his need for a money-laundering service. There was little doubt that he would be convicted after an arrest was made.

What happened next is less certain. In mid-June the Hetrick file was opened. The DEA, working in cooperation with the FBI, was going to gather proof of Morgan Hetrick's money-laundering activities. In addition to his work on the Hetrick case, James Hoffman began making contact with me, though the reason remains cloudy. According to government agents who have since talked with me and my attorney,

Hoffman was attempting to show how easily he could bring down a celebrity. If this was true, my involvement was by chance. Hetrick later told me that he believed I was the primary target from the beginning. Hoffman had mentioned my name and the names of entertainers such as Johnny Carson for no reason other than we were both in the news. In fact, long before he ever phoned me, Hoffman had read about my company's problems and at that time had told agent Gerald Scotti, who was "baby-sitting" him in another trial, "I met DeLorean, and as bad as he needs money, I can deliver him to you." If circumstances had been different, Hoffman could have targeted any other prominent American under financial stress.

Perhaps the most frightening thing for an innocent man in this whole thing is the scanty coincidence that prompted Hoffman to say he knew me—frightening in the sense that it shows how a chance intersection of two lives could destroy a man's reputation, family, company, and career.

At one time James Hoffman had worked for the pilot of Fletcher Jones, the same man Cristina once dated. Hoffman also rented a house in Pauma Valley, California, where I, too, had a vacation home. His son, Tom, had gone motorcycle riding with my son Zachary one Easter vacation, but since his son was much older than Zachary, no friendship had ever developed. In fact, my brief encounter with Hoffman happened during the nine days we spent in Pauma Valley over Easter vacation in 1980.

Because of business travel commitments, I spent only three days of that vacation time with Cristina and the children, and on one of those days, the Sunday after Easter, Hoffman and his wife had taken Zachary and their son, Tom, to a motocross race. When they brought Zachary home, Hoffman and his wife and Cristina and the two boys and I chatted for about ten minutes on the driveway in front of our house. Although Hoffman didn't discuss his business, I was under the impression that he sold used airplanes for a living.

That was my only contact with James Hoffman before June 29, 1982, when he called my office and talked with my secretary, Carole Winkler, who made notes (later introduced into evidence) concerning the call. As he introduced himself to Carole, Hoffman went to great lengths to explain who he was. Her notes confirm that he was sure I would not remember him, and indeed I did not. Once he got through to me, he talked extensively about some investors who might be interested in my company.

He asked, "Can your company be saved, or is it too late?"

I assured him it was not too late, that it was eminently salvageable. I said our people from our Orange County office could meet with his investors immediately.

He said, "No, I want to talk it over with you personally."

On July 9, we sent Hoffman a package of materials concerning the car company, addressed to the address he had given, a post-office box in Escondido, California. This package included everything an investor would need to know if he were considering putting money into our firm. It was the standard material we showed to anyone who expressed an interest in investing. I frankly did not expect to hear from him again; he sounded like dozens of other promoters we had heard from.

On July 11, I received several telephone calls from Hoffman at my Pauma Valley ranch, insisting that we meet that night. However, I wanted some of our staff people to screen him before I spent any of my time pursuing the matter.

But he was persistent that we meet and said, "My investors are ready right now, just awaiting my meeting with you to set the terms."

I had previously planned to meet Roy Nesseth, a friend and business associate in the company, at the Newport Marriott Hotel that day. I suggested Hoffman come to my hotel room there, where he and Roy and I could meet. I was in California for only a day of dealer meetings, I said. Roy, who lived there, would be the one following up with Hoffman if the investors were really interested.

Hoffman refused to come to the room and said he

wanted to discuss his commission with me one-on-one, without Roy. He wanted to meet me in the hotel bar, a place called the Main Brace. I finally agreed.

When I met him there, Hoffman promptly led me to the back of the room behind a folding screen, away from the bar. There was no one else in the section, so it was a quiet place to talk.

There were many tables in the back room, and I picked out one under an overhead light so we could both see the hundred or so pages of financial information and programs I had brought. Instead, Hoffman led me to a very dark booth. I thought it was odd at the time, and I told him we should sit in the light so we could review the documents. He insisted intensely on the dark booth. I did not argue. The man was a stranger, a bit eccentric in his actions, but by this time I had seen just about everything (I thought). If he had investors and wanted to sit in a dark booth to make a deal, that was fine with me. What mattered was getting help for the company to stem our cash problems.

During our conversation, I provided him with approximately 160 pages of documentation concerning the company. He glanced at them, then said that the people he had in mind could provide the $15 million we needed urgently. From this he wanted a 10 percent commission for acting as middleman, $1.5 million, and he wanted $300,000 for expenses. He was insistent about both amounts, never wavering from his demand for a total of $1.8 million.

I suppose I should have been surprised by Hoffman's behavior. But physically and emotionally I was exhausted, never knowing where to turn. Also, I had been contacted by dozens of investment middlemen who hoped to reap a commission from our plight. Hoffman was no different. There were fifteen or twenty middlemen calling me regularly, giving me progress reports on their "investors."

Whenever I was in New York, I went to St. Patrick's each day, listened to the Mass, and lit a candle to Saint John, "my saint." I also called Sonja every day and regularly read my horoscopes in some of the magazines to which we subscribed. I didn't really pay much attention to their predictions, but found myself checking them habitually as though they were Scripture. Each of these patterns became part of an overall daily ritual.

Cristina, too, was feeling the tension, although we did not discuss it as much as we should have. While I tried to isolate her from the problems, she was not unaware of my distress and was concerned about my spiritual state. Her sister and brother-in-law had recently become Christians and were anxious for us to have the same experience. Their words had had an effect on Cristina, and she began stressing to me, "John, Christ lives in your heart, not in St. Patrick's Cathedral."

Despite her advice the rituals continued, as did my search for ways to promote the company and raise money.

Even though I was in trouble, a number of advertising agencies wanted to use my high-profile celebrity status to sell their products. There were clothing lines, sunglasses, liquor companies, tire companies, and others. I listened to each presentation, then made my demands. I would appear in the advertising provided they stressed the DeLorean Motor Car. I would wear their sunglasses, for example, if the photograph included the car as the primary image. This was not what the companies wanted for their product, of course; so in the end I did only two advertisements: one for Goodyear and the other for Cutty Sark. In both, the DeLorean car was featured prominently and I took no money for my involvement. Every car we sold would be my reward as it helped stabilize the company.

During this period we also considered other projects, including the manufacture of buses. Bill Haddad encouraged us to undertake this project, saying that with his powerful Washington friends, we would be given contracts and could fill our Belfast Plastics plant with orders for bus side panels and help cover our overhead costs. If there was a way to improve our operations, I listened, but nothing he proposed proved practical because Haddad's Washington contacts either did not exist or chose not to get involved.

We needed working capital, nothing more. There was no cushion of money to handle the problems. As a result, I was willing to go anywhere and explore any avenue to legitimately finance the business.

James Hoffman was just one more lead. He called; he wanted to talk company financing; he responded positively when I named the size investment I needed. In my mind, he was as valid as any one of a dozen others who had come along. We would see if he could deliver the goods.

21

Meanwhile, unknown to me, on Hoffman's side, quite another scenario was taking place.

Hoffman had told the DEA agents of his first phone call to me. Supposedly, this call went unrecorded, a fact that allowed Hoffman and, later, the agents to say anything they wanted concerning what had happened. What they said was that Hoffman had called me to get my ten-year-old son Zachary's phone number for his sixteen-year-old son Tom and that I had asked him if he could arrange a heroin deal for me. Notwithstanding the fact that his son had run away from home and was a constantly drugged punk rocker in San Francisco with pink, blue, green, and purple hair, the FBI and DEA believed him.

When Hoffman and I met for the first time in the Main Brace bar, he had forced me into the dark booth because there was a hidden microphone installed there to pick up our conversation. I am convinced that the tape recording made of that session has never been made public because it would prove my innocence. According to investigators, this was also the story around the Department of Justice.

Despite this, Hoffman supposedly convinced the federal officers that I had long known him to be in the drug business and that it was very "obvious" that I was thinking of a heroin deal in meeting with him.

Oddly, the ridiculousness of this allegation was never analyzed. For example, Hoffman had not seen me in over two years, and at no time did anyone ever show that we were acquainted outside of that ten-minute casual conversation. Yet the contention would be made in court that when Hoffman and I talked on the telephone, Hoffman was certain that I knew he was heavily involved with narcotics and wanted to obtain money through a narcotics deal.

In reality, it would have been insane for Hoffman to have ever told me anything about his work in the manner in which he claimed and which the government later wanted the jury to believe had been done. No professional in the narcotics business, and Hoffman was a long-time professional, wants to go to prison. So if he meets someone casually, as even the government admitted was the only way I knew Hoffman, he is not going to discuss criminal activities that are the source of his income, for there is no way of knowing how the other person will react.

In this instance, I was a well-known corporate executive. If I chose to mention that I had a neighbor bragging that he was in the narcotics business, I would not be considered a crackpot. I would be taken seriously, and an effort would be made to see if the person making the comments had been serious or just trying to shock me.

I later learned that it was during this period that the DEA agents were still trying to determine whether they could entrap me with drugs. Some of the agents claimed to be unfamiliar with me. Others admitted they knew who I was but did not take Hoffman's charges seriously at this time.

Hoffman was working with a special agent named John Valestra, whose cover name was Vicenza, a man with whom he had worked closely in the Boukaram case. Valestra was one of those who said he did not know who I was. (A story written by Valestra's former DEA partner in *Rolling Stone* indicated that they engaged in every kind of illegal entry, frame-ups, planting evidence, drug dealing, and perjury.) Valestra would later give the impression that the July 11 meeting in the Main Brace bar was not recorded because there was not enough time to set up a recorder. Yet Hoffman's first call to the DEA on July 11 was at 8:30 in the morning. Our meeting was at 10:00 in the evening. Clearly, they not only had enough time and without doubt did record the meeting, but they destroyed the tape because it was exculpatory; it proved I was innocent. Word around the Federal Building was that it was indeed recorded and, like a dozen other exculpatory tapes, was destroyed.

22

In the business world there is an unusual breed of "middle" men and women. These are individuals who know people who may prove to be of value to others, though how and when is never certain.

For example, suppose that at a party you meet someone who is wealthy and may have several million dollars available for investment. Now, you may not know of any investment opportunity at the moment, but in your mind you file away the fact that this person may have money available.

Weeks or months go by. Then one day you learn of a company in trouble. The business is sound; the management knows what it is doing but needs money. If you can find someone interested in investing in this specific company, you will be paid what is known as a finder's fee. This might be an agreed-upon sum or it might be a fixed percentage. In addition, the investor may pay you a fee for providing information concerning the specific business he has been seeking. Often the finder specifically requests that neither the investor nor the investee mention the payment arrangements so that he can collect from both sides without either party knowing compensation has been provided by the other. In fact, this compensation may even be built into the amount of money requested.

This scenario is completely legal and quite routine on Wall Street. As far as I could tell, James Hoffman wanted to make such a deal. In fact, as time progressed, he made it quite clear that he would collect from both sides. During our first meeting on July 11, I tore a page from my pocket calendar and drafted a simple commission agreement with Hoffman, which I signed and he initialed. (This document has been verified by a top handwriting expert and would have been introduced into evidence if I had testified.)

I did want to run a check on the man, however, since I had no knowledge of his personal finances. At Hoffman's suggestion, I contacted his "banker," James Benedict, who confirmed that Hoffman had a bank account in eight figures. This meant he had at least $10 million on deposit and probably had many wealthy contacts. I was surprised by this, but accepted it; I had met others as sleazy as Hoffman who had tens of millions.

7/12/82—Telephone call tape recorded between James Benedict and John DeLorean. From Government Wire Tap Transcripts (partial quote):

DeLorean: "He [Hoffman] says that it may be possible that you could do some financing for us. . . . We have some cars in inventory that we would like to finance, and what I would like to do is figure out if that's a possibility."

Benedict: "Do you have anything, specifics or generalities, as to amounts or . . ."

DeLorean: "Well, in the States we have a total of about 1300 cars and we would like to finance either nine or all 1300 of those at about $13,500 a piece."

Benedict: "Okay, let me discuss this with our president, and maybe we can set up a meeting for you to come in if that would be . . ."

The remainder of the tape discusses the meeting and when it might be mutually satisfactory.

The money I was seeking from Eureka Federal would be for what is known as "floor planning." Essentially, this is money loaned to dealers for cars in their inventory. The dealer pays off the floor-plan loan on each car when he sells the car. With adequate floor planning, I could continue my operations, meet our obligations to the British, and buy time until they settled the insurance claim.

It is hard to know what the government agents were thinking during the two months that followed, July and August of 1982. Drugs were never mentioned in my conversations with Hoffman and Benedict. I discussed my car business and provided documentation concerning the company, its sales, and its needs. I was pushing for investment, desperate to keep going. Part of me was encouraged because I was meeting with the head of a major bank (Benedict), and a wealthy man (Hoffman) was calling me regularly to keep me comfortable with what was happening. Yet I still had no money. All that kept me going was the positive feedback from Sonja.

She assured me that this time the money would come; the financing would be there; the deal would work. "They have the money. They will invest," she said.

To me, Sonja's comforting words had to be coming from God because she said they were.

There was another motivating factor in all this, too, a factor I have only recently faced.

I took pride in building my own car company. The idea of stopping, of admitting I had failed, was untenable. I loved the Irish people who were working for me. I delighted in seeing my dream develop into reality. But if those had been my only reasons, I should have stopped the project any

183

number of times, at least temporarily. I pressed on, however, talking with characters such as Hoffman. Why? I didn't know then, but I do now. It was pride that would not let me quit. I had succumbed to the most insidious seducer preying on man—his pride. As C. S. Lewis commented, pride is "the essential vice, the utmost evil." I had yielded to the deadliest of sins, and I justified it by believing that my only motivation was to save the jobs of the people who worked for me. Even my sincere gesture of giving up control of the company to the British was more an act of pride than a meaningful self-sacrifice. Subconsciously, I did not want to see the end of the monument I had built to myself.

23

In September 1982 everything began to change. Hoffman began saying some unusual things during our telephone calls, although at the time the hint of menace in his words meant nothing to me. I gave courteous but nonspecific answers to most of his statements only to keep the dialogue going. I was not looking for hidden meanings; I was not trying to read between the lines. All I could think about was the money I needed. That was all I could talk about; that was all I heard.

Looking at this period objectively, it seems as though no rational man could have become so involved with such disreputable types without realizing that something was wrong. The idea that I would talk with them day after day, eventually feeling so threatened that I would give up all rights to my own company, seems impossible. But I was not a rational man at that point.

First, there were the telephone calls to and from Hoffman, Benedict, and others. Between July 12 and October 18, there were almost 200 calls, an average of two a day. There were promises of money, constant reassurances that I would receive what I needed, offset by endless delays, threats, and the eventual discovery of their narcotics deals in which they wanted me to participate. I was like a donkey whose driver forever dangles a carrot on a stick.

In addition there were other potential investors. Some were "crazies," men and women who believed they had millions but who might be using their last few pennies to make the call. There were people who wanted to negotiate just because they could brag to their friends that they had met a "famous" person. And there were legitimate investors who seriously considered giving me money. Yet there was no way to tell who was rich, who was poor, who was crazy, and who might supply me with the capital I desperately needed. As a result, during that ninety-eight-day period I made almost 3,000 telephone calls and traveled to almost a hundred cities around the world.

The Seconal I took to sleep at night was never meant to provide complete rest. In fact, a drug-induced sleep prevents complete rest. I later learned that the quantity of Seconal I was taking could have increased the anxiety I was trying to fight. My confusion and fuzzy thinking were probably made worse by the drugs, yet because I had an open prescription and my doctor had no idea how much I was taking, I did not stop. I would knock myself out with the drug, then use caffeine, another anxiety-producing drug, to fight to stay awake after only four or five hours of rest. I will never know how I avoided a heart attack or a complete breakdown during this period.

I got a call from Hoffman telling me to meet him in Washington on Saturday, September 4; he had good news for me, he said.

When I arrived at the L'Enfant Plaza Hotel in Washington, D.C., about noon on September 4, 1982, I called Hoffman's room.

"Come up in a half hour," he said. "I've got some good news for you. I'm going to invest my commission in a deal that will provide all the money your company will ever need."

I was pleased at his positive assurance, but I did wonder how it had suddenly become "his" commission—he had not earned it yet. Later our brilliant investigator, Jack Palladino, was able to show that this unearned commission technique was one Hoffman used all of his life. Frequently, he sued his "marks" for unearned commissions.

When I got to Hoffman's room thirty minutes later, unknown to me, the meeting was videotaped with hidden cameras and was the culmination of careful preparations on the part of the government. (This was the first videotape.) For almost two months I had been manipulated into believing that Hoffman represented legitimate investors. During this same period, Hoffman had prepared Morgan Hetrick for a possible involvement with me.

Hoffman began the discussion by explaining that he had run into delays regarding the financing but that he had put together a possible interim deal involving some Colombians. He explained that these men had the ability to come up with anything desired and could certainly put together at least $30 million by the following Tuesday.

I didn't know what Hoffman was talking about, and I did not care. All I could think about was that he might be able to bring me $30 million! He didn't suggest that I had to do anything. All he said was that the Colombian group could bring in as much as $30 million.

I suppose that the mention of Colombians should have been a clue as to the true purpose of the "business deal." Colombia is one of the major suppliers of illegal drugs being brought into the United States, and the very mention of the country gains the instant attention of drug-enforcement agents. But I was not in the narcotics business. I was an automobile manufacturer who had previously been a top

187

executive for a company with branches and sales forces located internationally. No matter what illegal activities take place in a particular area, no matter what corruption might exist, there are also legitimate business people, and they usually constitute the bulk of the people within the country. They may not be as well known as the criminals; they certainly do not make the same headlines. But they do dominate the business world. So when Hoffman mentioned Colombian business people, to me it sounded as legitimate as if he had said they were French or Swiss or Canadian. Not every French connection is a heroin manufacturer from Marseilles.

Later, watching the videotape of that September 4 meeting, I was able to see the way Hoffman was trying to set me up. He stressed that the Colombians wanted to make a cash investment and that they did not want to sit on the board of my company. He later stated that Benedict would represent them on the board, which was legitimate enough. In the world of the rich, personal eccentricities are rampant and unpredictable. There is usually a point where a major investor wants to have some power to assure himself that only practical business decisions are being made. Again, the message that might have been obvious to a person living in the world of narcotics was completely lost on me, a fact I suspect Hoffman recognized, for he immediately approached the subject of drugs.

Hoffman told me that there were two ways to obtain the money for me. The first was what he had alluded to on the lobby phone, and it involved a drug deal in which he would invest his "commission" of $1.8 million, the profits of which he could use to buy stock in the company. This statement shocked me senseless. I mumbled meaningless words until I collected my thoughts. The alternative was to continue to pursue the interim financing that, he claimed, was still realistic so far as he knew. I immediately told him that the interim financing was the better way to go.

Hoffman did not seem to be surprised by my interest in pursuing only the interim financing. He did not push the narcotics deal but switched to a different concern. His investors were uncertain whether or not I could come up with the money desired. I would need to personally or corporately have some cash to show good faith. Since I had approximately $2 million available for an arrangement that would provide me with the financing, as I had told Hoffman originally, this did not seem to be a serious concern.

As Hoffman continued to talk, he stressed that one of his deals was going to be made regardless of my involvement. He explained that the dope deal had gone too far and would take place no matter what. Since this did not involve me in any way, I simply agreed with him, not certain why he was telling me these details. But I was deeply concerned.

Listening to James Hoffman in that hotel room that day, I suddenly realized that I might be in trouble. If Hoffman was to be believed, and I had no reason to doubt what he was saying, he was obviously actively involved with organized crime. Even more frightening was the fact that the president of Eureka Savings and Loan, James Benedict, was a close associate of Hoffman. The obvious implication was that they worked together and that the Mafia or some other organized crime group owned a multi-billion-dollar financial institution. If I could not find some way to rid myself of James Hoffman and his friends, I would be trapped in the midst of extremely dangerous, powerful criminals. At that moment, then, my only thought was that I had to try and scare Hoffman as much as he was frightening me; I had to make him think I represented some organization even more violent than his connections.

The answer was obvious. My automobile manufacturing company was in Northern Ireland, the home of the Irish Republican Army, one of the most feared terrorist organizations in the free world. People who did not understand the Irish presumed that the only way anyone could do business in West Belfast was to be a part of the IRA or at least pay protection money. I could only hope that Hoffman and his friends were as naïve as so many others. If they were, I could pretend to be directly connected with men so tough that even the largest organized-crime groups might be willing to stop putting pressure on me.

As these thoughts whirled through my mind, I was also trying to make sense of what Hoffman was saying. Apparently, he had a legitimate way to help me obtain the $30 million he had been discussing, and he also had a drug deal in which he was engaged with someone else. He made it clear that he and his partners had put up the money to buy drugs and were selling them at substantial profit. He showed me a paper related to that deal to prove that approximately the same amount of money could be obtained from it, but all I wanted was to get back to discussing interim financing. He then furtively burned the piece of paper in the ashtray. (A "copy" of this paper was later introduced into evidence in court, purporting to show my initials next to the $1.8 million, implying it was my "investment" not Hoffman's. My lawyer was able to show there were four different "versions" on pieces of paper and that the one introduced into evidence was actually dated a month after the Washington meeting in October by two different agents. Obviously, it was faked by the FBI.) Hoffman then stressed again that the deal was an accomplished fact, but if I would put up his approximately $2 million "commission" he would invest his profits in DMC.

Suddenly, I only wanted to escape.

I told Hoffman that I could not get involved in a drug deal, and I reinforced my stand with a powerful lie: I told him that I was getting my money for his commission from the IRA, that I couldn't act without their approval, and that they only did "legitimate" deals. All I could do was accept normal interim financing.

Why didn't I just say that there was no way I would involve myself with something illegal? Because I did not know how organized crime operated. Once an offer was made, did this mean they considered me involved? Perhaps I knew too much? I knew Hoffman; I knew his accomplice Benedict, the president of a bank with more than forty branches; and I knew Vicenza's name. Was this "the offer I couldn't refuse," as the joke goes? Had someone made a false assumption concerning my desperation, bringing up the drugs only when he was certain I was trapped? And even if I was being tested, didn't this still make me a dangerous witness against them?

I knew nothing about crime, criminal law, or criminals except what anyone learns from reading newspapers and watching television. If I walked out the door, refusing to have anything more to do with them, would they retaliate against me or my family? I did not know, and I did not know what to do. I assumed that by bringing in the IRA I could buy myself time. In fact, I claimed that it would be at least a week before I could make contact with them, hoping that the extra time would mess up their timetable and I would be "forced" to avoid this "opportunity."

I have never feared for my own life. Somehow I think I was born without this fear. In fact, as I have mentioned, there have been times when I have deliberately tempted death. After Zachary and Kathryn entered my life, however, my attitude changed. I still did not worry about my own life, but I suddenly wanted to see Zach's graduation from college and give Kathryn away in marriage. Their lives were so precious to me that I would do anything to keep them safe. I was only vulnerable through them, and if someone recognized this fact, I could be controlled. I had to protect them.

My first concern was to obtain legal and spiritual counsel. The spiritual counsel came from Sonja, and for the legal advice, I turned to Tom Kimmerly, the lawyer for our corporation, who maintained offices in both Detroit and New York.

While I had never needed to be well-informed about the law, I did understand that a lawyer is considered an officer of the court. If he knows that a crime is being committed, he is required to tell you to report it to law-enforcement officers. The trouble was that I did not want to go to law-enforcement officers. I knew from reading about J. Edgar Hoover's attempts to destroy Martin Luther King, Jr., Jane Fonda, and others that all FBI people were not as pure as the driven snow. What if I picked the wrong person and found I was talking with someone who was on the payroll of Hoffman's organized crime ring? (I had no idea that the reverse was actually true, that Hoffman was being paid by law enforcement.) All I knew for certain was that the organized crime ring had apparently acquired a major financial institution, the one that had vouched for Hoffman. If they were big enough and rich enough to own and control a major savings and loan, it was highly probably that they were paying off a few federal agents too. I did not want to place Tom Kimmerly in a position where he had to tell me to do something I felt would be too dangerous. I wanted some other option, an option that might protect my family.

I called Tom and explained that I was being pressured to invest in an illegal transaction involving some extremely bad and dangerous people whom I thought to be organized crime. I did not tell him that I was being asked to become involved with a narcotics deal. I said I needed to know what I could do to keep from getting hurt. I was convinced they wanted DMC so they could use its resources to move money around the world.

Tom told me to call him when I got back to New York; in the meantime he would think about it and perhaps seek other counsel.

When I got back to Manhattan, I called him. Tom knew that I was talking to every potential investor who came along; he was often doing the same on behalf of the company. He had analyzed what I had told him and had concluded my best out was procrastination, not confrontation. He told me, *"Never commit to anything; never enter into any illegal agreement; never give them any money; never accept any money from them; don't give them anything of value."* He said, "Find ways to stall them, to put them off. Procrastinate." If I stalled them long enough, they would become frustrated and bored with me. They would look elsewhere for what they wanted. I could go to the police later, possibly in an anonymous way—but first I had to extricate myself.

Tom's advice made sense. Furthermore, it jibed with my own instincts in mentioning the IRA during my meeting with Hoffman, and so I followed it at once. I also sent copies of letters related to my Hoffman dealings to Tom, but these never indicated the exact nature of my problems. In essence, I followed his advice to the letter without forcing him into a legally compromising circumstance. (In the end it was good advice, and the jury found that indeed no crime was committed.)

I did tell Sonja, however. I needed to share with someone the entire story of what was unfolding, and I was not comfortable telling Cristina. I was terrified for my family, but I did not want Cristina to be terrified about something that at the moment was out of my control.

As ridiculous as it sounds, I even momentarily considered the Federal Protected Witness program. The idea was ludicrous, of course. I possessed a face readily identifiable throughout the United States, Canada, and Europe. Cristina was a much-photographed model. It was impossible to imagine us relocating to a tiny town where I would pump gas for a living and Cristina would work as a waitress in the local cafe!

The only answer was to stall but not confront.

9/15/82—James Benedict call to John DeLorean:

DeLorean: "Okay, how are we doing on the, ah, the investment, that's the thing . . ."

Benedict: "Okay."

DeLorean: "I'm desperate. . . ."

Benedict then went on to explain that there was a second person who "has some reservations." He wanted me to talk with the man directly, though he stressed that he knew the other person was interested. There was no mention of drugs, but there was a request for money. Benedict was now pushing me hard to put up the money for Hoffman's commission. He discussed this explicitly in some of the tapes that were destroyed, that is, in the supposedly "unrecorded" calls. (Incidentally, if we had presented our defense, our tape expert would have proved that Benedict's tapes were not only selectively culled and tagged illegally, but that those submitted to the court as evidence were not the originals demanded by law but cleverly rerecorded tapes.)

Benedict: "The first thing I gotta do with you, and it is also the very strong point with him, he says, is I want to see the color of the man's money. . . . For you and for him and for me, safety-wise, and his business end of it and your business end of it, I've got to have on your end in my bank . . . and I gotta go to him and vouch personally that it's there and it's on hand. . . . He'll pick up the products we need, and he'll front that end of it."

Again, this last statement referred to the deal taking place without my involvement. It was a statement of fact.

Later that same day I received a second telephone call from Benedict. This time I decided to bring in my so-called IRA "tough guy" contact again to keep me from having to make any deal. I explained that I had gotten hold of my IRA contact and that there was a serious problem: The IRA had given the $2 million to the British government on Friday via their New York law firm, Scadden, Arps, and there was no more money, no collateral, no anything. Just an empty shell corporation, DMC.

DeLorean: ". . . what he's [the IRA contact] done is he put the two million on deposit with the receiver [the British government, sworn enemies of the IRA], until we get some other investments. And so it's sitting there right now, and I honestly don't know what to do about it. In other words, we had to do that, or our whole deal was dead anyhow."

Benedict: "Right."

DeLorean: "So he had to do it. And there wasn't any alternative, and it's the only place there was any. So that's where it is, and we can only free it up by replacing it, you know, with actual investment in the company. It's in a deposit there now, and he doesn't think there's any way to get it back until the investment comes in."

Essentially, I told Benedict and company that I couldn't invest in their drug deal because I had no money and that the IRA couldn't get me money until someone invested in my company.

Benedict: ". . . you really put me in a bad spot now."

I regarded these words, said ominously, as a serious threat.

DeLorean: "I know that, but it wasn't a matter of choice, you see; it was the only alternative, and their [the IRA's] only interest is in keeping the factory alive. They're not interested in anything else. . . ."

In other words, I know you mob figures are bad guys, but I've got the IRA who are even "badder," and they want money for my company. They're not interested in your drug deal, just investment capital for the car company. If you have that kind of money, we can talk. If you don't, I have to yield to the "baddest" men who are pressuring me.

Benedict was extremely frustrated. He kept telling me what a bad spot I had put him in.

Benedict: "This is going to make us look extremely, extremely bad. And it puts me in a very bad position in general 'cause we committed ourselves on your behalf."

Now the threats seemed to be escalating. All the gangster movies I had ever seen became real to me. "You put me in a bad spot; I'm going to cause you grief like you've never known," was the message. I was going to die the death of a thousand cuts, have my feet encased in cement, or experience some other horror. Fantasy and reality blended together in my irrational state.

I explained that "their [the IRA's] interest is only in keeping the factory there." I stressed that "the people who put the money up are the Irish. It's an Irish group, and I told Jim [Hoffman] what they were." If the message about the IRA had not been clear, I wanted to further emphasize it. Finally, a frustrated Benedict said what I wanted to hear.

195

Benedict: "So what do you want me to do? You want me to kill this deal?"

DeLorean: "I don't see any alternative right now. Unless you got some other idea, unless we can get to him on the investment, and you're saying that's impossible."

In other words, either invest in my company or don't talk with me. I'm not going to do a drug deal.

But Benedict the agent could not let go. He finally returned to the talk about my company, explaining that maybe something could be worked out. The business had strong tax advantages, and maybe there was still a way to get me my money.

All my IRA talk was nonsense, of course. I just prayed it would work.

24

Under the laws of the United States, once it was obvious that I did not want to be involved with a criminal act, the FBI should have backed off and left me alone, instead of trying to find new ways to entrap me. Their job is to discover and prosecute crimes, not to create them. Even assuming they could digest that ridiculous IRA story, all the FBI had to do was check the Scadden, Arps bank account to see that no funds from the IRA went to the British government. But the agents and the prosecutors had already mentally received the praise, promotions, and bonuses for entrapping me, and they were not going to let the mere fact of my innocence louse up their plans. (As Prosecutor Walsh later boasted to agent Gerald Scotti, "Nailing DeLorean will put me on the cover of *Time* magazine.")

Looking back on those days, I am bothered by the way

all of this was handled by the federal agents. As I learned after my arrest, there were law-enforcement officers witnessing what was going on, recording my meetings and my telephone calls, reviewing the case as it was developing. It should have been obvious that I was trying to avoid any involvement with criminal activity. They knew I was not a criminal, that I was a respected corporate executive, a fact mentioned in the opening remarks by the prosecuting attorney at my trial. Yet this fact was totally ignored. Instead, the government chose to spend millions of dollars pursuing me, even after it was obvious that I was trying to avoid any involvement in the dishonest drug deal.

I believe the FBI had already contacted the British government and knew the truth: that I had no IRA contacts and that the "IRA man" I had mentioned was a prominent Protestant member of Parliament and former Minister of Industry. They knew I was lying about the IRA; it should have been obvious that I was deliberately trying to escape from their clutches. Why did they choose to ignore this obvious signal that something was wrong? They were no longer upholding law and justice but were using their powers as a license for moral corruption.

After Benedict's call on September 15, I got a call from Hoffman. "Benedict tells me you don't have the [commission] money and the deal's dead," he said. "Do you have any collateral?"

On this September 15 tape, my answer, which was absolutely true, "I have no collateral" was deliberately obliterated. Fortunately, through modern audio techniques, our brilliant tape expert, Anthony Pelicano, was able to reconstruct much of my side of the conversation. (If I had testified, we would have played the clarified tapes for the jury.)

I said, "I have no collateral. The banks have a lien on all of my personal assets and the British government owns all of the company's assets. There is no collateral of any type for a loan." This was true. As prosecutor Walsh testified in another deposition, the FBI checked and knew it was.

Hoffman then said, "You don't need any collateral. We just want it to look right so they [the "big boys"] don't get upset."

I said I was sorry, but there was nothing I could do. There was no collateral, no assets.

I'm out, I thought. I had held them off, and now I was certain they would drop me. I had broken free with minimal confrontation. I should have been relieved. Instead, I was extremely upset, even hyper.

At that time I was taking two Seconals every night to sleep. Later on that evening I took my pills and dropped into a fitful slumber. The phone awakened me, and I groggily answered. It was Hoffman. I was instantly awake, my stomach in knots, my breathing rapid, my heart racing. *No more*, I told myself. *No more.* I wanted it all to end. I wanted Hoffman to leave me alone. It was as though I was in the midst of one of those horror pictures where each time the monster is struck down, it returns bigger and stronger. Only this was real life. This man was flesh and blood, and the danger was all the more terrifying because of it. My movie was not going to end. The monster I was facing was not going to disappear.

This time Hoffman was harsh, profane, and threatening. "You know too much—you can't get out—if you try to get out there'll be a bloody mess—I'll send your baby daughter's head home in a shopping bag! When Benedict calls you tomorrow, you go along with whatever he says."

The unthinkable, the unspeakable, had finally been said.

25

The next morning Benedict called, and he immediately let me know where he stood. "Understand you *spoke* to Jim Hoffman," he said threateningly.

He then proceeded to detail a system by which I could provide what would seem to be collateral for Hetrick. Benedict knew there were no assets; he knew I was putting up nothing of value. But he stressed, "We just want it to look right," and that he would lie to Hetrick and tell him I put up some money.

By now I was totally confused and frightened. What in the world was happening?

On September 28 I was in Los Angeles and met with a man named Vicenza, who was introduced as being connected with Benedict's bank. (In reality, he was special agent John Valestra of the Drug Enforcement Administration and was considered Hoffman's "control." This meant that he was responsible for overseeing all of Hoffman's actions as an informant, especially when a sting operation was taking place.) Hoffman was also present for the meeting held in the Bonaventure Hotel.

I had talked with Sonja about the meeting, and she had assured me everything would work out in my favor. As unbelievable as it seems, I was still convinced that if I couldn't get the criminals to leave me alone, I would give them the entire company. Then, when and if they concluded their investment, legal or illegal, they could do business with the British government. And should they try to launder money through the company, the British government would soon put an end to their criminal activities.

For several minutes I gave Vicenza a review of the company's history, the promises of the British government, the auditing of our company's business practices by the respected Arthur Andersen Company, and related details. I also explained that the British government owed us $90 million, money that they refused to pay. I explained that we could sue, but there was a good chance it would take ten years in the courts, at the end of which time we could win but still have a bankrupt company.

I told Vicenza that I needed at least $30 million and that double that amount would give us a comfortable range of operating capital. I stressed that someone becoming involved in this way would have the potential to earn $100 million a year.

Vicenza said there was the possibility of throwing good money after bad, but I emphasized the popularity of the cars, the potential for future sales, and then detailed the success of BMW, pointing out that in 1959, BMW was in bankruptcy.

When I had finished, Vicenza and Hoffman began talking between themselves, discussing the money they were getting from a heroin deal and a separate cocaine deal. This was the money they would have for investing in the company, they said.

All my nightmares returned. The September 15 late-night call from Hoffman. The threat to my daughter. *You've put me in a bad spot. . . . There'll be a bloody mess. . . .* I was sitting with two men who were discussing profits from drugs that exceeded the gross incomes of many respected businesses. But I did not believe they were really in the drug business. The "deals" they discussed changed every minute and made no sense. I was convinced they had created this entire scenario to make me feel "involved" and that their true motives, which they would not disclose to me, were to take control of my company for a massive, international money-laundering scheme. I was certain they were underworld criminals, living lives filled with violence and unexplained death. I had already seen that a major financial institution had been corrupted. I wondered how the depositors in Eureka Federal Savings and Loan would feel if they knew they were investing with organized crime. I had sensed Benedict's and Hoffman's anger when I failed to deliver money for any deals, knowing that I did not feel their wrath because they had believed my story about the IRA giving my money to the British government. And now I was in the midst of their world, hearing about their crimes, gaining information that, if revealed to the proper law-enforcement officers, could result in their being jailed. I was being dragged into a circle I did not want to be in. If anyone was expendable, I was. If someone had to die to insure that their activities could continue, I was undoubtedly going to be the victim.

9/28/82—Meeting with Hoffman, Valestra, and DeLorean:

Hoffman: "Now then, in about five weeks after we pay all expenses of, of the Thai heroin deal, we're going to have approximately thirty-six to thirty-seven million dollars available. Now if you need that amount now, that's about what you need right now, or you can have ten extra million right now. I'm not trying to jump ahead of you John, I'm assuming, I shouldn't do that, so I apologize. Whatever you two decide on the $10 million that's coming up here today, there's those funds available and there is approximately thirty-seven available from that, and as of three days ago, I mean we're firm on the disposition of the Thai product, all right, so there's approximately $47 million gonna be available."

Valestra: "Not overnight, let's put it that way. Within at the outside six weeks, ten of that being available in the next forty-eight hours."

Hoffman: "What I'm concerned with now is the initial transaction which we're hours away [from]. I have to be told. You know Mr. Hetrick, and I won't bother him until the mechanics are ready to go, the money is in place, and basically it would behoove people to move quickly, and I can't control that end of it."

DeLorean: "Right."

Valestra: "And I want you to know that from that particular cocaine purchase you look at within forty-eight hours initial payback probably, now I'm including my share of this too, we're looking at a figure of $10 million initially. Now part of that would normally be mine, what I needed from you is the assurance and the partial percentage of the company was what, fifty I think, is very generous. I'm certainly not that down."

DeLorean: "No, I think if we could get it funded so it's on a good solid basis, then it's 50 percent, fifty-fifty deal everybody's got everything."

The talk continued. Whatever they said, I agreed that it made sense. I did not commit to anything, just played along with whatever they said. Then I suggested that any money provided come through a legitimate source such as the Eureka Savings and Loan.

At some point in our conversation, Hoffman decided to take things a step further. He brought up the idea of laundering money through my company. I wasn't certain just what was happening, but I also knew I couldn't tell him how I truly felt. Instead, I just discussed routine investment that would be open to anyone, hoping that he and Valestra would become bored.

DeLorean: "... if you had a tremendous amount of money that you wanted to bring in as a long-term capital gain, it could be worked out in a way that you know maybe two or three hundred million dollars could be handled that way, but to do it properly should be planned at the beginning about what the magnitude of it is. For example, say that this first ten million was regarded as a prime initial investment in this company and with the repurchase at the market value of the other stock, that means what you do is that as additional funds come in, the original investor then could get ten or fifteen times on his money, paid back as a capital gain as soon as the capital-gain period went by, and you could do that once as long as you knew about what the magnitude of the whole thing was so the whole transaction would track. And that would be straight up. It's been done. It's just like Arthur Rock and this Apple Computer. He put in a couple of million bucks and took out fifty, sixty million."

Hoffman: "In this Andersen outfit [refers to Arthur Andersen, our auditors], they're not going to let him dig into the origin of these funds?"

DeLorean: "Not if it comes through the Eureka bank."

Always I was trying to give myself an out. They were talking laundering money so I switched the subject to legitimate investment. Although I didn't think they realized it at the time, I was also trying to keep my company from being in the middle of improper deals. If they wanted to put money in the Eureka bank and then make a legitimate investment in my company, they would know the potential return. All I was certain about was that I needed to keep stalling, keep from making a commitment to work with them on their terms.

During this videotaped meeting, I was also asked to call Morgan Hetrick. (Since I had only met the man a week earlier at a Benedict-arranged [videotaped] meeting at the Bel Air Sands, I assume this call was supposed to somehow solidify my involvement with him for the government agents, though this fact was not known to me at the time.) I was to tell Hetrick that the deal was going along and that the cash was available. But I couldn't force myself to say I would put up the money when I knew I wouldn't; I was ever mindful of my lawyer's advice to "make no deals."

Everything that was said set me up as the middle man, relaying messages to both parties. I was so frightened that I would have gone along with anything they requested short of actually getting involved with their deal. If they thought it would help them to have me relaying messages, then so be it.

As I thought it over, I became convinced that I had to give up the company to save my life—give them 100 percent of it. I had already offered them 50 percent of the company, as was mentioned to Valestra and Hoffman in the hotel room. Giving them 100 percent would force them to work directly with the British government. No matter how large an organized crime operation Hoffman and his friends represented, it would never be big enough to successfully tackle the British government. Yes. I would give up the entire company. When they had 100 percent they would no longer have any use for me, and there would be no point in threatening my family. I would have no power in the company, not even a job. It would be theirs.

9/28/82—Telephone call Benedict to DeLorean:
DeLorean: "And the trust would have 100 percent of the shares of the company, both Vicenza's and mine. And they would hold the votes of the company, I mean 100 percent of the shares and the votes, for some period of time."

My fears, however, were still compounded by telephone calls from Hoffman (these were unrecorded—naturally!). After the September 4 conversations, he regularly alerted me to the fact that he and his partners were extremely powerful organized-crime figures. He wanted me to know the danger I was facing. He also continued threatening my children, especially Kathryn, implying she would be hurt or killed if I did not cooperate.

The pressures building inside me were enormous. I wanted to be free of these people. At the same time, I was driven to continue my search for investors, trying to keep the business moving (we were down to a skeleton crew in West Belfast, but were still operating).

I was out of control. Nothing made sense any more. Nothing seemed to work. I lit my candles, attended the masses, talked with Sonja, yet constantly avoided the one commitment that could have brought me true inner peace. I had too much pride to stop.

I was going to succeed. I *had* to succeed. And in my strivings, I was losing everything that mattered.

26

On October 5, 1982, I received a wire from the British government. It was both a nightmare and a blessing, for it meant that my cash needs were critical, but it also meant an exit from my involvement with Hoffman and Benedict and their criminal schemes. The wire stated, in part: "Unless by 18:00 hours our time tomorrow, you provide us with independent confirmation that not less than $10 million is available to DMCL as working capital and will be paid into that company's account at the time the agreement for the acquisition Northern Ireland assets is completed, we shall inform the government that we cannot be satisfied about the financial arrangements for the new company and shall announce a consequence final closure of the facility."

It was signed by Paul Shewell, the joint Receiver.

(Later we would learn that the British had given the

company a number of short extensions, each coinciding with a meeting I was to have with the agents—clear indication to me that there was a deep and coordinated two-government conspiracy to entrap me.)

Should Benedict and his people give me a letter of confirmation concerning their intention to provide legitimate funds, I could still save my company. If they did not, there was a good chance that all would be lost, but I would no longer be of interest to the criminals. My pride told me that it was important to have my company survive at any price. My common sense told me that perhaps I was at last going to be free from the pressures of organized crime.

But these were not the only pressures bearing down on me. Various creditors were beginning to bring lawsuits against the company. Some had potentially valid claims if the company went under. Others had invested in ways that they knew were of high risk and unfortunately were going to take a loss. But it seemed as though everyone was out to destroy John DeLorean, and there was no place to turn except to Sonja and her constant reassurances. Yet Sonja kept assuring me that I was acting properly, that everything would work in my favor. She and her "church" group were working for me through their prayers; the checks I was sending her were proper payments for what she was doing; and all would be well. I just had to have faith in her.

Suddenly, Benedict was the one who was stalling. He was being backed into the corner, though I failed to realize that this was because of the government's case, not because I was triumphing over organized crime. So I continued talking with him about financing through his bank, playing along with him, emphasizing that it was his company now. I kept stressing the long-term value of this legitimate business deal and the need for them to take it seriously.

10/7/82—DeLorean to Benedict Telephone Call:
DeLorean: "We're scrupulous in our business here to be sure that we follow the exact rules precisely in every single

way. You gotta do that." [This refers to SEC, auditors, and British government supervision.]

By the evening of October 18 I was near the end of my physical and mental resources. Sonja was assuring me that all was well; Benedict was discussing contracts; and Hoffman was threatening that my family would be hurt if I did not cooperate. Everyone apparently believed that I did have the muscle of the IRA behind me, but they were not afraid. Through the haze of physical, emotional, and mental exhaustion, all I could see was the destruction of everything I held dear.

I was convinced I would never leave California alive. There might be a tragic accident. I might just disappear, buried in some remote area. Or I might be tortured, my mutilated body left where it would appear that I had been killed by a sadistic mugger, the truth of the killing being known to other organized criminals who would take it as a warning.

I was the man who knew too much. But I was not going to let the people who murdered me go unpunished.

With that resolve, I sat down and wrote a letter to my lawyer, detailing everything that had taken place. If I called him, he might advise me not to go, might want me to tell my story to potentially corrupt law-enforcement officers instead and further endanger my family. By writing the letter I would have some power over the gangsters, some possible leverage to protect my family or even gain revenge from the grave if the worst happened.

10-18-82

Tom—

I'm going to L.A. tomorrow to accomplish a minor miracle! I will have induced organized crime to literally donate $10 million to reopen the Belfast plant—and when they figure it out they cannot do anything about it!

Hoffman, Benedict, Hetrick, and Vicenza are not what they pretend to be—(don't be shocked) cocaine dealers! Too many things they have told me are literally impossible. They have also engaged me in a play-acting scenario that is so Mickey Mouse I have trouble keeping a straight face. Hoffman, Hetrick, Benedict, and Vicenza have known each other for years—I don't even know Hoffman or Benedict's home phone numbers—but Hoffman constantly calls me on the phone and tells me to call Benedict or Hetrick and then proceeds to tell me exactly what to say to them—word for word. Without any question they are part of organized crime and Eureka Federal Savings and Loan is a front they use for laundering money. Their cocaine charade is designed to make me feel implicated so that I won't look too hard at their source of funds.

Tomorrow when they put the $10 million into Eureka and Benedict wire-transfers it to Cork-Gully, the mob will own 100 percent of DMC, Inc., a corporate shell with no assets! The Stoy-Hayward client will control the plant that the U.K. government still owns. The DMC shareholders will continue to own the American company and control everything. In effect, the mob will have donated $10 million to the Belfast plant and have gotten virtually nothing for it—a minority position in a government-owned factory in war-torn Belfast! Obviously, they wanted to control the motor co. to use it for moving and laundering money. When they find out they own and control nothing, they will be very pissed! The reason I'm convinced they won't do anything about it is that to take any kind of action—against the company or myself—will blow their whole money-laundering operation at Eureka Federal. When they start to push I will tell them that there is a letter that is to be opened in the event of my death. They will just take a walk.

If I'm wrong, and my death is from any but absolutely natural causes, take this letter to the police, otherwise destroy it. Tom, take care of my family.

God bless you,
John DeLorean.

I addressed this to Tom Kimmerly and his law firm, Kimmerly, Gans and Shaler, with the following instructions: "This sealed letter is to be held in trust by you for two years, to October 18, 1984. In the event of my death within that two years, open the letter and follow the instructions. If I am alive and well on October 18, 1984 return the letter to me unopened. John Z. DeLorean, October 18, 1982."

On the morning of October 19, I personally delivered the letter to Tom's Manhattan office before I caught the plane for Los Angeles and what I thought was certain death.

Hoffman and Benedict met me in a white Cadillac (a car I later learned Hoffman had purchased with the government's "expense" money!) and drove me to the Sheraton La Reina Hotel near Los Angeles International Airport. We had been scheduled to meet in Orange County at DMC's Irvine headquarters so that I could introduce Benedict as the new owner to the management there. But that morning before I left our Fifth Avenue apartment to drop the letter at Kimmerly's office, I had received a call from my secretary telling me that Hoffman had just phoned and requested that I meet them in Los Angeles instead. He said he would meet me at the airport so we could get to the banks before they closed.

It's about over, I thought when Carole gave me the message. This last-minute change of plans to a neutral site just confirmed what had kept me awake the night before. *They're going to kill me. But I'll have the last laugh. The company and the British government will have their money, the people will have their jobs, and there's nothing these creeps can do about it. Poetic justice.*

I was almost too numb to be scared, yet the way my mind was racing indicated that deep inside I was out of control.

We got out of the car at the hotel. *They aren't going to kill me in the parking area, are they? Perhaps the elevator . . . the room . . .*

Inside, Vicenza was waiting. Was he the hit man? Or did they really want to talk business? Had I convinced them I would go along with their schemes? I would follow Kimmerly's advice to talk business, agree to anything, but stall. But I was convinced in my heart that this was the end of the line for me.

After the preliminary banalities, Vicenza asked me about my company.

"We sold about a thousand cars in the last three months, so that part of it's okay," I told him. "We're right at the end of the line now with the guys in Ireland. They sent me a telex [October 19, 1982] saying that because we didn't show the required amount of money, they were going to let the people go on Friday. The people working in the plant."

"The reason I asked," said Valestra. "I heard something on the radio about . . . ah . . . shutdown."

"Well, that's what this is unless we, unless I show them that I've got the money between now and Friday, they're going to do it," I replied. (Again the British had adjusted their plant-closing deadline to suit the FBI schedule.)

"We're not too late?" asked Valestra.

"No, you're right on time," I said. I knew that if they made their $10 million payment to the British government, the company would stay open. "This is what they call in the nick of time."

I explained that everyone just wanted to get the money and get everything completed. But I also stressed that this was a legitimate business deal, not a laundering scheme or anything else.

"You recognize that none of the money goes anywhere but in working capital of the business anyhow, you know," I added. "You're not doing anything with it, but [it] *stays right in the business*. They just want to know that enough is there for the company to take over." In other words, none of the money would go to me—it all went to Benedict to be given to the British.

Then Valestra asked about the laundering scheme Hoffman had discussed. He wanted to know about the "conduit for funds, getting it out of the country." He wanted specifics, and I knew that the truth might cost me my life.

We haven't done that." (I understand the Department of Justice was really upset when I said we hadn't done any money laundering; they knew they had no case at all against me.) Then, not wanting to totally alienate him, I told him it could be done. "It's easy because you're in international trade all the time. We can, we can accumulate the money anywhere you want. Switzerland, in a trading company, in a Bahamian insurance company or anywhere else. It's very easy to do."

Actually, it wasn't easy to do with my company; it was impossible. There were American auditors, the Securities and Exchange Commission, Northern Ireland auditors, British auditors, and most of all the British government, who monitored every penny we spent or made. The nature of the company was such that laundering money would be impossible. But they didn't know that, and I wasn't about to tell them. They didn't know much of anything about the realities of my business. All I hoped was that I could fool them enough to invest the money. This would save the company and give them 100 percent control, but they would have to work through the British who owned all of the assets and controlled the entire activity through loan covenants. It would serve them all right.

Please, God, let me get out of this alive. And I kept talking.

"I need ten or twelve [million dollars] right now, and then that will keep it all together," I said. "And then we go into a mode where you really don't need any more money for, oh, thirty-five, forty, fifty days, of any, you know, consequence, 'cause now you're in a position where you're getting everything together and basically in the planning stage. And then I just pay the ongoing operation of a limited number of people of which is, oh, about 10,000 pounds a week or so."

Keep talking business. I've got to keep talking business. Bore them. That's what Kimmerly said. Bore them. Procrastinate. Just let me get out of here.

And then it happened. For some reason Benedict brought a suitcase of what he said was cocaine from the closet. I couldn't understand why. I wasn't buying any. I wasn't selling any. *They're trying to impress me,* I thought. *We've got the drugs, John. We're the big time. We've got the billion-dollar bank under our control. We've got the guns. And we've got you, John DeLorean. Welcome to the Twilight Zone. Only this isn't television. Rod Serling isn't going to come out, wrap up the ending, and break for a commercial. You're either one of them in their eyes, or you're a dead man.*

And then I somehow knew I wasn't going to die. These crazy mobsters were convinced I was in sympathy with them. Everything had become so crazy that I could only laugh and say, "It's better than gold. Gold weighs more than this for God's sakes." It was total insanity, yet somehow I knew I was going to walk out alive. *Let 'em think they've got me—I'm going to live!*

They ordered champagne. A toast to our new partnership! *My family is safe.* In the madness of the moment I had never been happier. My carefully constructed world—my company, my pride, my future—had been shattered, yet I was grinning like a fool and joining in the toast.

I told them we were on our way. I was filled with relief, tired, no longer terrified, yet feeling as though I was living in never-never land. Nothing made sense except that maybe I was not going to die, and for some reason, several kilos of cocaine had been brought into the room. And then the door opened and a new man entered.

"Hi, John?" he said.

"Hi," I replied, uncertain who the man was or why he was smiling. *Does a hit man smile?* (I later learned that Jerry West knew that this scene would be on national television, and he had rehearsed his speech, his walk into the room, and his smile dozens of times to get it right for the cameras and the audience.)

"Jerry West with the FBI," he said. "You're under arrest for narcotics laws violation." As he continued talking, his words were a blur.

"Okay, before we ask you any questions, you must understand your rights. You have the right to remain silent. Anything you say can be used against you in court. You have the right to talk to a lawyer for advice before we ask you any questions and to have him with you during questioning if you wish. If you cannot afford a lawyer, one will be appointed for you. If you decide to answer questions now without a lawyer, you still have the right to stop answering at any time. You also have the right to stop answering at any time until you talk to a lawyer. You understand that?"

"Yeah."

"Okay. And there's a waiver here if you wish to waive those rights. It says, 'I've read this statement of my rights and I understand what my rights are. I'm willing to make a statement and answer questions. I do not want a lawyer at this time. I understand and know what I'm doing. No promises or threats have been made to me and no pressure or coercion of any kind has been used against me.' You understand?"

"Yeah."

"Would you like to sign the waiver?"

"No. I'll want to call my lawyer."

DELIVERANCE

27

Shock. Numbing shock. The reading of the rights. The search for weapons. The handcuffs. The walk to the car.

When we got downstairs and into the car, probably less than five minutes later, an agent turned on the car radio, and we could hear the FBI already holding a press conference announcing my arrest.

I was a celebrity on parade. John DeLorean, the wonder boy of General Motors, the toast of Manhattan, the glamor kid of the automotive industry was now a pariah.

Exactly what happened at first remains a blur in my mind. The shell was tightly in place, protecting me from everything, even my own feelings. I was shifted from jail to jail; I was locked in one cell, then moved to a different building, a different cell; eventually, I ended up on Terminal Island, the federal holding facility. These movements appear to have been orchestrated to keep Cristina, my lawyers, and my friends from reaching me. My lawyers were told I would be one place, then at the last minute I was sent to another. There was no one to question, no way to think ahead, even to the next few minutes.

When reality finally filtered through, my anguished thoughts focused on Zachary, Kathryn, and Cristina and what they must be suffering as they heard the news of my arrest. Dazed though I was, I understood very well what was happening. I had been framed, and my fighting spirit boiled. But out there somewhere was my family, and they knew only pain. Inside, my life was on hold; outside, the world had gone mad. What horror my family must be experiencing!

As I learned later, Cristina was at home in New York with our two children, the children's nanny, and Maur Dubin, our dear family friend. Cristina had planned a birthday party for Maur that I had expected to attend until I was forced to fly to the West Coast to meet Hoffman and Benedict because of the financial deadline imposed by the British government.

It was October 19, at precisely 8:15 P.M. While everyone was seated at the dinner table, a telephone call came from a *New York Post* reporter. The reporter asked to speak with Maur Dubin whom the reporter knew. Because of the dozens of business calls I regularly received in the evening, our family had a house rule that we normally did not take any calls during the dinner hour so we could have a quiet time together.

The *Post* reporter insisted on speaking with Maur, who finally took the call in the pantry. The reporter told Maur of my arrest, which Maur considered to be a practical joke in bad taste that the reporter was playing because of his birthday. He hung up and returned to the table, saying nothing.

The reporter called again, this time asking to speak to Cristina. Maur suddenly realized that the reporter would not carry such a joke that far and took the call again. At that point, the reporter said, "They've got him locked up in L.A."

By this time Cristina knew something was wrong and she ran to Maur's side at the phone. "It's John," she said. "Is he dead?"

"No," Maur said, "but he might wish he were. You'd better get the kids to bed quickly. All hell is about to break loose. It's a drug bust."

All the tears Cristina had came at once. "They set him up," she cried. Seeing her mother so distraught, Kathryn, too, began crying. Zachary's face was ashen.

"Is he okay? Is he okay?" Cristina cried as she flew through the apartment. Three frantic telephone calls were made—to her mother, to a friend to meet her in Los Angeles, and to the airline. By 8:45 she was out the door and in a cab. With the birthday cake still uncut and the candles unlit, the scene of happy celebration was in darkness.

The arrest of John Z. DeLorean had been carefully arranged so that press conferences could be held, television programs interrupted, and the media exploited to the fullest. The federal agents had gathered reporters so that they could announce what was happening the moment FBI agent West burst into the hotel room. It was showtime, a three-ring extravaganza; it was a happening, an event, a magical moment of media history. The Justice Department was ringmaster, and I was the trained goat.

Of course, by generating all that publicity, the law-enforcement officers orchestrated media coverage so that there was a presumption of guilt. "They never would have made such an arrest unless they were certain he's guilty," said the viewers and readers. "After all, he's so prominent; they wouldn't dare arrest him unless he was guilty."

We were told by an agent who didn't like my frame-up that the FBI called in certain key media people, often called FBI stringers, and showed them the arrest videotape so they could spread the word to the other reporters not to embarrass themselves by taking a stand that I might be innocent. We were also told that the government was shocked by the initial public reaction. The typical reaction was rather sympathetic: "This poor schlump was trying to save his dream so desperately that he did something stupid." The government immediately initiated a "poisoning propaganda" campaign through their stringers. One of these stringers, a well-known television newsman, reportedly received an $89,000 "student loan" to buy an apartment in New York. The newsman had not been a student in twenty years.

Prosecutor Walsh did a number of other "staged" PR stunts that were designed to hurt me. For example, long after he got the U.K. and FBI reports showing I had no IRA contacts, he made court statements about my dangerous IRA connections. Later on when the trial was delayed, the FBI decided to quit paying Hoffman. Since Walsh knew Hoffman would disappear back into the underworld, Walsh lied to the court to have Hoffman put into the protected-witness program because of my "IRA connections." That way Hoffman would be paid through the trial and would still be around.

But such reflections on the inequities of the media—justice-system relationship were slow in coming. My first concern was getting a lawyer, and my second concern was trying to understand what had happened to me. Somehow my daily visits to St. Patrick's and my consultations with Sonja had failed me. To aid me in the latter, I asked Cristina to bring me a Bible. I began to read it. There is no doubt that this began my pilgrimage to understanding.

At Terminal Island I had an easier time than when I was first arrested. In the first jail cells, I still wore the clothing I had on at the time of my arrest and had neither a razor nor a toothbrush. I felt terrible, looked terrible, and went around in a daze. But at the federal holding facility, I was allowed to wash, brush my teeth, and change into a clean uniform, which made me feel a little more respectable.

One of the things that shocked me most was the camaraderie within the prison. My first cellmate was an intimidating figure. He was tall, strong, and accused of murdering several people, a charge that apparently was valid. Yet despite his violent past, he was concerned that I had enough soap, that I knew how to get breakfast cereal, and that I understood how to maneuver my way through the living conditions.

I found several others I met to be both contradictory and fascinating. One young Swiss man was accused of stealing computer secrets and selling them to a foreign government. Another was an Armenian college professor accused of conspiring to bomb the Los Angeles International Airport as a way of calling attention to the massacre of the Armenians by the Turks back in 1917.

The professor was an intelligent, compassionate family man who had, in his mind, been driven to the most heinous form of terrorism, the killing of innocents, to bring world attention to his cause. We argued and debated for hours. While I couldn't condone his actions, I said, I could understand his attacking a perceived enemy; but the murder of uninvolved innocents was not only senseless brutality, but would backfire and polarize world opinion against his cause. My logic and arguments were all wasted. He was inflexible. But I did gain a deeper understanding of the frustrations of an oppressed people. Here was a man who was noble in many senses. He had a good life with everything to live for. Yet he was willing, indeed anxious, to brutally sacrifice that life and the lives of many others for a cause about which the world knew little and cared less.

There were also a number of prisoners involved with the drug trade. One was a long-time narcotics smuggler who had been caught with the drugs—Roger Reeves, the legendary "Redondo Beach Fireman." The prosecutor, Layne Phillips, plea bargained his case, and Roger ended up serving two years of a four-year sentence on the mildest of charges and tax penalties so that Phillips could move on to something else—the publicity of being on my case! Reeves' "continuing criminal enterprise" charges were dropped, and he paid an effective tax rate of less than 10 percent. Reeves later called my lawyer and thanked me for getting him off; he laughed about it. Without my case as a distraction, he would probably have done twenty-five years.

My next cellmate was an uneducated Colombian youth who had been paid to swallow rubber bags of cocaine, get on a plane to Los Angeles, and then call a certain number when he arrived. The person he called would meet him, give him a laxative to help him pass the balloons filled with narcotics, and he would then be sent back home. All the kid wanted was to accumulate enough money to buy a house for his family, he said. He was sentenced to seven years in prison. Although he probably didn't realize it, he was lucky. Had the balloons burst, the drugs would have killed him. I later learned that he was released upon review of his case.

But the most important person I met was a young black man who was one of the guards. He was working his way through seminary and was on duty late afternoon until around midnight. He had a missionary zeal and had organized a Bible-study group for those prisoners who were interested. He asked me if I would like to attend, which I did. This young man's training and enthusiasm made even what I had thought were fairly simple stories, such as the Old Testament one about Jonah and the whale, take on new life and depth. He told me Jesus loved me; he repeated this over and over again with many scriptural proofs.

I made the Bible the focus of my daily activities. During the ten days I was held in prison, there were three reasons for this: first, I had nothing else to do and this seemed to be an ideal way to pass the time; second, I had an intense and growing curiosity about God and needed to find answers; and third, I was finding that everything I had valued, everything I thought I understood, was no longer clear. Without a doubt, something was wrong in my life.

For example, just the seemingly simple task of locating a lawyer was becoming extraordinarily complex. I was a celebrity, the star of the evening news. The lawyer who took my case would have instant access to radio, television, newspapers, and magazines. Every big-name attorney and every new attorney who hoped to become important seemed to want the case. None of them were particularly interested in my innocence or guilt. They didn't seem to care whether the government had a fraudulent case or whether I was the arch villain of the eighties. What mattered was the publicity. Defend John DeLorean and become a star.

I was angry, frustrated, and scared. If I thought I was out of control before the arrest, now I was no longer in charge of anything. My strength, my "steel trap" mind, my arrogance and pride, all meant nothing. And my "spiritual guide" Sonja? Well, she had disappeared the day of my arrest, probably able to travel in luxury to her next location with all the money I had paid her. I had learned firsthand what the Bible means when it talks about "false prophets."

The only pleasures I had were from the one-hour volleyball game I enjoyed with my fellow inmates each day and my intense study of the Bible. In fact, I found myself reading, thinking, and praying from six-thirty in the morning until it was time to turn out the lights at at night.

In addition to my personal study, the young seminarian—who was so determined to help those of us who would listen understand the Bible, the Word of God—would visit me each day that he could. In a simple manner he talked with me about Jesus Christ, the Son of God, telling me the story of His life on earth as a man and His death that was a once-and-for-all payment for the sins of mankind. There was no magic, no mysticism, no rituals. There was no blind devotion in his worship of Jesus. There was none of the exotic spiritualism Sonja had presented. He spoke of feelings, of course, but also of actions and a personal commitment that could be achieved in prison as well as in a palace. When he spoke of Jesus, his face would glow—a characteristic I was to later recognize in other devoted Christians.

As he spoke, I came to the slow realization of how wrong my past had been. Who I had been did not matter. My money, my success, or lack of it, my business reputation—all these superficial values were meaningless. I did not have to be special to obtain God's love. I did not have to do a certain number of "good works" to earn God's approval, nor was

227

there some form of special payoff God made when my actions somehow met with His approval. I was loved as a child of God. I was accepted, as God accepts all of us, and loved by Him without condition. All I had to do was ask for His forgiveness and His salvation and they would be given.

This message was so simple. It was also a little frightening. I had spoken rather glibly of Christianity for many years without truly letting myself be open to Christ as a person I could know, as the Son of God who was my personal Savior. I had always felt that being a Christian meant acting in a special manner to somehow earn His love. At the same time, I had been so arrogant; I wanted to be in charge of my life. I was the classic example of a person who saw himself as "captain of his fate and master of his soul." And hadn't I done a great job of it! Of course, the reality was that I never had to do it alone. God was there all the time. I had just refused to reach out and let Him give me what is available to all of us if we only ask.

And perhaps equally disconcerting was my new understanding that a commitment to the Lord does not necessarily mean that all will go well in life. But a commitment ends the fear, the searching, the foolish attempts at self-reliance when we should be giving ourselves completely to Christ.

In my Bible study I began to focus on the New Testament, studying the four Gospels, Romans, Hebrews, and several other books. And as I studied I sought to understand what Jesus was saying to us through these Scriptures and how to adapt His Word to my life.

I thought about the term "born again." I had never seen myself as a sinner or a bad man. I thought of myself as honest. I had never viciously tried to hurt anyone, and I had frequently gone out of my way to help others. I often gave and never asked for anything in return.

Yet as I reflected, I also began to think about the times I had wronged people. I remembered an incident that occurred when I was young. I had bought an old used Ford V-eight. It was a well-used car, but the body looked great, and I proudly began driving it. Unfortunately, it wasn't long before

I realized that the dealer had not been honest. The car had a poor quality engine that had only been fixed well enough to get the car off the lot. Irate over being cheated, I returned to the used-car dealer and demanded that the car be fixed. He told me that I had bought it as it was and essentially kicked me off the lot. I was not about to keep a car for which I had spent my last $500, only to find that it did not run, but I also had no legal recourse against the dealer. As I saw it, the only answer was to sell it to someone else, which I did, aggressively, never revealing the problems I had been having.

It was a minor thing, I rationalized. But why would I be reminded of such a petty incident from my past? Other people did the same kind of thing all the time. Besides, it happened years ago, and I never did it again. Yet as I read the Bible, meditated, and prayed, I realized that God was using the incident to show me how guilty I was. I had been guilty of dishonesty; beyond that, He showed me that I was responsible for my actions. I had been dishonorable with someone who was probably in no better financial circumstances than I had been when I bought the car. It was an immoral action, and I was truly sorry for it.

I also began to look at how I had lived before my arrest. Weak, exhausted, both physically and emotionally, I had been taking a painkiller called "222," which contained codeine and was sold over-the-counter in Canada. It was not available in the United States because it was a combination of an extra-strength aspirin and a mild narcotic. I couldn't sleep at night, so I would take sleeping pills, then drink endless cups of coffee to try and stay awake in the morning. I was racing from fire to fire, never able to get ahead, never able to plan, always reacting to crises, always in a panic. When one pressure disappeared, another pressure arose. And always I would ask, "Why me, God? I never did anything to deserve such trauma. I never . . ."

But now, for the first time, I really began to be open to answers. As I meditated about what had happened, I realized that I, John DeLorean, was a proud and arrogant phony. I had told myself that my objectives were noble. I had pontificated about my love for the Irish people. Everything I said sounded right and made my motives seem pure and good, but deep down inside, I was really doing it all for myself. For John DeLorean. I was living a lie. I was an egomaniac, out of control.

I thought back on my years with General Motors and to the policy confrontations that became legends to which older executives still refer. I thought about how I had always picked a principle over which I couldn't lose because it would be politically impossible to attack. Sometimes it was minority hiring. Other times it involved policies that were not in the best interest of a liberal democratic society.

As I thought about my actions, I came to see that I wasn't really a "do-gooder" at all; rather, I was trying to gratify my own ego. I always acted in a way that would force men I considered a pain in the neck to sit up and take notice. I was taunting them without even admitting my motives to myself.

My problems with Cristina also seemed to be a part of this. If I had a beautiful wife at my side, everyone would be envious. They would never know the difficulties in our relationship; they would only see that they had to go home to women who often were less attractive or desirable, yet whom they would never divorce because the settlement would cost them millions of dollars. I was showing them that I had taste, style, and the good life that they would never understand, just desire from afar.

Cristina had become a part of my vanity. She now says, "You only wanted a trinket for your arm." But I know I loved her when I married her—as much as I was capable of loving anyone at that time. And later I desperately needed and wanted her support during my ordeal. I know those feelings were sincere. Yet I now recognize that even in my personal life my motives were never what they should have been. They were all mixed up with arrogance, pride, and similar sins that were all too easy to avoid facing.

I sat in my cell hour after hour, reflecting, understanding, and seeking forgiveness as I came to see myself for what I really was. For the first time in my life, I was ready to stop playing the control game. I was ready to stop insisting on myself, my strengths, my desires. I was going to turn control of my life over to the Lord and let Him lead me instead of having the arrogance to try and make my own way, expecting God to follow. For the first time in my life, I was truly ready to follow Christ, no matter what that would mean, no matter where that would take me. I was a broken man, struck down, a humbled man with no place to turn.

When the essence of this finally got through to me, I was standing in my cell with the Bible open on the upper bunk. I alternately read and reflected upon my life, truly repentant for where I had failed and determined to change. For the first time in my life, I was open to the Lord. And then I felt His presence.

A powerful warming embrace engulfed my body from the soles of my feet to the top of my head. I was a man chilled from the elements, but suddenly wrapped in a comforting robe of strength and light. I was filled with a sense of being loved, protected, at peace. I saw no one, heard nothing, yet I knew at the very center of my existence that everything would be all right. I knew Jesus was talking to me, comforting me, telling me everything would be fine. The trial, my family pressures, the life I had yet to lead would all work out in ways I could not yet grasp. I felt healed, safe, protected from evil if I would just continue the rest of my life's journey walking hand-in-hand with Christ. I had been given a freedom of the soul that the steel bars of my cell, the power of my accusers, and the greed of my corporate detractors could never capture or destroy. In the depths of my despair, I had been wrapped in a blanket of spiritual light, and I would never be the same.

Did His embrace last five minutes or twenty-five? I have no idea. Time was meaningless. Eventually, I was again alone in my cell, yet not alone. Safe. At peace. Filled with the love of Christ I had refused to accept for too many years. Happiness and relief overwhelmed my body. I felt physically drained, but my mind glowed in a new light.

Then, for the first time in years I began to cry, softly at

first, then racked with deep sobbing. After almost sixty years of arrogance and pride, of trying to be in control, I had finally accepted the love of God that had always been mine for the taking, regardless of success, failure, triumph, or tragedy. Everything was going to be fine. I need never fear again. And I have not.

I was still in jail. I still had the ordeal of a criminal trial to face. My company was still destroyed. But none of that mattered now. By giving control of my life to the Lord, I had taken a major step forward; I had gained new life that no amount of personal striving could ever have achieved for me. And then I slept. Deep, restful sleep, warmed with the inner glow of the Lord.

The next day in the visiting room, Cristina looked at my face, and before I said a word about what had happened, she said, "What happened to you? You look twenty years younger. You're glowing. You don't look worried or concerned at all!" She seemed thrilled when I shared what had happened in my cell.

I don't know if either Cristina or I truly understood the depth of the change that had taken place inside me, but the peace in my heart radiated through my entire existence. My headaches disappeared, never to return. I have slept soundly ever since. I was a changed man, a new man, a man who, because everything had been stripped from him, could finally face God as He really was.

Despite the problems that I faced, I was so filled with joy that I wanted to run through the streets and declare the power of Christ. But I knew I could not. To go public with my testimony before the trial would create a mockery of my new life. The message would be misunderstood. I had to prove my innocence in court—and let my actions be my testimony of change and let my deeds speak louder than my words—before I could freely share my faith in the healing power of Christ.

And whether justice was to be done now or in the life to come, I could rejoice with King David as he exulted in God's promise to him so many centuries ago:

The LORD is my light and my salvation—
    whom shall I fear?
The LORD is the stronghold of my life—
    of whom shall I be afraid?
When evil men advance against me
    to devour my flesh,
when my enemies and my foes attack me,
    they will stumble and fall.

Psalm 27:1–2

28

I was released after approximately ten days. The bail was an outrageous amount—$10 million—a sum meant to strip me of all money to defend myself. (When the FBI arrested the five top Mafia dons in early 1985, men who had been involved in every conceivable kind of crime, the highest bail was $2 million.)

In trying to make bail, I was forced to liquidate my securities and real-estate holdings at horrendous losses and a tremendous income-tax penalty. Many of my other assets—such as car dealerships, my favorite cars, my real estate, and worst of all, my stock in the New York Yankees—had to go. When we had moved to New York, Bunker Hunt and George Steinbrenner were in the process of acquiring the Yankees from CBS. I bought a small share as a way of becoming part of my new city. When Cristina was desperately trying to raise bail money, Steinbrenner graciously offered to buy my shares, then sell them back to me when my ordeal was over. I hope and pray that someday I can. I love the Yankees.

Once outside the prison, we had to run a gauntlet of photographers and reporters, their flashbulbs and questions searching out new images and stories. As we drove down the L.A. freeway on our way to the Beverly Wilshire Hotel, where I was staying until the press stopped harassing me, some government agents suddenly swerved into our path and created a minor traffic accident. I felt as though everyone were trying to unnerve us (they call it "destabilization"), to make our lives as difficult as possible and upset us even further.

Then I began the extremely difficult task of selecting an attorney. As I talked with many of the major criminal lawyers from throughout the United States, I just got more and more confused. Finally, I settled upon a large, highly respected L.A. law firm, which seemed quite capable of handling the case. Two factors, however, forced me to go elsewhere after I had already spent a large sum of money on retaining the attorneys.

The first came to my attention during a conference of all five of my attorneys when the senior partner said, "The defense must be handled carefully so that the government cannot appeal and retry you if you're acquitted."

What he was saying, in effect, was that the government might be able to take me to court, lose the case, then charge me for the same crime and force me to go to trial on the identical charges. In other words, double jeopardy, a totally illegal situation under American criminal law. If you are acquitted of a crime, the identical charges cannot be brought against you again. This is a fact known to most people, including those who have never been in a court of law, yet my $250-per-hour attorney did not know it. He understood civil law but had no knowledge of how to defend a man accused of a crime. Everyone in the meeting, including two of his partners, were shocked at his statement. As I looked around at the ashen faces, I knew I had made a mistake; I had chosen the wrong lawyers.

Ultimately, I spent over $600,000 with this firm, and absolutely none of their work was useful at the trial. I still don't understand why such a fine man would attempt to handle my case when he knew he was not a competent criminal lawyer. What about my life?

The other factor that led to my decision was my introduction to Howard Weitzman and Don Re, two criminal-law specialists who were brought in by my law firm to prepare motions. The more I listened to my lawyer, the more I realized he knew nothing about criminal law but was, in fact, going to subcontract much of the case to Weitzman and Re. Once I felt that Weitzman and Re were better qualified for the job, and once I was certain the other attorney was not, I decided to go directly to them. I told them in all honesty that I would probably bring in a name attorney for the trial. But I never did. It was a decision I have never regretted.

After carefully reviewing all of the evidence, Weitzman and Re both said, "This case is an absolute travesty. You did not commit any crime. You did nothing illegal." They were truly outraged by the government frame-up.

In a moment of candor, Howard thoughtfully told me, "I've only had two clients in my entire career who were innocent; you're the second. The other innocent man was convicted and is still in jail." This revelation shook me a bit, but I soon saw that both men had extensive experience in criminal trials and trials involving narcotics violations, and that both were firm believers in the law and working within the legal system for a fair trial.

Weitzman and Re ran a relatively small office. Larger operations used law clerks—recently graduated attorneys who start out by working for a firm to learn the business before either moving up in the practice or going out on their own. In a complicated case, these clerks read all the details, then file reports with the lawyers going into the courtroom. If they are not experienced with what they are reading, and if they do not have strong instincts for the material, they may overlook a critical aberration or conflict of evidence in the prosecutor's case. When that happens, the client suffers, while the senior lawyers never know what might have occurred.

But Weitzman and Re knew what to look for. Both men personally reviewed the entire case. They analyzed hundreds of thousands of items and computerized all the material for easier cross referencing. By the time they were ready for court, they knew the case backward and forward. There would be no vital information lost because some clerk had not thought it was important.

There was a third lawyer who worked with Weitzman and Re, a young woman named Mona Soo Hoo. She had worked in the county prosecutor's office and had now gone into private practice to gain more experience in criminal law. She did not do preliminary research for them, as she was not a clerk, but she worked closely with Howard and Don and sat with me during the trial. Mona was a great comfort to me during that ordeal and a great help in explaining the points of law that were being raised.

As I said earlier, I had told Howard Weitzman that I wanted them to handle the motion phases of the trial but that I expected to bring in a name attorney to manage and defend the case. Don Hewitt of "60 Minutes" called me excitedly after a conference at Princeton and suggested Gerry Spence, a brilliant powerhouse of an attorney, who Don said hadn't lost a case in twelve years. By contrast, Howard told me that he hadn't won a case in twelve years, and indeed he lost the Louie Dragna and Grandma Mafia cases while working on mine.

I also spoke several times to Jim Neal, a truly incredible man, and "Racehorse" Haynes, a Texas legend, and dozens of others. More than one expressed a willingness to handle the case for little or no money. But the Lord told me to stick with Howard and Don.

Sometimes when the Lord does His incredible work, He likes to do it through an unlikely vessel so you will know it is His work. I heard an interesting illustration of this just this past Christmas. . . .

Over the Christmas holidays I took my kids skiing at

Vail. It was the first time I had been there since I married Cristina twelve years ago. While there, we spent New Year's Eve with musician Henry Mancini and his wife. As the kids played, we adults talked about the movie *Amadeus*. I explained that I have a recording of virtually every work of Mozart's that has ever been recorded. I have always felt that his work is in a class by itself—far above any other composer who ever lived.

"Yet this film portrays Mozart as a capricious practical joker . . . a supercilious buffoon," I said to Henry. "How do you account for that?"

Henry said something I'll never forget: "Mozart is a demonstration of God's grace—his music could only have come from the Lord—and the fact that it was delivered to us by such an unlikely human is proof."

What a powerful statement of faith! And somehow I felt that the same grace led me to stay with Howard and Don and not bring in one of the legal greats. Today, of course, because of their victory in my case, Howard and Don are considered legal greats themselves.

Although I had turned the control of my life over to the Lord, I had not suddenly become some strange new personality. There was a still a part of me that wanted to be in charge of something. I believe God enabled me to channel this in a positive way by becoming involved with my own defense. After all, since my life was on the line, I wanted to do everything I could to help my attorneys.

At Howard's suggestion I set up shop in the conference room just outside his personal office, tracking down whatever information was needed, reviewing the tapes over and over again to reconstruct what was going on. During the two years that I made that room my headquarters, I derived great inspiration from an old Irish saying tacked on the wall: "For those who fight for it, life has a flavor the sheltered will never know."

In effect, I became my own private detective, a fact that

eventually proved helpful when James Hoffman was on the stand. Using evidence I had gathered, we caught him in a seemingly small lie that began to unravel his credibility with the jurors, as they later told us.

I experienced many conflicting emotions during this period. First, despite all the activity that was whirling around me, including my own involvement in the legal work, I was extremely calm about the outcome of the trial. I knew that ultimately I would be vindicated. I had not been dealing in narcotics; I had never seen cocaine except for those bags the government took out of their safe, thrust in front of me, and then put back in their safe. I had not committed any crime. Although I did not fully understand the reasons for my indictment at first, I knew that whatever they were, they were completely false.

Since the government was using me as a celebrity prosecution, they could not afford to lose my case. They had already done every bizarre thing in the world to set me up. They wouldn't stop now. No matter what they had to do, be it destroy evidence, back-date documents, commit perjury, or intimidate witnesses, they would try to win this case.

I was innocent when I was arrested. I was innocent when I was handcuffed and driven to the jail. I was innocent when I was locked behind bars. I was innocent when I was paraded on television news and humiliated in newspaper headlines. But being innocent did not assure me anything. What gave me peace and assurance was the knowledge that the Lord was with me. Christ was in my heart, and He was walking side by side with me. He would walk into that courtroom with me, and He would sit beside me as surely as Howard, Don, and Mona. No matter what I might have to face, it would be fine. I might still have to continue through my personal hell, but I would never be alone. Whatever happened, it would be right.

The emotion that tore me apart was my concern for my children. They were being teased unmercifully in school. Zachary never told me what was said to him; he loved me too much. But some days he would come home too upset to eat.

(In one instance, which he did not mention until long after the trial was over, he returned to his classroom after gym to find a message on the board: "Zachary's dad is a cocaine dealer.") I wept for him.

Both children were also hearing their father torn apart on radio and television. I was famous, a name everyone knew, and so I became fair game for comedians and cartoonists. There wasn't a television talk-show comedian who didn't tell jokes about John DeLorean or the DeLorean car. Editorial cartoonists delighted in ridiculing my "career" as a cocaine dealer. Even Gary Trudeau lampooned me in his popular satirical comic strip "Doonesbury." Some of the jokes were deliberately vicious. Others might have been funnier had I heard them spoken about a stranger. When you are your own man and you stumble, every conformist moves in to kick you. While nobody enjoys being kicked when down, I knew I could bear the bruises. I wasn't sure that Zachary and Kathryn could.

But my actions, innocent or guilty, had nothing to do with Zachary and Kathryn, yet children and many adults do not differentiate. A child has enough trouble developing a positive self-image, but when that child's parents become the brunt of constant ridicule, the difficulty is compounded. My children were humiliated, ashamed, but still not willing to talk it out as much as I wanted because they did not want to hurt me any further. They had to grow up faster than any child should have to, and I know that their feelings about what happened to our family may not be resolved for many years.

And finally, there was my concern for Cristina. During this high-stress period of our lives, I knew that our relationship would be challenged and possibly even destroyed. I also realized that my notoriety placed an unfair stress on her career.

Cristina had never devoted the time to her career that many models and actresses do, but she was a working professional. Although she always worked under her maiden name, it was no secret that she was my wife and was well-known as Cristina Ferrare DeLorean.

Suddenly, she was not getting bookings. Few of the companies for whom she had modeled had the maturity to separate her life from mine. The fact that I was a "notorious criminal" translated into the message, "stay away from his family." Cristina was tainted by my arrest, and her career was endangered by being married to me. The fact that no one admitted this did not matter. She and I both knew that contracts would be canceled, other models hired, and her future jeopardized.

I also recognized that the stress of the trial, the press, and the other concerns could be too much for her. I would have understood if she had said to me, "John, the pressure is too much for me. I love you, but I can't take the pressure. I have to get out." I didn't want her standing by me out of a sense of duty or a show of concern she felt I might need.

Unfortunately, Cristina's supportive actions during the trial were juxtaposed to statements that caused me discomfort. On one hand, she was going to court with me each day, standing by as my loving, faithful wife; on the other hand, her actions contradicted this and focused solely on herself.

One morning, just before we left our New Jersey home for the trial, Cristina became extremely concerned about finding our prenuptial agreement. She hounded her secretary to locate it. I didn't pay much attention. At that point, in the midst of all that was happening, I didn't examine her actions too closely, probably because I was afraid to face the possibility that Cristina might be thinking of leaving me.

I was also somewhat bothered by the fact that Cristina seemed to view the days in court as an advertising showcase. During the trial, Cristina wore a new and different outfit to the trial each day, clothes supplied by her friend, Albert Capraro, a dress designer who specializes in clothing for the higher-priced stores such as Saks Fifth Avenue. In essence, Cristina was modeling Capraro's fall line of designs, and the press treated her daily change of garb as part of the sideshow. In fact, she regularly treated the trial as she would a modeling booking, rising two hours early to wash, set her hair, and fix her make-up.

There was another incident that should have rung some loud warnings about the basis of our relationship and where it was headed. Cristina had taken some one-and-a-quarter-million dollars' worth of jewelry out of the family safe-deposit box, giving her exclusive access to it. During the trial, Howard ran out of money and told me he needed $50,000 to finish the case, bring in our expert witnesses, and provide transcripts. I went to Cristina and said, "Cristina I know you dislike certain of your jewelry. Would you be willing to sell $50,000 worth and give it to Howard so he can finish the case?"

She looked at me with hard eyes and said, "That's your problem. I'm going to keep the jewelry."

Her strangest response, however, occurred at one of my emotional low points during the trial. This low culminated in my thinking I might lose the trial and have to go through a second one on appeal. Deep inside I understood that whatever happened would come out all right, but that did not necessarily mean it would be in my lifetime. I was beginning to better understand the workings of the Lord, and part of that was accepting the fact that there is human time and God's time. God's time is always right, but it does not mean that we won't have to endure unpleasantness far longer than we might desire.

I believed the outcome of the trial would be God's will, no matter what that meant, but I was still an executive, a man accustomed to taking charge. God had become my Chief Executive Officer, but as His administrative assistant, I needed to be aware of all aspects of the case and trial. I needed to spend time with the kids. I needed . . .

What I really needed was rest. Although I was sleeping deeply and fully without pills, I was still keeping ridiculously long hours. I had not given my body a chance to convalesce from the months of abuse it had endured, and as a result, I remained unusually emotional and on the edge of exhaustion.

One aspect of my exhaustion was a feeling of great depression. Depression over the pain my family was endur-

243

ing on my behalf. Depression that my children were being taunted in the schoolyard. I felt that perhaps the greatest love I could show my family would be to give my life for theirs. If I were to die, the wounds could begin to heal.

Exhausted, I studied the Bible and thought about what would be right. Should I end my life for my family? But if I took my life, would those who knew me think my new-found faith a hoax? Would they say that if I had truly found God, I would have had the faith to endure, knowing that God never gives us a greater challenge than we can handle? Even worse, would they be right? Would I have found Him only to turn against His loving grace?

The answer was obvious. I had to live this life with all its uncertainties, go to court, and endure the trial. If I truly loved and trusted the Lord, I must face whatever the future brought and trust Him to heal the hurts of my family.

The one irrational thought that remained was that God might have prepared me for death by entering my life. If this was true, I could die in the midst of the trial since this would be His plan. If that happened, my family had to be protected.

When I was arrested, I had a $10 million life-insurance policy; to keep it in effect I had to borrow large sums of money to cover the premiums—$40,000 a month. It was a stupid decision, but at the time, exhausted and hurt as I was, it made sense. It also made sense to Cristina who undoubtedly was experiencing the same type of strain.

I had discussed my possible suicide with Cristina before my meditating on God's word convinced me of my foolishness, and she and her mother became quite concerned that the policy would not pay off should I commit suicide. I calmed Cristina and her mother, Renata, by explaining that the policy was over two years old so the suicide clause did not apply. Her mother seemed relieved. Instead, I should have asked myself why they never said a single word to dissuade me. Not once did either one say, "John, don't be silly. That's no answer. Don't do it."

Today the idea that I would willingly destroy God's handiwork is appalling to me. Then it made perfect sense and was proof of how disturbed I had become from the exhaustion of the trial and the stress that went with it.

Shortly before my trial was scheduled to begin in August of 1983, Don Hewitt of CBS contacted Howard Weitzman and told him that Larry Flynt, the publisher, had shown him the videotapes related to my case. Hewitt told Howard that their local CBS station was going to put my videos on the air. After a flurry of legal machinations, the U.S. Supreme Court ultimately ruled that CBS could show the tapes on the basis that the first amendment of the Constitution did not allow stopping the broadcast. If there were to be legal repercussions, they would have to follow the broadcast. They already had them and therefore could not be stopped. CBS was widely and severely criticized for showing stolen videotapes for purely sensational reasons. I was angry, however, because the tapes would soon have been shown in court anyway (and in their proper context), at which time CBS could have legally obtained tapes without tainting the minds of prospective jurors.

Judge Robert Takasugi, who was to be the judge for my trial, questioned Larry Flynt about how he had obtained the trial videos. Flynt initially said he paid a large sum of money to a certain FBI agent for them. At this point, the FBI announced an investigation of the tape matter, and that same day NBC carried a story in which they quoted an FBI source as stating that the FBI suspected our tape expert, Anthony Pelicano, of being the source. Again, this was a pure "poisoning" propaganda tactic meant to imply that my attorney, Howard Weitzman, was involved, and it was a violation of Justice Department guidelines.

Flynt later admitted that he bought the tapes for $5,000 from the office manager at my first law firm, Huffstedler, Miller, Carlson and Beardsley. After questioning, the manager admitted he gave the tapes to Flynt and said that Flynt welshed on paying him the $5,000. Suspiciously, the government elected not to prosecute.

In any event, the subsequent national television show-ing of the videotapes, particularly the carefully orchestrated arrest tape, led Judge Takasugi to delay the trial until the following February to permit an extensive questioning of proposed jurors and minimize the effect of this television-induced bias. Working cooperatively, both sides prepared an elaborate questionnaire, and the 177 members of the jury panel filled it out.

In February we started the process of jury selection. I was to be there to study their attitude toward me, their responses to the questions, and to make the final determina-tion.

As the first sixteen candidates were seated in the jury box, I was filled with a strange uneasiness and foreboding. At that moment, the irony seemed overwhelming to me. Here I was, a man whose company had been in deep financial trouble largely because of my inability to select good people and recognize troublemakers. I was in trouble with the government because I had not immediately recognized Hoffman for the scoundrel he was. Throughout my life I had been cheated dozens of times and lost millions of dollars to people I thought I could trust. I had even been horribly misled by the first law firm I had hired to handle this case. Here I was, the world's worst judge of character, and I was expected to play a major role in determining the honesty, integrity, and objectivity of the jurors who would determine my fate!

Ultimately, twelve jurors were selected on the basis of their intelligence and honesty in answering the questions that had been compiled by both sets of attorneys. We knew the government had a totally fabricated case and would try to confuse the jury by obscuring the truth. But we had to believe that we had chosen people who would understand the case as it was presented and would think objectively.

During the months I spent in the courtroom, I devel-oped the peculiar feeling that I knew the jurors despite the fact that we were not even allowed to speak to each other if we met accidentally in the hall. I watched their reactions. Occasionally, their eyes met mine. They were good people, conscientious and clearly attentive. I realized that, for me, they were the most important people in America because they were my only protection from unscrupulous government agents and prosecutors.

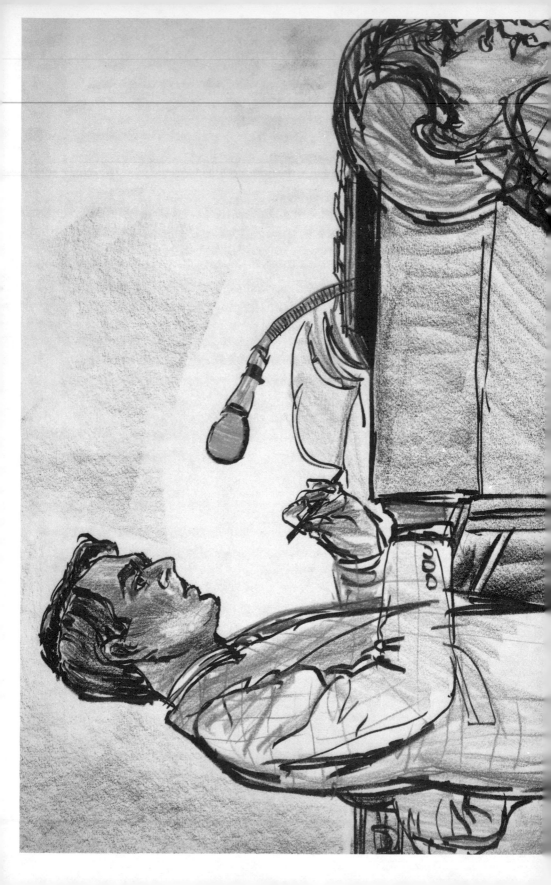

10-18-'82   TOM- I'M GOING TO L.A. TOMORROW TO ACCOMPLISH
A MINOR MIRACLE! I WILL HAVE INDUCED ORGANIZED CRIME
TO LITERALLY DONATE $10,000,000 TO REOPEN THE BELFAST
PLANT --- AND WHEN THEY FIGURE IT OUT THEY CANNOT DO
ANYTHING ABOUT IT? HOFFMAN, BENEDICT, HETRICK AND
VICENZA ARE NOT WHAT THEY PRETEND TO BE --- (DON'T
BE SHOCKED) COCAINE DEALERS! TOO MANY THINGS THEY
HAVE TOLD ME ARE LITERALLY IMPOSSIBLE. THEY HAVE ALSO
ENGAGED ME IN A PLAY ACTING SCENARIO THAT IS SO
MICKEY MOUSE I HAVE TROUBLE KEEPING A STRAIGHT FACE.
HOFFMAN, HETRICK, BENEDICT AND VICENZA HAVE KNOWN EACH
OTHER FOR YEARS --- I DON'T EVEN KNOW HOFFMAN OR
BENEDICT'S HOME PHONE NUMBERS --- BUT HOFFMAN CONSTANTLY
CALLS ME ON THE PHONE AND TELLS ME TO CALL BENEDICT OR
HETRICK AND THEN PROCEEDS TO TELL ME EXACTLY WHAT TO
SAY TO THEM -- WORD FOR WORD. WITHOUT ANY QUESTION
THEY ARE PART OF ORGANIZED CRIME AND EUREKA FEDERAL SAVINGS
AND LOAN IS A FRONT THEY USE FOR LAUNDERING MONEY. THEIR
COCAINE CUMRADE IS DESIGNED TO MAKE ME FEEL IMPLICATED
SO THAT I WON'T LOOK TOO HARD AT THE SOURCE OF FUNDS,
TOMORROW WHEN THEY PUT THE $10,000,000 INTO EUREKA AND
BENEDICT WIRE TRANSFERS IT TO CORK-GULLY THE MOB WILL OWN
100% OF DMC, INC, A CORPORATE SHELL WITH NO ASSETS & THE
STOY-HAYWARD CLIENT WILL CONTROL THE PLANT THAT THE U.K GOVERN-
MENT STILL OWNS. THE DMC SHAREHOLDERS WILL CONTINUE TO OWN
THE AMERICAN COMPANY AND CONTROL EVERYTHING. IN EFFECT, THE MOB
WILL HAVE DONATED $10,000,000 TO THE BELFAST PLANT AND HAVE GOTTEN
VIRTUALLY NOTHING FOR IT -- A MINORITY POSITION IN A GOVERNMENT
OWNED FACTORY IN WAR TORN BELFAST! OBVIOUSLY, THEY WANTED TO CONTROL
THE MOTOR CO. TO USE IT FOR MOVING AND LAUNDERING MONEY. WHEN THEY
FIND OUT THEY OWN AND CONTROL NOTHING THEY WILL BE VERY PISSED?
THE REASON I'M CONVINCED THEY WON'T DO ANYTHING ABOUT IT IS THAT
TO TAKE ANY KIND OF ACTION - AGAINST THE COMPANY OR MYSELF WILL
BLOW THEIR WHOLE MONEY LAUNDERING OPERATION AT EUREKA FEDERAL.
WHEN THEY START TO PUSH I WILL TELL THEM THAT THERE IS A LETTER
THAT IS TO BE OPENED IN THE EVENT OF MY DEATH. THEY WILL JUST
TAKE A WALK.
      IF I'M WRONG AND MY DEATH IS FROM ANY BUT <u>ABSOLUTELY</u>
<u>NATURAL</u> CAUSES TAKE THIS LETTER TO THE POLICE OTHERWISE
DESTROY IT. TOM, TAKE CARE OF MY FAMILY. GOD BLESS YOU,
                                    John DeLorean

DE LOREAN MOTORS HOLDING COMPANY
280 Park Avenue
New York, New York 10017

To: T.W. KIMMERLY
KIMMERLY, GANS AND SHALER
100 W. LONG LAKE ROAD
BLOOMFIELD HILLS, MI 48013
      THIS SEALED LETTER IS TO BE HELD IN
TRUST BY YOU FOR TWO YEARS, TO OCTOBER 18,
1984.
      IN THE EVENT OF MY DEATH WITHIN THAT
TWO YEARS OPEN THE LETTER AND FOLLOW THE
INSTRUCTIONS. IF I AM ALIVE AND WELL ON
OCTOBER 18, 1984 RETURN THE LETTER TO ME UNOPENED.
                              John J. DeLorean
                              OCTOBER 18, 1982

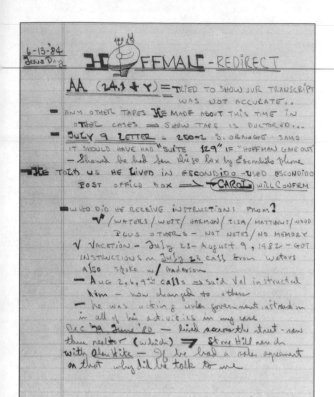

6-13-'84
Jesus Day

HOFFMAN - REDIRECT

AA (24.1 + Y) = TRIED TO SHOW OUR TRANSCRIPT
WAS NOT ACCURATE..

- ANY OTHER TAPES HE MADE ABOUT THIS TIME IN
  OTHER CASES ⟹ SHOW TAPE IS DOCTORED..
- JULY 9 LETTER - 250=2 S. ORANGE - SAYS
  IT SHOULD HAVE HAD "SUITE 129" IF "HOFFMAN GAVE OUT"
  — Should he had San Diego box by Escondido phone
- HE TOLD US HE LIVED IN ESCONDIDO - USED ESCONDIDO
  POST OFFICE BOX ⟹ CAROL WILL CONFIRM

- WHO DID HE RECEIVE INSTRUCTIONS FROM?
  √ /WATERS / WEST / HARMON / TISA / MATTHEWS / WOOD
    PLUS OTHERS - NOT NOTES / NO MEMORY
  √ VACATION - July 23 - August 9, 1982 - GOT
  INSTRUCTIONS on July 23 call from Waters
  also spoke w/ Anderson
  — Aug 2, 6, 9th calls ⟹ said Val instructed
  him - now changed to others
  — he was acting under government instruction
  in all of his activities in my case
  Dec '79 June '80 — lived across the street - saw
  three realtor (which) ⟹ Steve Hill ran in
  with Alan Kite — If he had a sales agreement
  on that why did he talk to me

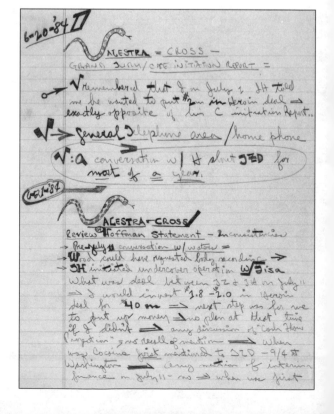

6-20-'84

ALESTRA = CROSS —
GRAND JURY / CASE INITIATION REPORT =

➡ √ remembered that I in July 1 SH told
me he wanted to put #2 in Heroin deal ⟹
exactly opposite of his C initiation Report..

√ ⟹ General Telephone area / home phone

√ : A conversation w/ H about JED for
most of a year.

6-21-'84 ⟶

ALESTRA - CROSS √
Review Hoffman Statement - Inconsistencies
⟶ Pre-July 11 conversation w/ waters =
⟶ Wood could have requested body recording ⟶
⟶ SH initiated undercover operation w/ Tisa
What was deal between JZ & SH on July 11
⟹ I would invest $1.8 - $2.0 in Heroin
deal for 40 m ⟹ next step was for me
to put up money ⟹ no plan at that time
if I didn't ⟹ any discussion of "Cash Flow
Projection" ⟹ no recall of mention ⟹ when
was Cocaine first mentioned to JED - 9/4 in
Washington ⟹ any mention of interim
finance on July 11 - no ⟹ when was first

29

On the opening day of the trial, April 18, 1984, the courthouse was a controlled mob scene. Reporters were everywhere—in the courtroom, outside the courtroom, and outside the building itself. Cameras, microphones, video equipment, notebooks, and all the other tools of their trade were thrust at me wherever I went. Some reporters even followed me into the men's room. Others hovered around Cristina. We had no privacy, no opportunity to even think about the questions they asked.

With the jury selected and all the preliminary motions made, it was now time for the lawyers to enter the arena. For the prosecution: James Walsh, Jr., and Robert Perry, both Assistant United States Attorneys working under Robert Bonner, the United States Attorney in Los Angeles. For my defense: Howard Weitzman, Don Re, and Mona Soo Hoo.

The opening statement by James Walsh was a calm, controlled, subtle twisting of facts and innuendo meant to establish my guilt. No anger, no dramatic presentation, just a simple statement explaining their case in detail. He began by explaining my background at General Motors and then moved on to the prosecution's views of my actions.

"This case is a story of a man with a dream, John DeLorean, and how he turned that dream into a nightmare, a nightmare composed of failure, jail, drugs, disgrace," Walsh began. "The evidence in this case is going to show that John DeLorean left a successful career at General Motors to found his own car company, to build his own car.

"In early 1982, he was facing the prospect of failure. His car company was in the first stage of bankruptcy, and John DeLorean needed money, lots of money, millions of dollars, to save it.

"In June of 1982, John DeLorean received a chance telephone call from a former neighbor, a man that he believed, with good reason, to be a drug smuggler, and John DeLorean saw in that telephone call an opportunity, an opportunity to raise the millions that he needed to save his dying dream. The opportunity was risky, for John DeLorean's bold gamble was this: that he could reach down and snatch the millions that were needed to save his company from the grimy underworld of narcotics and get away undetected.

"So he offered to invest in a load of narcotics, but DeLorean's plan to save his company was flawed from the outset, from the very start, because the man that he thought was a drug smuggler was in fact an undercover narcotics informant. Two other men that he believed to be criminals turned out to be undercover federal agents.

"From July through October of 1982, John DeLorean pursued the drug deal that was to save his company, the company that he built, the company that bore his name, the DeLorean Motor Company. That pursuit is captured on videotapes and audiotapes and recordings of telephone calls and tapes of meetings.

"On those recordings, John DeLorean, in the words of Alan Funt and Candid Camera, is caught in the act of being himself, in unguarded and spontaneous conversation about drugs and money and money laundering with men that he believed to be criminals.

"Now, this melancholy trail ended near where it began, a few miles from here where we now gather, I to prosecute and you to sit in judgment, with John DeLorean to face your judgment here in this courtroom.

"At the end of that trail, federal narcotics agents seized fifty-five pounds of pure Colombian cocaine worth tens of millions of dollars, the dollars that were to save John DeLorean's company, save his car, save his dream.

"So this case, reduced to its essentials, is about drugs and money and pride and ego. It is about a man whose driving need to succeed at any cost led him into the dirty world of narcotics and thence into this courtroom."

In this last statement, perhaps, Walsh was more accurate than he realized. My story *was* about pride and ego; my actions had frequently gone to an extreme because of my compulsion to be in control of my life, taking actions for reasons that were frequently reprehensible. But my failings as a man had nothing to do with criminal actions, a distinction I fear prosecutor Walsh will never understand until he evaluates his life as I have had to do with mine.

He then proceeded to detail the charges against me.

"The first charge, conspiracy to possess and distribute cocaine. Counts Two and Three are related to that. Those three grouped together are the narcotics charges.

"Now, conspiracy is nothing more and nothing less than a partnership with a criminal purpose. It is an agreement among two or more people to break the law.

"The evidence will show in this case that John DeLorean agreed with an individual known as William Morgan Hetrick and others to possess and to distribute cocaine, and the purpose was to make a lot of money.

"Counts Two and Three charge possession and distribution respectively of fifty-five pounds of cocaine.

251

"The evidence will show William Morgan Hetrick and an individual named Stephen Arrington did in fact possess and distribute fifty-five pounds of cocaine as part of the conspiracy of which John DeLorean was a member. That was done on October the eighteenth, 1982. And even though John DeLorean was not present, indeed he was not in California, indeed he wasn't even in Los Angeles, he was in New York on the evening of October eighteenth, the evidence will show he is equally responsible with Mr. Arrington and Mr. Hetrick for the possession and distribution of that cocaine, as it was done in furtherance of the conspiracy of which he was a member. They were his agents, and he theirs.

"Counts Four and Five and Nine deal with the same kind of violations. It is called the Travel Act. It involves the interstate travel to facilitate unlawful activities, in this case narcotics trafficking activities. (After the opening arguments, Judge Takasugi threw out Count Four.)

"Those counts describe three separate instances where John DeLorean traveled from New York to the Los Angeles area to facilitate the conspiracy involved in this case, and those dates range from the eleventh of July, when the plan first began to be formed, until October the nineteenth, the day that John DeLorean was arrested here in Los Angeles.

"Counts Six, Seven, and Eight charge violations of the statute which makes it unlawful to use any communications facility in interstate commerce to advance or facilitate a narcotics felony violation, and the evidence will show that John DeLorean used the telephone on two occasions and the Federal Express on a third occasion in order to facilitate the conspiracy with which he is now charged. A narcotics conspiracy is a felony.

"So, you have three groupings of charges. You have the conspiracy and related offenses of possession and distribution, the narcotics charges, if you will; Four, Five, and Nine, which are the interstate travel charges; and Counts Six, Seven, and Eight, which are the use of a communications facility charges. That's the charge of the indictment."

252

There was still a part of me that could not believe these charges were actually being read out and leveled against me. How had the skinny engineer from Detroit ever come to this? Harry Bennett's goons seemed mild by comparison with the forces I had encountered.

Walsh then moved to James Hoffman, laying out the man's criminal background and weaving his version of my involvement with Hoffman and Morgan Hetrick. When Walsh made incorrect statements or lied outright, I noted them on a legal pad before me. I filled endless numbers of these pads with questions and suggestions for my attorneys—and with my doodles. The latter are a constant part of my note taking, ranging from caricatures of the men on the witness stand to highly stylized letters reflecting my mood.

Even when Walsh's statements were correct, he often took the information out of context so that it would appear damning. But there was nothing I could do. No witnesses had been called. The prosecutor was simply laying his case before the jury, just as my attorney Howard Weitzman would present his own statement regarding what had happened.

It was at that point, however, that I began to form the opinion that James Walsh was the most dishonest person in the courtroom. Even before we entered, Walsh had to have known I was innocent. As will be evident later, he tampered with the facts and, in my opinion, was guilty of suborning perjury before the Grand Jury. As agent Gerald Scotti would later testify, Walsh's ambition and lust for promotion made him sacrifice his oath to uphold the law. His overwhelming desire became "to make the cover of *Time* magazine," no matter how he had to bend the law to do it.

30

"What this case is about or not about, rather, is the war against drugs," Howard Weitzman began in his opening statement for the defense. "It doesn't involve John DeLorean as a drug dealer. It doesn't involve a known criminal, by the government's own admission. What exactly does it involve?

"Well, I think the evidence will show you for openers it involves a man whose dignity and self-respect agents and an informant attempted to strip away from him by battering him, pushing him, cajoling him, coercing him, and putting him into a position to make it look like he was committing a crime."

Then Weitzman dropped his first bomb.

"The government here created everything you see in this case. That's what the evidence will show. There is no one except John DeLorean, no one except John DeLorean, that isn't attached to, attenuated with, or provided by the government.

"What must be foremost in everyone's mind, when you consider the evidence and what I believe it will show, is what in the world was going on here? What are these people doing? Where is the war against drugs that we heard about? What are they doing spending two months attempting to see what a man's intent may or may not be? Your money, my money, their money—we're paying for it. What is going on here?

"You will see the evidence show you that this case is solely a government creation, a government product, run by an unsupervised miscreant—that's a kind word for James Timothy Hoffman—the con man, the criminal, the cocaine smuggler.

"If during my opening statement I appear to be a little bit emotional, I guess it can best be described as quiet outrage, and I believe that's what you are going to feel as this case progresses.

"You have already been enlightened as to what this case is as compared to what you all thought it was. I venture to say more than a few of the jurors were shocked and surprised to learn what this case involved.

"The evidence shows that it does not involve John DeLorean trafficking cocaine, and there are some in the panel that thought it did. The evidence will not show that John DeLorean was supposed to buy cocaine as some of you thought, and the evidence will not show that John DeLorean sold cocaine as some of you thought.

"What the evidence will show is that James Hoffman not only put the big con on John DeLorean, but I think the evidence will show that he started out doing it on the government. And I want you to know the evidence will show this case was not just run by Hoffman, but that some of the agents got involved and that they knew what was going on, and a lawyer for the government was involved in part of the supervision in this case, James Walsh—I know you didn't hear that in opening statement, but you will hear about it as the evidence progresses.

"Now, we are told that the case started by a chance phone call by James Hoffman. James Hoffman, a man we are told—I would just repeat it once, because I don't think any of you will fail to remember—James Hoffman, the admitted perjurer, the admitted cocaine smuggler, the admitted con man, the admitted liar."

Howard continued his impassioned statement, concluding with the comment that eventually reflected the feelings of many: "This case is a sick case. It is a tragedy and a travesty of justice, and the evidence will show you that. These are not my idle words, and I'm not arguing the case. That's what the evidence will show."

He then presented the same series of events that the government had, providing the facts omitted or ignored by the prosecutor. Step by step, for an hour, he covered the circumstances. And when he was done, I was relieved that he was my lawyer. Howard understood the case and was ready to counter false statements made by the government. I had made the right choice when I decided to go with him.

Benedict Tisa was the first witness for the prosecution. This was the man I had known as James Benedict, the "crooked bank president" connected with Eureka Savings and Loan. I don't know what I expected to hear when this experienced FBI agent took the stand; I guess I assumed he would be honest, professional, and present a well-reasoned case as to why I had come under the scrutiny of the FBI. Instead, as time passed, I saw a flustered, often-confused man who was determined to interpret whatever happened in the case in the manner that would be most beneficial to the government. And in some instances, it was clear to me that he was providing false information and perjuring himself.

For example, Tisa claimed that he had never heard of me before. In fact, he claimed that he had no idea how to correctly pronounce my name when he first became aware of

257

my existence. To bolster this statement, the earliest telephone recordings had identification tags in which my name
was mispronounced.

Each time a tape recording was made of a telephone
conversation, the agent or informant making the call would
add an identification tag. This was a voice-over statement
after I had hung up the telephone indicating the date, the
agent, and the caller involved, and a brief statement about
the call. At first, the tags Tisa made had my name mispronounced. When the jury heard the actual tapes, however, it
was obvious that Tisa could perfectly pronounce my last
name when asking for me and talking with me. It was only
on the voice-over tags that he mispronounced my name.
When speaking with me or my secretary, he pronounced my
name perfectly; only on the tags, tags that, by his admission
under cross-examination by Weitzman, were added later,
sometimes minutes, sometimes days, did he mispronounce
it. The implication was that he was trying to adjust evidence
to fit the story he was telling. This blundering attempt to
doctor evidence was a shocking revelation—the first of
many.

The most important phone call of the entire investigation was made by Hoffman to me on October 18 from the
airport-hotel surveillance room. This was the final call in
which Hoffman invites me to take them to Orange County to
introduce the company management to them, the new
owners. I had given 100 percent of the stock to Benedict so
they owned the company. I had done this to be sure that any
illegal proceeds went to Benedict, not to me—and hopefully
to position myself so they would no longer threaten my
children.

According to government records at least ten agents and
two video cameras monitored the call. Yet it went "unrecorded" in a deliberate forty-seven-minute "gap" in the tapes.
(Later, the joke in my lawyer's office was that the FBI had
hired Rosemary Woods to transcribe the tapes.) It is peculiar,
to say the least, that sophisticated equipment would result
not only in unintelligible sections but in sections that

somehow always related to statements further reinforcing my unwillingness to be involved with criminal activity.

The story of when I became a primary criminal suspect for the FBI was revealed when Tisa was being questioned by Assistant U.S. Attorney Robert Perry, who asked about the status of the Hetrick investigation in early August 1982.

Tisa stated: "Well, at that point in time, I was in the process of continuing to be involved in money laundering for the quarter of a million dollars in cash that he [Hetrick] had given me. I was involved in attempting to develop a plan or a scheme insofar as money-laundering techniques to get Mr. Hetrick's cash or cash from his cocaine profits from the Cayman Islands back into the United States.

"Additionally, we are dealing with Mr. Hetrick's capabilities and of supplying large quantities of cocaine that he wanted to sell."

"You were dealing with him. In other words, you were investigating him?" asked Perry.

"Yes, we were attempting to explore and expand upon that capability of Mr. Hetrick."

"By 'explore and expand,' you mean to gather evidence?"

"That is correct."

"So, is it fair to say that the Hetrick investigation was ongoing?"

"Yes."

"Now, by early August of 1982, you had had some contacts with John DeLorean, the two that we have played; is that right?" (This reference was to two of the telephone tape recordings. Throughout the examination of Benedict Tisa, both the prosecuting attorney and my lawyer would play the tapes where appropriate to discuss what was happening at the time.)

"That is correct."

"Were you aware whether or not Mr. Hoffman had had additional contacts with John DeLorean?"

"Yes, I was aware of the fact," said Tisa.

"Was an investigation underway of John DeLorean?"

"There was a narcotics investigation underway of Mr. DeLorean."

"What were the goals of the narcotics investigation of John DeLorean in early August of 1982?"

"We were attempting to find out who he was associated with insofar as the narcotics transaction, what his full intentions were, be in a position to possibly obtain and seize whatever he wanted to put up as collateral for this or invest in this drug deal."

"You say 'collateral.' Had there been any mention that you were aware of at that point in time about collateral from John DeLorean?"

"No. I meant to say 'cash,' which is at that particular point."

"Is it fair to say that by early August of 1982 that DeLorean was a suspect in an ongoing narcotics investigation?"

"Yes, it was."

"And that was based on contacts that you had had and contacts that Mr. Hoffman had had; is that correct?"

Tisa agreed that it was correct, then explained how the investigations were to be combined. "What I was to do was to go to Mr. Hetrick and Mr. DeLorean separately and ask them if they would be interested in meeting each other from the standpoint of mutual desires, needs, and intentions. If they were agreeable to that, then I would go ahead and arrange a meeting for them to sit down and discuss their mutual interests."

"What was the purpose in trying to put Mr. DeLorean and Mr. Hetrick together?"

"Well, on one hand, I had Mr. DeLorean, who, based on my understanding at that point in time, wanted to invest approximately $2 million in a narcotics transaction to generate money for his company and also having an immediate need for a lot of cash, and on the other hand, we had Mr. Hetrick who had expressed his capability of supplying narcotics, cocaine, and also having this off-shore cash from his cocaine trafficking in the Cayman Islands and needing that to be brought back into the United States in some usable form.

"So, what I had was a willing investor, apparently, and a willing supplier, and by putting those together, they might come to some agreement along their mutual desires along that line."

Perry then asked Tisa why he had brought me into the scheme to gain Hetrick's drug money.

"We were trying to come up with a way to launder Mr. Hetrick's money in the United States," Tisa explained. "Using Mr. DeLorean's companies as a possible attraction to invest in or loan to, if we could convince Mr. Hetrick of that, then we would be able to get that cash maybe into the United States and, specifically, into the Eureka Federal Savings and Loan, where we could get our hands on it."

Tisa also added, "We wanted to possibly get our hands on Mr. DeLorean's investment into the narcotics transaction, seize any cocaine that was brought into—or brought into the country by Mr. Hetrick, seize any assets that we could identify that were purchased out of Mr. Hetrick's drug trafficking."

Tisa went on to explain that combining the cases would aid the government in bringing conspiracy charges against me. He also said that he did not know directly from me that I had $2 million to invest in the drug deal. That information had come from Hoffman, a trusted informant.

As I listened to this agent of many years experience, a number of emotions roiled within me. Here was a member of the most sophisticated branch of law enforcement in our country; he should have been worthy of respect. Yet his testimony was shocking and ridiculous. For instead of his case revolving around evidence obtained by trained and honorable investigators, it revolved solely around the statements of James Hoffman, a man who had previously perjured himself in court in other cases.

"Mr. Hoffman advised me that he had finalized what— both him and Mr. DeLorean had finalized the details of their narcotics transaction, and I was to play a part in that insofar as I was supposed to handle the financial end of it," Tisa explained. "Mr. Hoffman indicated that the transaction consisted of sixty-five—excuse me, thirty-four kilos of cocaine which was supposed to be sold at approximately $150,000 per kilo, an approximate gross profit of $5.1 million; consisted of fifty kilos of heroin, approximate cost of $800,000, approximate gross profit of roughly $14 million; and then an additional sixty-five kilos of cocaine at the same price, $30,000, with a gross profit, the number which I don't recall at this time, and I was to be involved in the same point, that Mr. DeLorean's involvement was to come to me, and the resulting profits were to be moved through the bank."

On the second day of the trial, April 19, 1984, during questioning by Assistant U.S. Attorney Perry, Tisa mentioned Robin Bailie and said, "That was the name of the Irish Republican Army associate of Mr. DeLorean who was coming in on this narcotics transaction."

As I have already mentioned, when I was being increasingly pressured to come up with the money for a narcotics deal, I had to find a "source," someone on whom I could blame my delays. I finally had settled upon Robin Bailie, though I don't remember exactly what I hoped to accomplish. It was the only name I could come up with.

Robin Bailie was one of the last men with whom the Irish Republican Army might want to conduct business. Given their choice, Bailie would be dead. Not only was he a former Protestant Member of Parliament, he was also responsible for seeing that several IRA terrorists were convicted by the British government. The FBI immediately checked out Bailie and myself with British Intelligence. British Intelligence told the FBI who Bailie was and that I had no IRA contacts.

31

In his cross-examination of Benedict Tisa, Howard wanted to show the court the way I had been manipulated by the lies of Tisa and his associates. He began his questioning in a way that, we hoped, would make this evident in the man's own testimony.

"What did John DeLorean do to cause him to be arrested?" Howard asked.

"Based on the evidence we have in this investigation to date, it was investing in a narcotics transaction with Mr. Morgan Hetrick who supplied it for profit."

Tisa was then asked what money I invested. "As of the day he was arrested, he had put up a promissory note with an indication that he was to pay me $2 million out of the profits from the narcotics transaction once it was consummated," was the reply.

Not satisfied with this answer, Howard demanded to know just what money I had invested.

"As of the day he was arrested, he had not put up cash," Tisa admitted. He also admitted that no one had checked to see if the promissory note I had given him was valid. No effort was made to verify whether my note was backed by corporate assets or whether I was bluffing. (Later it was shown that prosecutor Walsh had given a sworn deposition that the promissory note was valueless, with no collateral behind it. Again, this proved that Walsh knew I was innocent before the fact, yet allowed information he knew to be false into court.)

By his own admission, Benedict Tisa knew that I had never pledged any money or gotten directly involved in any way in a drug deal. Yet he had to be led through seemingly endless questioning each time before he would admit the truth.

At this stage in his cross-examination, Howard began probing the matter of Morgan Hetrick and how I had been brought to Hetrick's attention.

Tisa stated that he had indicated to Hetrick that I was attempting to invest in a narcotics transaction with James Hoffman.

"Didn't you tell Mr. Hetrick that DeLorean had given you $1.8 million to invest in a dope deal with Hoffman?"

"That is correct."

"And of course that was a lie, wasn't it?"

"Yes, it was, from the standpoint of cash, yes."

"And as matter of fact, in your role as a crooked banker, it was a lie for investigative purposes; is that correct?"

"We wanted to see—I didn't want to tell Mr. Hetrick that the—there was no cash on Mr. DeLorean's part at that point in time because it would allow him to continue to go out and obtain the narcotics as additional evidence of his drug trafficking activity, yes."

"So the answer is yes?"

"Yes."

"And you lied to Mr. Hetrick when you told him that

DeLorean had put the cash in for this deal with Hoffman, correct?"

"That is correct."

As the questioning continued, it was obvious that two themes were present in all that Tisa said: First, the government agents were not convinced of my guilt on the basis of evidence, but solely from the statements of James Hoffman, who told them that I had expressed interest in making a drug deal during our "unrecorded" conversations and that that was what I "really meant" when the recorded conversations had nothing to do with narcotics. Second, as reluctant as he was to admit it, Tisa always worked to convince me that somehow he, in his role as a bank executive, was going to help me find legitimate investors for my company.

For example, during his April 25 testimony, Howard asked him: "Did you tell John DeLorean, in getting him to come to the meeting on September twentieth, that this fellow Hetrick may want to invest or have some investors to put some money into his company?"

"I indicated that was a possibility."

Then a new twist was added, and the case became even more confusing. Although I was supposedly part of this deal, I was never to be involved.

"How come Morgan Hetrick was under the impression he was supposed to supply cocaine to James Hoffman?" Howard asked Tisa.

"Mr. Hoffman was supposed to sell the cocaine that Mr. DeLorean was investing in."

"But Mr. DeLorean didn't put up any cash, correct?"

"Not at that point in time. He had ...."

"He never put up any cash, did he?" my attorney interrupted.

"No."

"And you lied to Hetrick about that, correct?"

"That's correct."

Each time special agent Benedict Tisa was pressed, he admitted that everyone seemed to be misled about everything. The only thread linking all the criminal deals together came from James Hoffman.

As the testimony proceeded, I was increasingly shocked by the information Tisa disclosed. For example, his case notes. By law, notes made during an investigation must be retained, for they become a part of the evidence if a case goes to court. They can be subpoenaed and the investigator asked to testify about them.

Benedict Tisa, however, did not retain his notes. In fact, at some point he illegally destroyed them and "created" a whole new daily log, apparently to make a better case against me. This was discovered because he made mistakes on some of the dates and got some of the events out of sequence. In a daily log prepared between July and October of 1982, in a large number of instances he wrote the date as 1983. This was very telling with the jury since no one ever accidentally writes next year's date. His fabrication of evidence was devastating to the government's case. In fact, on the stand he admitted destroying the original notes; under Ninth Circuit law, this act in and of itself would be enough to throw the case out if it ever went to appeal.

Under Howard's questioning, making reference to his 1982 log, Tisa said: "Based on what I recall about this, I wrote it during 1982, and I might have gone back in 1983 to add or update with new information. I may have rewrote a page because I spilled something on it. Who knows?"

"So are you telling us that this log could have entries in it that were entered in 1983?" Howard asked.

"This log reflects events during 1982. I may have rewritten some of these entries in 1983."

"When in 1983?"

"Mr. Weitzman, I don't recall when I did that."

"Well, now, the investigation in this case terminated in October of 1982, correct?"

"Yes."

"And these are supposed to be your original notes, correct?"

"Yes."

"But they are not your original notes. You have indicated they were rewritten from other notes which have since been destroyed, correct?"

"It appears that a portion of them are."

"That is the truth, isn't it? That the original notes, or a portion of them, were destroyed, and this document indicates what you believe was reflected on the original notes, yes?"

"Yes, in this particular portion right here."

"And you are aware, are you not, that you are not supposed to destroy original notes?"

The outrageousness of Tisa's actions became even more blatant as he said: "I don't believe I was destroying original notes. What I was doing was taking the original notes and rewriting them and adding additional information to them to expand upon them."

"And then I presume that you either shredded up or crumbled up or threw away the original notes?"

"The original notes to this page right here, yes."

Then, on April 26 during the midmorning break, something absolutely astonishing occurred.

When everyone had left the courtroom except for U.S. Attorney Perry and Tisa, Perry began a loud verbal attack on his witness. His voice rose louder and louder in anger as he berated Tisa for the way he was testifying and the stupidity of his actions. And in no uncertain terms, Perry implied that Tisa should change his testimony.

What neither man knew was that on the table beside them was an open microphone that was wired to the press room for the hundred or so members of the press who couldn't fit into the courtroom. The press heard every word they said and were astounded witnesses to Perry's illegal act of telling his witness how to testify.

When Tisa took the stand again after lunch, Howard said, "Let me ask you something. Over the last recess, I was privileged or privy to a conversation you had with Mr. Perry in which he was kind of yelling and screaming at you, right?"

"You could say that," said an embarrassed Tisa as people in the courtroom burst into laughter.

"He was asking you whether or not you destroyed original notes, and you said, 'Well, I rewrote the notes,' and he said, 'Yeah, but you didn't destroy original notes, did you?' And you told him, 'Well, I might have rewritten some notes.' Is that correct?"

"Yes."

"Why do you think he was doing that to you?"

"Because he understands how I did those notes, and he realized I must have made a mistake when I said some of the things I said."

Tisa went on to explain that Perry was afraid that he may have given the impression that he had destroyed the notes. (Actually, Perry wanted him to lie and say he had not destroyed them.) Fortunately for us, Tisa had more trouble lying than the other agents. Not only had he corrected, recopied, and edited his papers, which is against the law, but he had in fact destroyed the originals so that important legal evidence was no longer in existence. I am certain that Tisa, as a twelve-year agent, fully understood the seriousness of the actions he confessed to. All that was certain was that the more he talked, the less professional he sounded. His testimony was a disgrace.

The next shock came when Tisa was asked, "What is your interest in this investigation, sir?"

"A successful prosecution."

"A successful conviction; is that right?"

"Yes."

"No matter what the facts are?"

"The conviction would be on the facts."

Notice what he did not say here. The purpose of the FBI, in the mind of special agent Tisa, was not to enforce the law or learn the truth. He was not sworn to determine right and wrong, to protect the public from criminals, or to otherwise uphold justice. Instead, his role was to prosecute.

"That is still your state of mind today, isn't it?" Howard asked.

"Yes."

"Now, your purpose was to gather evidence here to show John DeLorean's guilt, right?"

"Yes."

Then Howard said, "If you believe from the get-go somebody's guilty—and you told us that there was no doubt in your mind that John DeLorean wanted to do a drug deal—you go in looking for evidence that the person committed the crime you believe he wants to commit, right?"

"Yes, we do."

"And you believed from July 12, 1982, that John DeLorean wanted to commit the crime of dealing in drugs, right?"

"Yes," said Tisa.

These men had determined that at no point was I to be let off the merry-go-round. They had created a netherworld where black was white, white was black, and I was expected to find my way through the maze. I was expected to somehow disprove that I was a bad guy even as they were using every device to deceive me to prove that I was. Meanwhile, each day that they played at their charade in an effort to find reason to arrest me, millions of dollars worth of drugs were being brought into the United States and distributed on the streets to be smoked, snorted, and injected. But John DeLorean was their priority. John DeLorean was the name that could make headlines.

Tisa admitted that he had learned, before my arrest, that Robin Bailie could not be an IRA contact, that he was a Protestant Member of Parliament at the opposite end of the political spectrum, and that I had absolutely no contact with the IRA.

"So you knew before the investigation was completed that John DeLorean had lied to you when he said he had $2 million coming from Robin Bailie and the Irish Republican Army, right?" Howard asked.

"Yeah, I believe so, yes," Tisa said.

He then also admitted that he did not know if the promissory note I had given him was of any value.

"And of course, you believed that he was getting $2 million from the Irish Republican Army, right?"

"At that time, yes."

"And once you learned during the course of the investigation that he had lied to you about having $2 million from the Irish Republican Army, did it ever occur in your wildest dreams that he might have been lying to you about the worth of the collateral?"

"It didn't occur to me, but that is a possibility, yes."

With all the government's resources, with all its sophistication, Tisa and the men working with him checked everything I was saying and doing. They knew I didn't have any connection with the IRA and that the name I used was an obvious attempt to avoid their criminal suggestions. Yet they were so obsessed with gaining a conviction that they never looked beyond the headlines they would make if they proved me guilty, whatever the charge.

Even when he discussed Hoffman, Tisa admitted how little evidence he had had of my involvement in any crime.

"We have heard the tapes," Howard said to him. "Those conversations on their face involve nothing illegal or unlawful, isn't that correct? Yes or no."

"Yes."

"The only thing that makes them anything but what you said, that is that they appear to be illegal, is James Hoffman's input that this man [DeLorean] called and wanted to invest $2 million in some heroin deal, correct?"

"I think you have to take in mind, first of all, Mr. Weitzman, the context in which Mr. DeLorean made his statements, and combining that with what I knew about it, that seemed to in fact support Mr. Hoffman's statement."

"Mr. Tisa, all you know about in terms of context is what Hoffman told you; isn't that true?"

"That's correct."

"If Hoffman was lying, you made a mistake; isn't that true?"

"If he was lying, yes."

And how much contact had Tisa had with Hoffman? What reason did he have for trusting Hoffman?

"Mr. Hoffman has been a reliable informant in the past," Tisa explained.

"Has he?" asked Howard. "How many cases has he made for you?"

"He hasn't made any cases for me, but the information he has introduced, the people he introduced to me, and what he told me about he's been accurate."

"Really, who?"

"Mr. Hetrick."

"Who else?"

"That's the only one that I can—at this point in time."

Howard then said, "Now, the information you had from Hoffman was that DeLorean didn't have any background in narcotics, right?"

"Yes."

"And the information you had from Hoffman is that DeLorean came to him to put this together, right?"

"Yes."

"Didn't Hoffman tell you that DeLorean came to him, because he didn't know anybody else to go to with respect to narcotics?"

"I don't recall him saying that."

"Did you think that John DeLorean was in the heroin sales business?"

"I had no reason to believe that."

"Did you believe that John DeLorean was in the cocaine sales business?"

"I had no reason to believe that."

"Did you believe that John DeLorean was associated with heroin sellers or cocaine sellers?"

"I had no reason to believe that at that time."

Everything revolved around James Hoffman and his plans to get a big name in the middle of an arrest, regardless of the truth.

Tisa also was asked about my attempts to get out of the deal. He admitted that I kept telling him that I had no money. He seemed convinced that it was his duty to "help" me stay involved.

By May 2 Tisa's statements became even more absurd in terms of what I would have thought was rational law enforcement. That day Howard stated this conclusion:

271

"So let me see if I understand this. On September fifteenth it was your frame of mind that whether John DeLorean came up with the money or not, Morgan Hetrick was going to run in there with this cocaine, Jim Hoffman was going to pretend to take the cocaine and sell it, and you all were going to give John DeLorean money. Was that your frame of mind?"

"That was the intent of the plan at that point in time."

In other words, no matter what I did, they would get me. If they had to place money in my hands after completing their own deal, they would get me. There was no escape. I was their pigeon. As I listened to this I kept asking myself how such an attitude could have been allowed to dominate a legal investigation for so long? Were these men FBI or the secret police of some totalitarian country where the truth is what the government declares, not what people witness?

Howard then set about trying to learn how and why Tisa felt it was his responsibility to encourage criminal acts when he was playing the role of an undercover criminal. Howard did this by creating a hypothetical scene in which there were people planning to blow up a building and Tisa was to be a part of the gang, though secretly acting undercover.

"How about if the plan is: That we are going to blow up the building, you and I are terrorists, Irish Republican Army terrorists. We are going to blow up the building. Are you with me so far on that hypothetical?"

"Yes."

"And you are posing as an undercover crooked terrorist. And we are going to blow up this building. We get to the scene, and I turn to you and I say, 'I forgot the dynamite.' Are you with me?"

"Yes, sir."

"Now, at that point, we can't go ahead and blow up the building because we don't have the dynamite, right?"

"Yes."

"Do you think it is your responsibility to run and get the dynamite for me?"

"No."

"Do you think it is your responsibility, as an undercover terrorist, to come up with some alternative explosives, so that we can blow up the building?"

"I don't think you can—well, the answer is, no, because I don't think you can equate dynamite with a drug transaction in coming up with the money."

"Do you think it is your responsibility to come up with some alternatives to blow up the building if I forget the dynamite?" Howard repeated.

"No, Mr. Weitzman."

"Now, we come up to the building. We come up to the building, and we are sitting there; the man says, 'Gee, undercover crooked terrorist, I don't have any dynamite.' Are you with me so far?"

"Yes."

"Do you think it is your responsibility to tell me where I can go get the dynamite?"

"No."

"Do you think it is your responsibility to go get the dynamite for me?"

"No."

Howard then compared the actions described in the scenario with Tisa's actions in getting me money. The FBI special agent still did not see how they were related. He was convinced that I wanted him to find a way to participate in a drug deal. He was certain that since I obviously wished to participate in the criminal action that he had to help.

"Do you believe it was your responsibility, as an FBI agent, to develop an alternative for John DeLorean when he told you he didn't have the money to invest in the drug deal?"

"If it would be evidence of—if it would be further evidence of his intentions, and that is what he is asking me to do, then, yes, that would be my response to that question."

"So your answer is, yes, as an FBI agent, part of your responsibility was to create some alternative to keep John DeLorean in these discussions; is that your answer?"

"The responsibility from the standpoint that in my undercover role, Mr. DeLorean is asking me to do that. And he is asking me to do that as further intentions of his wanted to be in the drug deal, and if that is what he wanted, then I could suggest some other alternative to him."

"If he asked you to kill somebody, would you have done it?"

"I think that is a little far-fetched. No, I wouldn't have done that."

"Where would you have drawn the line, sir?"

Where would Benedict Tisa draw the line? How far would he go to gain the fame and possible promotion that could come from making headlines with my arrest?

John Dean, an associate of former president Nixon, discussed how he and others close to the disgraced chief executive deliberately committed crimes against the public in the name of "blind ambition." When I fought to build my company, my crime might have been called blind pride. Like Benedict Tisa, I avoided facing reality. I started my car company because I wanted to build a car my way; I wanted to craft something I could be proud of that might even successfully compete with my former employer. I had inadequate money for the project and was constantly trying to catch up with my debt. Although I knew that I should have temporarily abandoned my project, pride kept me going. Too many people had said I couldn't succeed. Pride said I had to prove them wrong. What drove me to the brink of destruction was pride, not my faith in the future, not a rational appraisal of the actions I was taking. I could not fail. I was going to have a successful company, seemingly at all costs.

Only in my prison cell did I finally face the truth about myself. Stripped of my business, my friends, my money, and my power, there was no more reason to be proud. By trying to walk alone, to live a life of foolish arrogance in pursuit of selfish personal goals, I had lost everything. And it was only in accepting my own powerlessness without the Lord that I became open to the healing, loving warmth of Jesus Christ.

By the time I walked into that Los Angeles courtroom, I had begun a new life, able to rely on and relax in the faith that comes from knowing all would be right so long as I stopped trying to be in charge.

Suddenly, I had a moment of déjà vu. In Benedict Tisa I came face to face with the old John DeLorean in all his prideful pursuit of fame, power, and glory. Here was a man who had all the power and skills of the United States government at his command, yet he was falling apart on the witness stand, destroyed by his own proud arrogance. That this could happen with the very first witness to give testimony against me seemed proof that the hand of God was evident in the trial. I was no better than my accuser. We were just being shown the penalty for our arrogance in ways that each of us could understand.

32

Benedict Tisa seemed to feel that since he was an FBI agent, I somehow should have reacted differently to him if I was honest. He kept ignoring the fact that I only knew him as a criminal aiding other criminals.

"Weren't you representing yourself as a crooked banker involved in criminal activities?" Howard asked.

"I was—yes. Well, not necessarily involved, but assisting other criminals in their financial dealings insofar as crooked deals."

"Gee, sir, in your twelve years as an FBI agent, if you were to catch a banker aiding criminals in criminal activity, would you consider arresting the banker?"

"Yes."

"Would you consider him to be a criminal?"

"If there was sufficient evidence of his crimes, yes."

277

"Were you posing as a criminal in your role as a crooked banker?"

"Yes, because it makes other criminals deal . . ."

"I don't care about the explanation. Just yes or no, were you posing as a criminal in your role as a crooked banker?"

"Yes."

"Were you posing, in your role as a crooked banker, as a criminal representing other criminals?"

"Not representing other criminals. I was a crooked banker who assisted and provided financial support to crooked transactions if they should come up."

"Were you representing yourself as a crooked banker associating with other criminals in your duties as a crooked banker?"

"Yes."

I hoped that the jury understood what Howard was doing because it never seemed to register with Tisa. But even with all I had seen and heard, I did not know how far he and the government were ready to go to put me in jail until I heard his testimony of May 3.

"Did you participate in the decision that DeLorean should be arrested?" my attorney asked Tisa.

"I was advised that he was to be arrested when he showed up on the nineteenth."

"Who advised you?"

"Once again, the agents I was working with, Mr. Weitzman, the same group of people."

"So, you knew when the man was going to get off the plane, you were going to arrest him, correct?"

"Yes."

"You had already concluded that he had been involved in and committed a crime, correct?"

"Yes."

"You believed he was guilty, correct?"

"I believed there was sufficient evidence, yes."

"Notwithstanding that, notwithstanding the fact that you thought a crime had been committed and not withstanding the fact that you had already decided to arrest him, you thought it was important for evidentiary value to have one last videotaping, correct?"

"Yes, from the standpoint that that was the decision that had been made by other people."

"So, was this another situation that you are merely following orders; you didn't participate in the decision?"

"Once again, I was made aware of the decision along those lines, and I just carried out my role."

"You will agree with me, won't you, that Mr. DeLorean did not know the cocaine was going to be in the room?"

"Yes."

"And DeLorean did not know it was going to be put in front of him?"

"Yes."

"Regardless of how he reacted, he was going to be arrested anyway, wasn't he?"

"Yes."

"I mean if he had attempted to run out of the room, would you have arrested him?"

"Yes, yes."

"If he would have fainted, you would have arrested him, correct?"

"Yes."

"And if he would have faked whatever reaction he faked, you would have arrested him, right?"

The question was an important one, stressing my desperate desire to stay alive. It was also a question to which the prosecutor objected. When the judge overruled that objection, Howard repeated it.

"In other words, it wouldn't have mattered what John DeLorean had done, whether he had bolted out of the room, taken you hostage, fainted; it wouldn't have mattered? He would have been arrested regardless, correct?"

"Once again, it would depend on . . ."

"Isn't the answer 'Yes, sir, he would have been arrested, Mr. Weitzman, regardless'; isn't that correct?"

"I would think I would have to say yes, but with an explanation."

"Wait a minute. Time out for a second," Howard said.
"John DeLorean would have been arrested, according to your testimony, no matter what he would have done, because the decision had been made before he came into the room, right?"

"Yes, but once again, with an explanation."

Judge Takasugi leaned across the bench and said to Tisa, "Why don't you give us the explanation, please."

Tisa replied, "Well, if Mr. DeLorean stood up in the room and said, 'I'm sorry. This is a complete utter mistake. I'm going to call the FBI or the DEA,' or walked out of the room, then he probably wouldn't have been arrested."

"He wouldn't have been arrested?" asked Howard.

"No, I don't know. But if that would have been his reaction, that would have been a consideration."

For me, this was one of the turning points of the trial, even though there would be weeks to go. By Tisa's admission, I was in a room with three men I thought to be closely connected with organized crime; two of these men had threatened me—one of them viciously through my family. Despite these facts, which Tisa corroborated, I was expected to prove my honesty by denouncing them and walking out to place a telephone call to the FBI or the DEA. They had shown me drugs, they had proven what they could do, and I was to assume that they would simply let me leave because I didn't like drugs? The mindset was a little like the tests for witches in medieval England: Since it was thought that a witch could not drown, the suspect was thrown into the water, bound hand and foot. If she floated to the surface, she was a witch. If she drowned, she was innocent. The fact that she was dead never seemed to enter anyone's mind, much as Tisa never thought of the illogic of the plan he was describing. Unless I had been willing to risk being murdered or having my family murdered, I was going to jail.

Tisa's suggestion is even more absurd in light of my emotional state at the time. When I viewed the videotape of that final meeting, I was amazed at the man I saw there. I had joined in their bizarre toast—obviously staged for its video value. While they were toasting my imminent arrest, I was toasting life, toasting my joy at still being alive. But there was even more going on behind the man on that tape. I had been on an emotional roller-coaster. I had gone from the extreme depression of the night before to a seeming euphoria just before my arrest—a result of what might be called a drug-induced psychosis.

According to the medical experts I have since consulted, the combination of Seconal, to which I now know I was mildly addicted, the caffeine in the coffee I drank constantly, the codeine in my headache medicine, and the wine I drank with dinner brought on the extreme emotions of someone who is seriously disturbed. I was actually in the depths of drug abuse. Being forced to stop cold during my time in jail probably saved both my mental health and my life.

Drug Enforcement Administration agent Gerald Scotti's name was brought into the trial on May 8, 1982. Scotti is one of the most courageous people I know. He was an aggressive Detroit police officer who proved his worth in an elite anti-drug unit working in some of the toughest areas of that city when he first came to the attention of the government. First, they made him a member of a joint federal-state task force, then offered him a job with the DEA. Being a respected member of law enforcement was all he ever wanted from life. Yet when he became involved with the case against me and discovered the truth about the way Hoffman, Walsh, and the others were setting me up, he felt he had to stand up against the improper tactics of men he once greatly admired. He would eventually sacrifice his life, as he wanted to live it, for my sake. He had both the intelligence and the courage to evaluate what was taking place and decided that the government was acting improperly. He left the DEA eventually and offered to testify on my behalf, a terrible embarrassment to the government. Even worse for their sake, he was a decorated, honored agent who had been involved with a number of important cases. And most telling of all, not one word of his damaging evidence was repudiated by the government; they didn't put up one rebuttal witness. Not one!

If Scotti was shown to be as honest as his record indicated, the fact that he was working with my defense would be extremely bad for the government. For that reason, Benedict Tisa, or those associated with him, decided that Scotti must be discredited. Tisa began this during his time on the stand by explaining that he had objected to Scotti entering the case against me. Howard asked him what his objection had been.

"My objection was that I knew of Mr. Scotti being under investigation for leaking information about a previous undercover operation for the defense attorney," Tisa said, "and I was very much concerned about the security aspects."

This was an opening Howard wanted. "Let's talk about that, Mr. Tisa," he said. "I want to know who you learned that from, that in October 1982 Gerald Scotti was under investigation for leaking information to an attorney. I want to know who you knew that from."

"I knew it prior to October eighteenth, 1982," Tisa replied.

"Did you also know that he had been cleared and that the investigation had been terminated?"

Prosecutor Perry was not pleased that such a contradiction would be presented to the jury. He tried to stop any further comments by shouting, "Objection; assumes facts not in evidence."

"If he knew it, he can answer yes," said Howard, and the judge agreed, telling Tisa to answer the question.

Tisa admitted that he did know Gerald Scotti had been cleared. It was obvious that he was only trying to create doubt in the minds of the jury as to Scotti's credibility if he eventually took the witness stand. (At that time we had no idea that Scotti might testify. He hated Howard and rebuffed all of our attempts to talk to him. Perversely, it was the government's attempts to discredit Scotti that prompted him to come forward. He saw he was being made the fall guy so he came forth with the truth.)

282

That same day, another situation arose and was presented to the judge away from the hearing of the jury. The previous week Howard, who was doing most of the questioning, had been stopped by Assistant U.S. Attorney Perry when they were away from the courtroom. The conversation was a quiet one but, when it was over, Howard's normal ruddy complexion was ashen, and he was visibly shaken. Don Re asked him what had happened. When he heard Howard's answer he felt the details should be presented to the judge.

In statements made as part of the court record but away from where the jury could hear them, Don Re said: "Your Honor, the defense, as I think I have indicated, is very concerned about the conduct that the government has engaged in with regard to defense investigators or defense experts, and we are also concerned because—and perhaps because it strikes closer to home—that it is something we want to put on the record, and I have virtually insisted that Mr. Weitzman allow me to put it on the record because I think it is a significant issue. We were going to do it last week, but Mr. Weitzman wanted to cool off, as they say, but I think it's appropriate.

"Last Thursday, during a conversation with Mr. Perry, Mr. Perry informed Mr. Weitzman that the FBI was upset with him for statements that he made, apparently, concerning Mr. Tisa's credibility and some comments he allegedly made on the courthouse steps.

"Mr. Perry's statement that the FBI is upset with Mr. Weitzman is something we don't take very lightly because I think a statement like that is akin to a statement from God if He doesn't like your attitude, and Mr. Weitzman, I think, is in a position where he has to watch what he does or watch what he says at this point, and I think that's unfortunate. The effect of that kind of statement is either, don't speak your mind or don't cross-examine effectively.

"I am not convinced that there is anything particular that this court can do to alleviate the effect of that kind of representation, but I think it's very, very important that this court be aware of it and that the public be aware of it, and my

283

concern is with regard to Mr. Weitzman. I don't want in the future, should there be any kind of activity to be attributed to the government as a result of this case, for it not to be put on this record at this time that these comments were made and that the FBI, for whatever bizarre, improper reason they may have communicated or wished to have communicated or feels it was appropriate for them to be upset with Mr. Weitzman for his representation of Mr. DeLorean in this case."

The prosecutor denied that he had meant to be threatening. Perry explained that he was just trying to "help" Howard.

I now assume this threat is used by the government many times when defense attorneys do too good a job. It was also true that intense investigation into some of our witnesses had become a frequent tactic. One of our key witnesses was to be the legendary Dr. David Raskin from the University of Utah whose polygraph test proved that I was absolutely innocent to what Dr. Raskin felt was a 99.9 percent certainty. Dr. Raskin, the top polygrapher in America, does extensive work for the U.S. Secret Service and the Defense Intelligence Agency. FBI agent Jerry West, using the stature of his organization, attempted to have Dr. Raskin's license revoked and his government contracts cancelled. West's conduct was an illegal and outrageous obstruction of justice.

The government's contention was that Howard was trying to unduly influence the case by having press conferences outside the courthouse each day. Yet the government itself had used the media to create tremendous adverse opinion against me from the time I was arrested; thereby, virtually anyone who was placed on the jury would have already seen the government's propaganda. There was no way to avoid it. It was impossible for a juror to enter that courtroom without at least a suspicion that I was guilty. For the public, Howard wanted to provide an opposite view based upon what was taking place in the courtroom each day. The jurors, of course, were prohibited from watching news media during the trial, so they were in no way influenced by anything Howard would have said to the press outside the courtroom.

The amazing aspect of the trial system is that the men in "high places" who engage in improper and illegal conduct like prosecutor Walsh, Hoffman, Tisa, West, Valestra, Waters, and their bosses—are not subject to any disciplinary action. The back-dating of documents sent former President Nixon's attorney to jail. Valestra, Waters, and their bosses did exactly the same thing, yet they admitted in court that nothing would happen to them. The bonuses they had received for arresting me would not have to be given back when they lost the case. If the government does not hold its own employees accountable for illegal acts and misconduct, such abuses of the public trust will never stop.

By May 10, Benedict Tisa had been on the witness stand for several days. He had been examined by the prosecution, cross-examined by the defense, then reexamined by the prosecution. Now, as Tisa's testimony wound to an end under the re-cross-examination, Howard was attempting to show just how badly I had been treated, how carefully I was misled, and how so much of the case against me was only believable if you accepted the word of James Hoffman in the first place.

Referring back to the earliest conversations between Tisa and Hoffman, and specifically to July 12, 1982, Howard said, "If Mr. Hoffman lied to you, if he lied to you, your whole presumption with respect to what Mr. DeLorean was talking about would be incorrect, true?"

"Yes, if he lied."

"All right. For example, if in the meeting with Mr. DeLorean, Mr. Hoffman told him that he thought he could help him get some financing, he'd go out and get some financing, and he wanted a finder's fee for it, if that's what they talked about and if, secondly, they talked about in that conversation that Hoffman had a banker that maybe would help or finance or get some interim financing for DeLorean Motor Company, this conversation would be totally different in terms of your interpretation than it is now, right?"

Tisa argued about this point, finally admitting that his entire understanding of what was happening revolved around his acceptance of Hoffman's claims concerning the unrecorded comments the day before.

"You told us before, when you were testifying under cross-examination, that you initiated this investigation based solely on the information given you by James Hoffman in a telephone call July twelfth, 1982, right?"

"Yes."

"And if James Hoffman lied to you about the subject matter of his meeting with John DeLorean on July eleventh, 1982, then this investigation would have been initiated—it would have been initiated for reasons that were not true, right?"

"Yes."

"And your interpretation of this conversation on the twelfth and the conversation on the fourteenth may have been substantially different, correct?"

"Yes, if Mr. Hoffman was not being truthful."

"Because you have told me that the words of the conversation do not indicate anything unlawful or illegal, right?"

"I had said on the surface, Mr. Weitzman."

"Right. In other words, if you and I were just to hear these conversations and we never met James Hoffman, we wouldn't think there was anything illegal taking place just by the nature of the conversation, right?"

"July twelfth?"

"Yes, July twelve."

"July fourteenth?"

"Yes."

"Those conversations only become—became illegal and unlawful to you when you plug in Hoffman, right?"

"Yes."

They only became illegal because of undocumented

information from Hoffman, a criminal and convicted perjurer who had become a professional informant. All my life I had driven myself to accomplish work worthy of respect. In fact, my life had been so public and well-documented that it could easily be checked. Yet no one bothered to try and learn the truth about me. Instead, they took the unverified word of a known criminal and then used him to destroy me. In effect, when a criminal lied, he was more believable than when an honest man told the truth. This was law enforcement by assumption.

"You must take Mr. Hoffman's words for what he says took place there, right?"

"Yes."

"And every other conversation held in July and August 1982 contained no words that indicate anything unlawful or illegal, correct?"

"Once again, on the surface, Mr. Weitzman."

"In other words, you need James Hoffman to relate back to what happened on July twelfth to interpret those conversations as indicating criminal conduct, right?"

"That's correct."

Without James Hoffman's interpretation, none of the words indicated any criminal actions or criminal intent on my part.

Again, the horrifying fact slapped me in the face! I was a dead man no matter what I might have said. Hoffman could claim that anything I said was in code, and therefore, anything I said could be accepted as illegal. In fact, Tisa himself claimed that "floor-plan financing" was a code, even though "floor-plan financing" is simply a standard term used by every car dealer and manufacturer in America. This was a clear attempt on the part of the prosecution to turn innocent words into illegal ones, hoping the jury would be fooled.

As the questioning continued, Howard was able to bring out the fact that Tisa led me to believe that it was important for me to meet with Hetrick because Hetrick could help me save my company. He admitted that he kept me constantly aware that there was a chance to have money for my company, which encouraged me to stay in the midst of criminals who were also talking drug deals. I was a fish being tantalized by bait hiding an unseen barb.

On May 11, 1984, the questioning of Benedict Tisa came to an end. During his prolonged period on the witness stand leading up to that day, Tisa was frequently confused and several times could not remember my attorney's name. By the time Howard began to cross-examine him, I believe everyone in court had lost all respect for the integrity of the FBI. Before Tisa left the stand, Howard stressed one more time the confusing money scheme.

"So, John DeLorean really had to come up with no money?" Howard asked. "Hetrick was going to front the dope deal, give it to Hoffman, sell the dope, give the money to you, and you will hold out $2 million for Hetrick, give it to him and give DeLorean the rest; was that the deal?"

"That's essentially the basics of it."

So why was I needed? Where did I fit into anything other than as a celebrity to arrest? My position seemed to be meaningless. It was as though my company was going to be a charity case for organized crime, and that made no sense at all. I was mad! I could not forgive these men for the nightmare they had created for me and my family in their desperate attempts to destroy me.

By the time Tisa left the stand, however, I felt that the case against me had been destroyed. There was no case, no crime, no criminal act. There was no reason for me to have been brought into a drug deal, absolutely no evidence that I was involved with narcotics, and so many contradictory statements by Benedict Tisa that I was amazed. The first witness for the government had made an excellent case for my innocence. Somehow I knew that the hand of God had to be working in my life. I felt like a member of a high-school football team playing against the Dallas Cowboys. And my team was winning.

33

James Hoffman took the stand as witness for the prosecution on May 17, to be questioned by Assistant U.S. Attorney James Walsh. It was then that I heard for the first time just how bad his background was. For example, in explaining how he had begun working for the government, Hoffman discussed a situation in Las Vegas where he had become involved with a man named Nathan Marx in an extortion attempt. All that had saved Hoffman from jail was his willingness to turn informant against Marx.

As Hoffman explained: "Mr. Marx said that he had devised a plan whereby—well, first of all, before he told me that, he told me that he had felt cheated out of a life in many respects, that he had not been successful, and that he had just gotten a lot of bad breaks out of life and he had devised a plan to straighten that out.

"He explained to me that the plan that he had had to do this was that he had sent—I forget the number, but—six or more letters to the major hotels and casinos in Las Vegas demanding that each of them pay him a million dollars or he would start systematically bombing those casinos until he received that payment from all the hotels."

"Did he have a particular hotel in mind that he was going to use first?" asked Walsh.

"Yes, he did."

"Which hotel was that?"

"Circus Circus."

"Did he tell you why he picked Circus Circus?"

"Yes. He told me that the reason he picked Circus Circus is he assumed they would not consider him serious, and that would be the first one he would bomb since it's the only one that had children in it, and he could probably kill forty or fifty children to start with."

Walsh asked Hoffman what it was that Marx wanted Hoffman to do to help him.

Hoffman replied, "He [Marx] told me that he wanted me to get a private aircraft, that he had a private airstrip staked out on the outskirts of Las Vegas, and after he had collected the moneys that he was going to be paid from this extortion plot, that he wanted me then to fly him out of Las Vegas and fly him out of the country."

According to his testimony, Hoffman chose not to contact the FBI directly, but rather to use a friend. His explanation made him even more obviously a man with a checkered past.

"It was at this time that I was aware that the two warrants were out for me in Houston," he said, "and if there was nothing to what he said or if he was just hallucinating over this, then walking into the FBI office and telling them who I was would have—at that time I assume that they would have arrested me on those warrants. And before I did that, I wanted to make sure that what he was saying had some merit to it." He then corrected himself, explaining that he was in Houston at the time but that the warrants for his arrest were in Tucson, Arizona.

As Hoffman discussed becoming a witness for the government in the case against Marx and some of his other work for the government, he also mentioned personal arrests and convictions relating to narcotics. The testimony indicated that he had been involved with drug trafficking since 1976 and detailed some of his past actions, including his work as a pilot in transporting drugs. I couldn't believe this was the man around whom the entire case against me had been constructed.

"In how many cases had you furnished cooperation by the time you were sentenced?" asked Assistant U.S. Attorney Walsh.

"Three."

"Can you name those cases? How would you identify those cases?"

"Yes. Faez Boukaram case, the Norman Bonner case, and Fred Beahm–Tom O'Neil case."

"What sentence did you receive in May of 1982?"

"Five years probation."

"Is it your understanding that your sentence reflected your cooperation with the government prior to that time?"

"Yes."

"Were you sentenced prior to beginning any work on the case involving John DeLorean?"

"Yes."

"Were you also sentenced prior to beginning any work on the case involving William Morgan Hetrick?"

"Yes."

"When you were sentenced in May of 1982, did that represent completion of your part of the plea agreement, in your mind?"

"Yes."

"Were you under any obligation to continue to work as an undercover narcotics informant after that time?"

"No."

"Were there cases that you were working on as part of your agreement which were not yet completed at that time?"

"Yes."

"And which cases were they?"

"Faez Boukaram, Norman Bonner, and the trial had not taken place in the Beahm-O'Neil matter."

Hoffman explained other types of work he had handled for law enforcement and that he had worked in exchange for expenses, though later it would be proven that the money he received from being an informant was substantially greater than his expenses and included a new Cadillac.

Among the things Walsh brought out was that Hoffman had perjured himself before the Grand Jury at least thirteen times. In some instances it was clear that assistant prosecutor Walsh knew Hoffman was lying to the Grand Jury. This made Walsh guilty of suborning perjury in my mind. It was also clear that the Grand Jury had at first refused to indict me; they asked to see Hoffman. If Hoffman had answered the Grand Jury's questions truthfully, I would never have been indicted.

I don't know what the jury thought of James Hoffman when he first took the stand, but my reaction was that he was not a good man to have making a case for the government. Prosecutor Walsh presented the litany of Hoffman's crimes so there would be no surprises, with us bringing Hoffman's past out as damning evidence in our defense cross-examination. But I certainly didn't see how it helped their case. In a sense they condemned themselves, for it was made eminently clear that the government had, for whatever reason, chosen to make a seemingly habitual criminal the mastermind of much of the case they were trying to build against me.

Walsh's direct examination of Hoffman took several days. Then on May 24, 1984, Howard began his cross-examination.

Howard's questioning elicited more negative information about Hoffman. For example, after discussing his income from various sources, Hoffman claimed that in 1980 he had made $16,000, though at the time he was leasing a house in Pauma Valley, California. "The first Pauma Valley residence, as I recall, was either fifteen or sixteen hundred dollars a month, and the second one was a thousand." This indicated that either he was lying about his income or was living beyond his means. Whatever the truth was, it also became clear that the IRS was not getting its share.

"Did you pay your taxes in 1980?"

"No."

"Did you file taxes in 1980?"

"No."

"Did you file in 1979?"

"No."

"'78?"

"No."

"'77?"

"No."

And on and on until he admitted that in 1973 he probably had filed taxes. He also filed in 1982, after his arrest, because he had received money from the government.

"How much money did you report as income that you received from the government?" Howard asked, concerning his 1982 tax return. Hoffman said he had been paid some $161,000.

"Net, I believe, was $253 or it may not be exactly—less than $300, as I recall, or somewhere in that vicinity."

Failure to file a tax return, regardless of the fact that you may owe nothing, is against the law. Hoffman not only managed to survive on what he claimed was very little money for his lifestyle, but also repeatedly violated the law by not filing his income taxes. Even worse, Hoffman stated that when he did file taxes, he was assisted by a representative from the IRS, who had him paying $253 in taxes on $161,000 of income.

Hoffman's finances were always a little vague. During his testimony on May 29, he admitted receiving rent money, among other payments, from the government. These payments were in cash, and just the amounts mentioned as living expenses seemed to indicate that he was holding back

293

a great deal. Yet he stressed that he was not working for the money; he was working because he felt that he was gaining respect and doing something worthwhile.

"What did you believe you were doing that was worthwhile?"

"Assisting the government in what they asked me to do, in investigations of possible violators."

"So you were like a quasi-investigator; in other words, your job was to act as an undercover agent would act; is that correct?"

"Not correct."

"What was your job in these investigations."

"To follow the directions of the agents and to take orders from the agents."

"You believed it was worthwhile to follow the instructions of the agents and take orders from the agents?"

"Yes, I did," Hoffman responded, later adding that he wanted to partially atone for his sins and partially gain the self-respect he felt when working with the government.

Hoffman was a real pro on the stand, never wavering into confusion the way Benedict Tisa had. Hoffman was a con man, experienced in convincing people to involve themselves with him. Telling falsehoods was his stock in trade, and this trial was no exception.

As Howard turned his cross-examination toward Hoffman's contact with me, Hoffman began discussing my involvement with drugs and how I had worked so hard to have him help me with a narcotics deal. Always he stressed conversations for which there was no record except his word. Then he discussed how my case was to be combined with that of Morgan Hetrick.

"Morgan Hetrick was a—they believed a willing and able supplier of cocaine," he said, referring to the government agents. "Mr. DeLorean being a willing and able investor in cocaine, and that a possible plan was being talked about to combine the investigations for that reason."

"Did you say Mr. DeLorean was a willing investor in cocaine?" Howard asked. "That's what you were told?"

"And heroin, but as it related to Hetrick."

Trying to clarify this, Howard said, "Was it your understanding that the government believed Hetrick was a willing seller and DeLorean was a willing buyer?"

"Yes."

"Was it your understanding based on what you were told that the government believed DeLorean wanted to buy cocaine or heroin?"

"I would say the word 'buy/investment,' whatever interpretation is made there; but my understanding was never that DeLorean wanted to buy cocaine physically. He wanted to invest in cocaine and heroin."

"And the cocaine was talked about at the meeting of July eleventh; is that right?"

"That's correct."

"How exactly did the conversation shift to large amounts of cocaine?"

"In an effort that I related per Mr. DeLorean's request to figure out something to generate funds prior to sixty days, and my statement that possibly that could be through cocaine."

Then Howard asked, "When did DeLorean raise cocaine?"

"July eleven."

"He raised it, you didn't, right?"

"He asked me what we could do to speed up the process of getting some money. I said to him—it would be my statement possibly I could arrange a cocaine deal. I would check into it."

The payment for the deal was a constant question. Hoffman insisted that I was going to spend $2 million. Then he said that he would not be paid the money but that it would go through Eureka Savings and Loan. He said that I would be using collateral once it was found that I did not have the money. Yet each time he explained the plan, my position became more and more unclear.

"So the plan was that Vicenza [DEA agent John Vales-
tra] puts in $5 million, Hetrick goes and gets the dope,
comes back and gives it to you, you sell it and give the
money to Tisa, and Tisa disburses the money; isn't that
right?"

Hoffman replied, "To Mr. DeLorean, yes."

"That was the plan, correct?"

"Basically, yes."

"And John Vicenza gets stock in DeLorean Motor
Company, correct?"

"Correct."

"After he invests $60 million, correct?"

"That's correct."

And once again Howard asked the most important
question. "Now, what did you need John DeLorean for?"

The response would have been humorous had it not
been so pathetic. "To provide an investment for the narcotics."

Yet Hoffman had just described the plan for the purchase, never mentioning me. Vicenza was putting up the
money, Hetrick was putting up the drugs, Hoffman was
selling the drugs and giving the money to Tisa, and Tisa was
disbursing the money.

"On June eleven, are you telling us that John DeLorean
came up with a plan where you, James Hoffman, would get
stock in his company for investing proceeds from the
narcotics deal?"

"Yes."

Howard continued, "John Vicenza put in $5 million, you
were going to sell the dope that Hetrick provided and
deposit the money in Eureka Federal Savings and Loan, and
it would be given to John DeLorean in exchange for stock; is
that right? Is that true?"

"Yes."

"What did you need John DeLorean for in the dope
deal?" Howard persisted.

"For an investment." But there was no investment. The
drug deal was to be financed by Vicenza, the man who was

working undercover as the big criminal connection of James Hoffman.

By May 30, Hoffman was back to his old statements.

"The basic deal was: Mr. DeLorean was going to put up $2 million in cash for the purchase of narcotics, primarily heroin and possibly cocaine, and that he was going to receive the full cash profit and proceeds out of the sale of those narcotics. It was my understanding that those proceeds would be used for the purposes of the car company and that I would receive stock in lieu of a normal narcotic profit being paid for my participation for helping."

Howard introduced the grand-jury testimony Hoffman had made, pointing out that many of the statements were perjurious. He discussed the fact that the timing Hoffman claimed for the alleged deals was wrong.

Everything had to be explained by Hoffman. According to him, nothing was quite the way it seemed. I felt as though the whole world could only be understood when defined through Hoffman's eyes. Everything had a hidden message, a hidden meaning, and only Hoffman had the key. Everyone involved with my arrest and indictment needed to put their logic, their common sense, and their inherent good sense aside to know "the truth." We had gone back through the looking glass; we were in Wonderland with Alice.

"So what did you need John DeLorean for in this dope deal, sir?"

"Didn't need him at all."

"You didn't need him at all?"

"He was there because he wanted to be."

"You didn't need him for the dope deal, right?"

"Right."

"But you were willing to loan him the money, so he would stay with you and promise him he would get thirty or forty or fifty million dollars to invest in his company; right?"

"Forty or fifty."

"You have indicated to us that you didn't need him in the dope deal; is that right?" Howard repeated.

"That is right."

"And when he told you he didn't have the money, you went after him to propose an alternative, didn't you?"

"Yes."

And back in Wonderland, the Queen of Hearts was shouting, "Off with his head."

Hour after hour my attorney questioned James Hoffman. Unlike Benedict Tisa, Hoffman would not admit to making many mistakes. He was a skilled witness, able to speak convincingly. He constantly tried to twist reality so that it would fit with previous testimony. Whenever a tape recording was played and the dialogue did not use the exact words necessary to prove I was a master criminal, Hoffman would explain that there were hidden meanings related to earlier, unrecorded statements.

His skilled performance went off without major errors on his part until June 5 when Howard questioned him about his post-office box. This was the box to which on July 9 my office sent the documents concerning my company, the documents Hoffman requested during that infamous, unrecorded first telephone call when he was talking investment in my business, but later maintained that I talked drugs. This mailing showed that I did not expect to see him in the near future, and certainly not on July 11, since the mailed materials could never have arrived by then. In other words, my mailing the materials basically proved that his statements about the key July 11 meeting were lies.

Under Howard's questioning, Hoffman testified that he had retained his box at 250-2 South Orange Street in Escondido, California, only until January of 1982. But it was to that box that I sent a letter and the materials on July 9, 1982, a copy of which Howard had in court.

Howard asked, "Do you remember receiving a letter at that box dated July ninth, '82, that read as follows:

" 'Dear Jim: I am enclosing descriptive and financial information on our company. Today we have the newest and most modern assembly plant in the world with the most advanced product, and we are essentially free of debt. We are poised to become another BMW fully capable of earning 150 million to 200 million per year. Sincerely, John Z. DeLorean.'

"Do you remember getting that document addressed to 250-2 South Orange Street in Escondido?"

"No, I never received that."

"Would it help refresh your memory if you saw the document?"

"No. I have never received that. What was the date on it?"

"July ninth, 1982."

"I wasn't even there. I didn't even have the box."

This was an important slip on Hoffman's part. I knew that I had sent the letter, and I was certain that Hoffman had given us the post-office box address. My secretary, Carole Winkler, later testified that she typed and mailed the letter to Hoffman's Escondido box on July ninth.

"Now, this post office box that you said you got after you moved to Valley Center, what is your recollection as to when you got rid of it?"

"As I recall, I got rid of that or didn't return—I may have returned there once after January, maybe in February, but I think I went back one time. And as I recall, I didn't return there again."

"Did you give John DeLorean that address to mail you anything?"

"No."

"Your recollection is it was 250-2 South Orange Street, Escondido, California, 92025, correct?"

"That is, as I recall, was the address, yes."

The box was a private rental, and Howard again asked about when he had last used it.

Hoffman said, "Last time I recall I went there was—I am not exactly positive, but I may have gone back once in February. But after then, I did not return to that box."

Howard pressed the point: "You didn't use the box after you gave it up in '82 and you haven't used it since, have you?"

"No"

"Did you give that number to Mr. DeLorean?"

"No."

Howard asked, "You gave John DeLorean that address when you talked to him on the thirtieth and told him to mail you the brochures about the investment of the company, Mr. Hoffman, didn't you?"

"Couldn't have done that."

"You certainly could have, Mr. Hoffman. The question is: Did you?"

"The answer is: I did not." He also claimed he did not remember the name of the company from which he rented it and did not know if he had rent receipts.

For a number of years, I had been a very wealthy man. One of the tactics the government used against me was to reduce my ability to defend myself by taking my money from me. They tied everything up in litigation and bail so that I could not mount an effective defense, or so they hoped. What they did not realize was that for once in my life, I was going to fight back. Despite my involvement in controversy from time to time, I had always avoided negative experiences and confrontations, as I have said. Yet now I knew that I was not fighting alone. The Lord was a very real presence in my life, and I had experienced the joy of knowing that. While I knew He had asked me to turn over the control of my life to Him, I was certain that He did not want me to lie down and not participate in the clearing of my name. Since I could not afford to hire a private investigator, I decided to do the work myself.

When I was not involved with the court proceedings, I took it upon myself to call Escondido. Using the telephone directory, I located the private mail box companies and called each in turn, pretending to be James Hoffman. I explained that I had a box with them and couldn't remember if I had paid my rent to date. In just a few minutes I was able to learn exactly where James Hoffman had his box and to confirm that he still had it. Thus, we were able to subpoena the records to prove the man was a liar.

As it turned out, the box was rented so that four names could receive mail. James Hoffman was listed, as was a company called Windjammer, a Danny James, and most improbable of all, Veronica Rand! The names were obviously aliases and indicated that Hoffman was engaged in a number of personal scams unknown to the government.

When confronted with the truth about the box, Hoffman tried to bluff his way out, saying that a friend, a man named Bill Nash, was the person who used the box. Nash paid the rent and picked up mail, even though his name was not listed, which of course made no sense at all. Nash was also an ex-convict, and Hoffman's association with a fellow ex-con would be grounds for revoking his parole. Hoffman's thin excuse was an obvious falsehood, but it also raised some serious questions about potentially illegal schemes with ex-con Nash, if that person did exist and was picking up mail under one of the pseudonyms.

At one point prosecutor Walsh asked Hoffman if he hated "the defendant." He wanted to know why he chose to testify against me.

Hoffman, sounding almost sincere, said that he wanted to change his life, to do that which was right to restore his self-respect. Howard was able to destroy the credibility of these statements completely.

First, Howard found that another of prosecutor Walsh's informants had used exactly the same speech, word for word, in another case. Clearly, Hoffman had memorized Walsh's standard "repentant sinner" speech.

Next, we had finally obtained a document, a telex to Washington, that Walsh had illegally kept from us. Under past Supreme Court rulings, Walsh was legally obliged to deliver it. He deliberately hid it from us. When Perry saw the Walsh misconduct all around him, he delivered it to keep his own skirts clean. It was from the heads of the DEA and FBI to top justice officials in Washington and said, "Hoffman has demanded moiety. He wants 10 percent of all the assets confiscated in this case or he says he'll blow it sky high." Walsh had this telex in his possession, so again he was perjuring himself. When this came to light, Judge Takasugi blew his top. "Hoffman is nothing but a hired gun," he said. "He will say anything for money!" The judge was also extremely critical of prosecutor Walsh for illegally withholding this vital piece of evidence.

In other instances of evidence tampering, Tisa had admitted to back-dating records and "altering" notes when by law they should have been left exactly as they were when he first made them. Government agent Valestra had even apologized to the jury for the "misleading" statements that had been made. Lies!

Don Re and Howard Weitzman are extremely competent defense attorneys, but as highly trained government agents seemed to fall apart on the witness stand, there were times when I felt as though I was being defended by Perry Mason, the famous fictional attorney who always won his cases in dramatic fashion.

Hour after hour, day after day, the truth unfolded. The ordeal was all-consuming. I would sit and listen, make notes, talk with Mona, watch Howard and Don in action, hope that the jury was witnessing the same discrepancies, lies, and outrageous statements I was catching. When we did take breaks, reporters were usually waiting, trying to accompany me everywhere. Outside the courtroom the newspapers often portrayed me as the most despicable man in America, and the television coverage placed me on a level only slightly below that of some notorious mass murderer. Most of them portrayed me as a guilty man.

Yet I was never nervous or concerned. I knew the Lord was there. The warmth of the light that had cradled me in my darkest hour remained in my heart. I was in His hands. No matter what happened, His love for me would endure.

34

Carole Winkler, my former secretary, was our first witness. She confirmed that the sets of documents she had mailed Hoffman and Tisa were the same as those sent to dozens of other prospective investors and that the telephone log entered into evidence was hers, in her handwriting.

Carole was wonderful. Walsh attempted to discredit her on cross-examination and only managed to alienate himself with the jury. Carole was so open and honest that everyone fell in love with her.

Gerald Scotti, the second witness for the defense, took the stand on July 31, 1985. Scotti had been DEA co-case agent along with Valestra, but had resigned after he had been viciously attacked because he had expressed reservations about my case.

Scotti's courage on the witness stand was amazing. He

303

had been a successful, decorated agent who had had some problems after he was accused of discussing a case with a defense attorney. It was assumed that his actions were improper, that he had threatened the outcome of a trial by being too free with information. The pursuant investigation indicated that Scotti had done nothing wrong and appeared to have been feeding the attorney information as a way of gaining the attorney's confidence for a broader investigation. He was cleared of any wrongdoing and then ordered to become involved with my investigation.

The prosecution tried to imply that Scotti had resigned from the DEA because of the charges that had been brought against him. But that incident had occurred some time before Scotti was assigned to my case. The attacks against him were all personal, never against his professional competence. The government never rebutted one word of Scotti's testimony about the case against me. They could not refute his work or his word, so they attacked the man.

Early in his questioning, Howard asked Scotti how he had first learned about the case against me. Scotti said that it had come to his attention during a conversation with James Hoffman.

"Well, we had been talking about a lot of different things, and I asked Jim if he was working on anything else currently. He said to me, 'You know I'm going to get John DeLorean for you guys.'"

"Just out of left field?" asked Howard.

"It wasn't really out of left field. We had been talking about narcotics trafficking in general leading up to that, and I asked him what else it was he was doing, working on."

"Did you know the name John DeLorean when you heard it?"

"Yes, I did."

"What did you know about it?"

"I grew up in Detroit, and I knew he was involved in the auto industry with General Motors. I heard the name before."

"Did you have a conversation with Hoffman specifically

304

about what he had said in terms he was going to get John DeLorean for you?"

"Yes, I did because when he said that I didn't believe him. It was incredulous."

"Tell me about the conversation."

"Well, I told him, 'What do you mean you're going to get John DeLorean? How would a guy like that—why would a guy like that have anything to do with drugs?'

"He told me, he said, 'Listen, this guy is in a lot of trouble now with his auto company. He's in a lot of financial trouble,' and I remember he was bragging because he was indignant about the fact that I didn't believe him, and he kept saying, 'I'm telling you, Scotti, I'm going to deliver John DeLorean to you guys.' He said, he told me, 'You know me.' He said, 'I can do it.' " (This conversation between Scotti and Hoffman took place before Hoffman called me the first time.)

Scotti continued: "I said to him, 'How are you going to do that?' and he told me about some problems he was aware of with Mr. DeLorean in financial states, and he said, 'The problems he's got, I can get him to do anything I want.' "

"Is that the phrase he used?"

"He used words to that effect. I wouldn't say those were the exact words"

Then Scotti added: "I continued to express doubt. I really still didn't believe him. I said, 'You are going to get this guy involved in a drug deal?' and he said, 'I think I can,' and he told me that he knew him before, knew him from his past. He said he hadn't had any contact with him for a while.

"I asked him, 'Does he know about your involvement with drugs?' He said, 'No,' no he didn't."

At last the truth was out. A Drug Enforcement Administration agent involved in the case from the start admitted having been told that I had no awareness of Hoffman's drug dealings. Hoffman himself had admitted early on that I did not know what he did for a living, yet everyone had been accepting Hoffman's later claims that I had called him to handle a drug deal. While Scotti was not particularly appreciated by his colleagues for questioning what was taking place, no one questioned the honesty of his statement that, according to Hoffman, I had no knowledge of his drug dealings.

Scotti continued: "I said, 'Well, how are you going to bring drugs up to him?' He says, 'Well, I'm not going to bring drugs up to him. That would scare him off if I did that initially.' Then he kept on more or less—'You just leave it to me. You know me. I can handle it,' and he was kind of half laughing, kind of cocksure of himself, and I really didn't take it all that serious."

Scotti explained that after that conversation he did not see Hoffman for several weeks. Then he was asked to begin paying Hoffman money he was earning for acting as an informant. When Scotti learned the payment was for the DeLorean investigation, he was surprised.

"He [Hoffman] had a very boastful manner," Scotti said. "He referred back to the conversation we had had earlier. He said, 'You didn't believe me, but, see, I told you I was going to do it.'"

"Do what?" asked Howard.

"Deliver DeLorean, get DeLorean."

Scotti had then asked Hoffman how he had accomplished his boast. "He repeated the fact that he knew him [DeLorean] previously. He said that he went to see him several times, that he had approached him, and that he had used the lure of bailing him out of his financial troubles with the auto industry. I remember on more than one occasion he said, 'This guy is really in trouble financially, and he needs a way out.'"

Scotti said that he had had the impression that the approach Hoffman used in trying to convince me that he had the contacts to save my car company was a lure. "He said he had talked with him [DeLorean] a couple times, I believe a couple times. I asked him 'Do you have anything?'—I think I challenged him. I said, 'Well, you don't have a case on the guy yet,' and he said, 'No, this is a tough nut to crack. I'm having a little trouble,' but he said, 'I'll get him.' He said, he told me that he [DeLorean] was very reluctant."

I had long maintained, and Cristina and Zachary confirmed, that, before his first contact with me concerning the financing I so desperately needed, my total involvement with James Hoffman had been a ten-minute conversation on our driveway with our wives and children present. The claims I had made were called lies by the prosecution, and James Hoffman's testimony naturally went against me. When Jerry Scotti took the stand, however, he stated that Hoffman had told him that I knew nothing of Hoffman's drug dealings. Hoffman had explained to him how carefully he would manipulate me before he ever mentioned a possible drug deal. Scotti not only confirmed the truth of my entrapment but was never contradicted by the other agents. They attacked Jerry Scotti's personal life but none of them even tried to refute his testimony, which cleared me of being a willing participant right from the start.

The prosecutor cross-examined Scotti about when he and Hoffman first talked about the possibility of involving me in a drug deal. Scotti was skeptical, explaining: "He [Hoffman] said, 'Well, you know this guy's in a lot of trouble with his auto company.' He said—he was cocky about it. I remember he had kind of a haughty attitude. He said, 'You know me, Scotti. Just leave it to me.'"

"Anything else?" the prosecutor asked.

"That was the essence of it. We talked more about the same things, me telling him in so many words I thought he was full of it, I didn't think that was possible, and him continually saying, 'No, no. I'm going to do this. I'm going to deliver John DeLorean for you guys.'

"And I remember asking him, trying to identify—'Are we talking about the same guy, the guy who's involved in the auto company?' And he said, 'Yeah, that's the guy.' He seemed to have a lot of knowledge of the situation. He asked me, 'Haven't you heard? Don't you read the papers or something? He's in a lot of financial trouble.'

"He said—he mentioned—I asked him something to the effect, 'How are you going to get next to a guy like this?' He said that he had known him in the past.

307

"I asked him, 'Well, does he know you were involved in drugs?' And he said, 'No, no. He wouldn't have anything to do with me. If that was the case, it would scare him off.'"

"He said that?" asked the prosecutor.

"He said, 'It would scare him off.'"

Scotti was then questioned about the videotaped meeting between Hoffman and me on September 28. The meeting had taken place in a hotel room that, unknown to me, had a hidden camera connected to a monitor and videocassette recorder in the next room. The moment was apparently an extremely exciting one for the law-enforcement officers involved with the case. They had a celebrity, a man who could place them in the headlines, and they were delighted to watch what they believed would be evidence leading to my destruction. Members of the police, FBI, DEA, and the U.S. Attorney's office had crowded themselves in the monitor area, watching the television screen, smoking cigarettes, and making jokes about my downfall. They were on their way to being media stars. They were going to have promotions, awards, a future brighter than would have been possible from any other case on which they had worked. What happened next would have made a hilarious silent movie if the scene hadn't been such grim reality.

The law officers were so thrilled with what was taking place in the next room, so preoccupied with the glory awaiting them, that they ignored the increasing build-up of smoke from dozens of cigarettes. As the smoke grew thicker and thicker, filling the room with a dense grey cloud, it set off the smoke detector in the ceiling and triggered the alarm. The blaring siren startled the agents who desperately opened windows and fanned the smoke, trying to silence the noisemaker.

Next door, Hoffman and I were startled by the noise. We looked around the room, trying to determine what was making the commotion. I assumed that it was a police cruiser or ambulance on the street below and returned to the discussion.

To the agents, that meeting seemed to confirm their

success, because I did not storm out, insisting I wanted nothing to do with any dastardly deeds Hoffman was planning. In reality, I was stalling for time. I had no intention of getting involved. I was following the advice of my lawyer because of my fear of these men, but to a casual observer, it appeared that I just might be willing to commit myself to the drug deal.

Scotti described how he, assistant U.S. attorney Walsh, FBI special agent Mike Harmon, and DEA agent John Valestra, along with three or four other men, decided to celebrate what they thought was going to be my involvement in narcotics. "I think we ordered something like three hundred dollars' worth of wine [paid for by the government]," Scotti said, describing toasts that were made, including Walsh's self-serving pronouncement that he would make the cover of *Time*.

Scotti said he had questioned Walsh's meaning at the time. "He mentioned the impact of an individual in a high corporate-executive level, and this is the stuff that *Time* magazine or something like that would really go for. He made some comment about, 'We'll all get into *Time* magazine.'" And this was the same man who was now present in the courtroom as part of the prosecution team.

Now it became even more evident that Perry and Walsh had been so confident that they had not adequately prepared their case. To discredit Scotti, Perry confronted him with the hotel bills to show that they did not itemize $300 for wine. But I remembered seeing Valestra on the videotape paying his bill with hundred-dollar bills and tipping the waiter in cash. After we adjourned that day, I dug out the tape and showed it to Howard. There was Valestra paying in cash. Later Howard showed the film on redirect and made a complete fool of Perry, who had not done his homework.

As the questioning continued, Scotti was asked about how his role in the investigation had changed before my arrest. He explained that he was assigned the task of coordinating the DEA's efforts in the financial investigation for seizure of assets. This meant that if they were successful

309

in entrapping and convicting me, there was a chance that they could take just about everything I owned if they could relate it to the drug deal I was supposed to be handling. In their minds, this could mean millions of dollars in cash and property, the type of haul that would make their supervisors extremely happy and help everyone when promotions were being considered.

Scotti also told about the arguments between officials in New York and Los Angeles as to where I should be arrested. Each wanted the extensive publicity that my arrest would generate; each wanted the glory. Eventually, the West Coast won, which made Assistant U.S. Attorney Walsh extremely happy.

Howard wanted to make certain that the jury knew of Scotti's past and fully understood the attempt that had been made to discredit his reputation. Scotti had been cleared of any wrongdoing, but in March of 1983 Assistant U.S. Attorney Perry, the co-prosecutor in my case, reopened the matter. It was clear that the case was reopened because Scotti had begun questioning the actions that led to my arrest.

Scotti's testimony regarding these matters led to one of the most dramatic events of the trial: the deliberate attempt to emotionally destroy him.

When Howard examined Scotti again, he asked him about how he had been pressured to plead guilty to allegations of which he was innocent.

"I had been on limited duty for nine months," Scotti said. "While I was theoretically under investigation for a second time for an item I had been cleared on earlier, during that time the government had made repeated offers to me, saying—they offered me a misdemeanor. They said, 'Plead guilty to the misdemeanor. We won't seek any time. We'll drop any consideration of indicting you. If you don't agree to that, we're going to indict you.'

"And I recall then on each occasion, every occasion—

my attorney was present every time—that offer was made, Mr. Drooyan [of the U.S. Attorney's Office] insisted that the following Wednesday—I guess that's when the grand jury met—he said he would indict me that day, that Wednesday.

"So, when the offer was first made, I consulted with my attorney—he gave me a week to think about it—consulted attorneys I knew to get an opinion on it, tried to lay out everything there was to them—"

Scotti continued: "And I came back the first time with my answer to Mr. Drooyan. This was in about May of '83 after I had been on limited duty. The first time, I told him, 'No, I can't accept your offer for a misdemeanor. I can't admit to anything I didn't do. If you've got to indict me, go ahead and indict me.'

"The indictment never happened. About three different times we went to his office, maybe two additional, two or three times more. There were about three times, maybe more. He repeated the offer. In fact, Mr. Trott [formerly of the U.S. Attorney's Office and now Assistant Attorney General of the United States and in charge of the Criminal Division] got involved to communicate the offer to my attorney.

"He literally begged me to take the offer. He said, 'Take the misdemeanor. It's the easy way out. There won't be anything brought against you.'

"He kept reminding me, he kept driving it in, about how serious being indicted was and of what I had to face. He talked about, 'You may have to do time if we convict you on this. Can you imagine what it would be like to serve time in jail for an ex-agent?' He went through a lot of stuff like that. And I told him the same thing, 'I didn't do anything wrong. If you have to indict me, indict me.'

"As a matter of fact, one time he pounded his fist on the book, and he said—on the U.S. Code book—'Please, Jerry, I want you to take the misdemeanor.'

"And I told him, no, I couldn't do that. Again, every time, it was the following Wednesday they would indict me. They kept passing it, and it never happened.

"Finally—well, through all this, I pretty much realized I didn't have much of a career left with the government. And I had begun to form this business with my partner [Scotti was referring to a part-time business in which he helped produce a baseball-trivia radio show with a man in Detroit]. And finally, in November of 1983, my attorney, Mr. Twitty, told me, 'Jerry, they don't have anything here, and they know they don't have anything here.' He reminded me, 'If they ever do indict you, it's going to be a tremendous expense.' He says, 'They can indict you. They can indict just about anybody they want, but I don't think they can convict you. They don't have the facts. It's a tremendous expense, it's a tremendous hassle—' in so many words— 'to suffer an indictment.' He says, 'I think, if we make an offer to resign and drop the matter, they'll go for it.'

"I said, 'Okay.'

"He made the offer, and they went for it. And that's why I made this agreement, and I had resigned."

Howard then brought out the way in which Scotti's personal problems had been presented to the courtroom; the way, in effect, that former DEA agent Gerald Scotti had been placed on trial for telling the truth. Those personal problems had been known by only one man, his superior Bill Waters, a person whom Scotti trusted completely. The problems had been presented to him in strictest confidence and did not affect his work with DEA. They were not a part of some permanent file readily available to the prosecutor, nor did they have a bearing on the case the government was trying to bring against me. The only reason for mentioning them was to hurt Scotti and to hurt his standing as a witness for the defense. To accomplish their own ends, the government had betrayed a loyal and valuable member of their own team. Even more hurtful, the personal betrayal came from Waters, whom Scotti considered a close personal friend.

Regarding this friend, Howard said, "Scotti."

"Yes, sir."

"Does that surprise you, that he would relay that information?"

312

There was a pause, and Scotti's face revealed the deep and disquieting emotions he was experiencing. Then, quietly, he said, "I'm not sure I know him anymore."

"What do you mean?" asked Howard.

The courtroom was silent, the jury obviously moved. Then the mood was broken by the word "objection!" The prosecutor did not feel that the comment was relevant to my case. But I suspect he was afraid of the impact on the jury if the drama was played to the end.

Judge Takasugi overruled the objection, and Scotti said, "I knew from a long ways back I thought that the government would go to any length to prosecute Mr. DeLorean, but I always thought that there was a limit to it, that there was a bottom to it. Now I'm not sure of that anymore."

35

Gerald Scotti and Carole Winkler were the only witnesses appearing on my behalf. Obviously, we had originally planned for a much greater defense. We had carefully documented the fact that audiotapes provided by the FBI and the Justice Department had been extensively "doctored." We had documents signed by Hoffman proving that he had been giving me the impression that his only interest was in establishing a business deal for financing my company, not involving me in drugs. We had witnesses and documents to prove that the government knew I was innocent from the start. We had the letter I had written to my lawyer before my arrest, which so clearly showed that I believed I was being threatened by members of organized crime. We had polygraph-test results and proof of perjury by prosecutor Walsh and others when presenting the case to the grand jury. In a conference call with Howard Weitzman, investigator Palladino, and me, Kenneth Kidwell, the chairman of Eureka Federal Savings and Loan, had admitted that he had information that would "blow away" the government's entire case against me and prove it was pure fabrication. Had we presented our defense we would have subpoenaed him as a witness. There were literally thousands of pages of documents that would have so shattered the arguments of the prosecution and so thoroughly proven my innocence that even my worst enemies would probably have had to vote for acquittal. But after Gerald Scotti was finished on the stand, none of that was needed.

Benedict Tisa had shown the jury that an FBI agent was willing to alter records in pursuit of my conviction. John Valestra of the DEA had apologized to the jury for lying. Valestra had also back-dated a critical document. James Hoffman had lied under oath about what I sent him and had revealed that he continued to engage in apparently illegal scams even while working as an informant, scams that his controls within the government did not know were taking place. We didn't need our extensive defense plan. My enemies had destroyed themselves in their efforts to be my undoing.

I must admit I identified with King David when he wrote the Third Psalm:

> O LORD, how many are my foes!
>   How many rise up against me!
> Many are saying of me,
>   "God will not deliver him."
> But you are a shield around me, O LORD;
>   you bestow glory on me and lift up my head.

By August 6, 1984, all the witnesses had been heard. In attempting to unravel the knots of truth and falsehood, reality and fantasy, I felt that my lawyers had proven my innocence far beyond a reasonable doubt. I felt that the jury had heard the truth. Yet I did not know for certain that my ordeal was going to end. All I was certain of was that I could remain calm in God's healing love, that He would be with me. But inside, as the closing arguments were presented, I could only pray that when the prosecution and defense attorneys were finished, the jury would believe me and find me innocent.

Robert Perry gave the prosecution's closing argument to the jury, placing his own interpretation on the events.

"Now, ladies and gentlemen, when you look at the evidence, you know that John DeLorean saw the opportunity to make millions in narcotics, and he accepted the risk.

"I would ask you to think of the time and the money that John DeLorean spent in chasing this opportunity to make money from narcotics. This internationally reknown [sic] businessman, a man whose daily decisions must have affected the lives of hundreds if not thousands of people. This man made time from his schedule for the likes of Hoffman, Tisa, Valestra, Hetrick. He made time to take telephone calls and to make telephone calls. He took time to travel thousands of miles, to meet in dimly lit hotel rooms to talk about narcotics.

"He took time to go to Morgan Aviation. He took time to take Hetrick and Tisa and their girl friends out to dinner, a dinner that he paid for, a dinner that he brought his wife to.

"Think of the time. Think of the time that he gave to men that he believed were in the heroin and cocaine business, and think of the money he spent.

"When you look at the exhibits, you will see that there are in evidence the receipts for travel expenses, American Airlines, bills for his hotel expenses while he was out here attending meetings with these men that he believed were narcotic traffickers, and you will see that the receipts total more than $4,000. John DeLorean in four months spent more than $4,000 chasing this narcotics deal.

"Oh, how he chased this deal. Valestra asked him, 'John, what's your schedule?'

317

"DeLorean answered, 'I got all the time in the world. The most important thing in my life is to get this thing done.'

"Ladies and gentlemen, when you look at the evidence, you will conclude that John DeLorean saw the opportunity to make millions in narcotics, and he accepted the risks. He designed his own disgrace. He and he alone is the architect of his own destruction."

It was a dramatic opening, as misleading as Hoffman's statements had been. Certainly, I had spent weeks chasing investors and badly needed capital. What was important was raising money, and I would travel anywhere to talk with anyone who seemed serious about investing in DeLorean Motor Company.

I could hardly restrain myself from shouting the truth at Perry, but I comforted myself with the knowledge that Howard and Don would have the final say in presenting my defense.

"We use informants," Perry continued. "You know we use informants, and it takes a crook to catch a crook.

"Mr. Waters [a DEA supervisor] gave me a great phrase. He said, 'For a plot hatched in hell, don't expect to have angels for witnesses.' And we don't. We don't vouch for Mr. Hoffman's past. We want you to be sure that you view his testimony at arm's length.

"Remember in jury selection I told you that he is an admitted perjurer, and I told you he made statements before the grand jury in this case that were not true, and I told you that he had been paid lots of money, one hundred fifty, one hundred sixty thousand dollars or more, for expenses to cover the medical expenses and the more than nineteen moves that he had with his family of four.

"I told you in jury selection, and I remind you now, that the testimony of an informer or a perjurer must be weighed with greater care than that of an ordinary witness. Remember we settled all this out in jury selection? You all told me that you would keep an open mind about Mr. Hoffman's testimony, that you would judge it based on the other evidence in the case.

"That is the point I am making here. Look for corroboration, look for support, for what Mr. Hoffman had to say. And I submit you will find support, you will find corroboration, for what Hoffman testified to in the record of this trial."

But there was no corroboration. Everything that was tried failed to work. And prosecutor Perry had to admit some of this made little sense, even to him.

"Mr. Hoffman, cooperating with the government, on June twenty-ninth called John DeLorean in New York City. Hoffman testified that he called because he wanted to see if he could get his kid together with John DeLorean's boy.

"Now, you've got to admit that sounds preposterous. It just sounds preposterous that someone would call someone three thousand miles away, somebody he hasn't talked to for two years, for the specific purpose of talking about getting their children together, particularly when you take into account that the children had a wide difference in age level, five or six years' difference."

Of course it was preposterous because the entire incident was a lie. This was a conversation that was conveniently unrecorded according to the prosecution, though I suspect that a recording was either not made because Hoffman knew it would reveal him to be a fraud or it was made, then erased by someone working for the prosecution because it would obviously have shown my innocence right from the start. I was outraged that such fantasies were given importance during the summation.

Finally, Perry summed up his argument:

"Now the defense is going to say Hoffman went for the big score; it was going to get John DeLorean. But wait a minute. Hoffman is going to induce an internationally reknown [sic] businessman to get into a narcotics deal? You've got to be kidding.

"He is going to pick up the phone, and he is going to say, 'Hey, John, we could make millions in narcotics. How about it?' Isn't Hoffman taking a risk that John DeLorean might go to the police, that John DeLorean might report that he had been contacted by his former neighbor, that the neighbor is talking contacts, and lo and behold, Hoffman's status as an informant is blown, blown up bigger than anything when the police back there arrest him?

"Furthermore, Hoffman is on probation. Maybe his probation is violated. Maybe he ends up being prosecuted for something. There were certain risks here, ladies and gentlemen, if Hoffman is doing what the defense is accusing him of.

"Also, if Hoffman is going to set up John DeLorean, why does he tell Valestra about it? Why does he tell Valestra right after the June twenty-ninth and June thirtieth contacts that he has had a contact with John DeLorean? Why does he tell Valestra before the July eleventh meeting that I am going to go see DeLorean?

"Hoffman is an intelligent fellow. If he is going to set somebody up, wouldn't it be a lot smarter to get the guy set up before he starts talking about it to the people you're working with, to the agents who are controlling it? But the bigger question here is what is Hoffman supposed to have set up DeLorean for? Dangle legitimate financing? Remember, the defense in the cross-examination of Hoffman suggested that Hoffman couldn't even pay his rent in 1980.

"No, ladies and gentlemen, what makes sense here is that James Hoffman called about the children, and John DeLorean brought up the idea of doing narcotics. He saw the opportunity in this contact from a man he hadn't spoken with for two years, but a man he believed was in the narcotics business. . . ."

Perry made no mention, of course, of the Scotti testimony that Hoffman knew I was unaware of his narcotics activities. He made no mention of the fact that there were no toll records, no tape recordings, of my alleged calls to Hoffman concerning drugs.

After those words, the court was adjourned for the day; the attack on my life and actions were the last words the jury would hear until we reconvened for Howard's statements on my behalf. As I went into the hall, I witnessed a scene that has haunted me ever since.

Many people have accused the contemporary news media of showing bias. Reporters play favorites, slanting the news in one direction or another. Two different reporters for two different papers will come to totally opposite conclusions when writing about the identical incident.

When I read the newspapers during my trial, it was obvious to me that some reporters thought I was guilty and others thought I was innocent, but in almost every case, when the facts seemed to belie their preconceived notions, the articles they wrote reflected the facts no matter what their opinions. One exception in the Los Angeles area seemed to be the work of John Kendall, a reporter for the *Los Angeles Times*. No matter what occurred in the courtroom, no matter how a witness might recant his testimony against me or admit to improper or illegal behavior, the news stories always seemed to indicate that my guilt would shortly be proved.

As I left the courtroom after Perry's summation, I spotted Kendall with the prosecutors. He walked up to them and embraced them, emotionally telling them what fine jobs they had done. It was a scene that shocked me because it indicated that the man was far from objective. Certainly, there is nothing wrong with being friends with one side or the other, but here was a scene that added weight to the implication of bias on the part of his reporting.

Such bias and manipulation of a few members of the working press came as a horrible shock to me. To me, this side of journalism was as ugly and frightening as the manipulation of evidence by government agents desiring to convict me. I can only thank God that the majority of writers, editors, and media personalities are honest, objective, and willing to present the facts.

During Howard's summation in my defense, he first highlighted the way the government had regularly withheld evidence that should have been provided to my attorneys, evidence provided only after courtroom reference was made to teletypes and other documents none of us had ever seen.

Then he moved on to counter the prosecution's "prize" witness, James Hoffman.

"Hoffman, the teletype shows, was a gun for hire," Howard explained. "Hoffman was a man selling himself, a paid-for informant.

"Now think for a moment what that demand was. The government plays that down. Here's a guy working full time for the government; they're supporting him full time for the government; they're moving him around. Whatever he wants, he gets—car, food, clothes, whatever he wants, and he still goes back to them, because he knows what this investigation means to them.

"Maybe they are not willing to admit it, but Hoffman even knows. 'I've got them where I want them because I'm the contact with DeLorean. DeLorean's talking to me. I want some money. I want a cut of the action.'

"The guy is right back in business again. He's wonderful. 'I want a cut of the action.'

" 'Well, you can't have it, Hoffman. Do your job, or we're going to put you out on the streets, and everybody knows who you are. We will make sure they know who you are. Do you want to be back on the streets, man? Do you want to be dealing dope with us looking over your head, or do you want to work for us? You know that heroin case we never prosecuted you for; is that in your agreement? Well, it might be, but if you don't work for us, pal,' . . . or whatever. Do you think for a moment that there wasn't a hold on James Hoffman? Do you think there wasn't some exchange here? Do you think the government didn't feel they had control of Hoffman? Baloney. You know it and I know it. It doesn't work that way. That's not real life.

"Let's talk about Hoffman, the grand-jury lie, the statement lie, the post-office-box lie. Lies to you in your face, as my kid would say sometimes, right to you.

"Unrecorded calls. Let's talk about unrecorded calls for a moment. I love it. 'I told Valestra about the unrecorded calls.'

" 'Mr. Valestra, when did you learn about the unrecorded calls?'

322

" 'Oh, sometime in June '83.'

"Oops, a mere slip. Why is it important that Hoffman lies to you that he told him [Valestra] about the unrecorded calls? It is important because otherwise his credibility is in question, and if his credibility is in question, his case is in question.

"He is allowed to plug in his own language, according to everybody, except Hoffman told the grand jury that the agents monitored everything he did and he didn't do a thing without talking to them except, of course, the agents telling you something differently."

Howard also brought out the many instances where Hoffman had lied. At one point, Hoffman said that he was making a key call in the presence of DEA agent John Valestra, but Valestra testified on the stand that he was not with Hoffman; he had not overheard anything. Hoffman also said that Valestra told him to tell me to go to Orange County for a meeting, but Valestra said that he never had any discussion with Hoffman concerning Orange County. He was even surprised by the reference to Orange County in one of the telephone calls.

In his part of the summation, Don Re also had harsh words concerning James Hoffman. He mentioned that Hoffman "was trapped by Mr. Weitzman about the post-office box. Do you remember the post-office box? The agents didn't know about the post-office box. Mr. Hoffman said that he didn't. They didn't, and who was at that post-office box? Mr. Hoffman and another person, Nash; a man who was in narcotics activity; a man who, according to Hoffman, was an informant and, according to John Valestra, was not an informant; a man who was sharing a business enterprise with Mr. Hoffman behind the back of the government; a man who I think the evidence shows with Mr. Hoffman was running a narcotic activity at the time that they were involved in this case or doing something behind the back of the government.

"That didn't come out from the government. That didn't come out from Mr. Hoffman until he was pushed and shown proof of the situation, and Mr. Hoffman, by the way, lied to you about when he terminated his relationship with that box, and the evidence is before you.

"You should also consider Mr. Hoffman is a man who used his children on runs to South America to pick up drugs. This is a man who uses family as a front on a dangerous trip so that he could make some money off drugs. He has made constant demands for money during the course of this case. He has misrepresented a situation to the government, and yet the government and Mr. Hoffman come before you and say that he is a man who is to be believed, and he is not to be believed, ladies and gentlemen, and he is particularly not to be believed in those situations in which he is the only one who was giving the information.

"The most telling thing about Mr. Hoffman is the fact that he can't keep his story straight."

During his summation, Howard also addressed prosecutor Perry's comments concerning the money I spent to obtain an investment in my company.

"Mr. Perry said to you, 'Can you imagine John DeLorean spent $4,000 to travel around dimly lit hotels, courtesy of the government, to meet with these people, courtesy of the government.'

"When he said that, did anybody think, I wonder, how much money the government spent on getting this non–drug-dealer, non–drug-smuggler—let me see. We can start with Hoffman. There's a few hundred thousand dollars. Then we start with the salaries of all the agents who were not fighting crime but dealing with this case. Then we can start with the hundreds of thousands of dollars it took to investigate this case worldwide, worldwide, and you wonder what is going on here. Why? Why?

"Now, is the government on trial here? Mr. Perry used the line almost every prosecutor uses because it's kind of a cute line, and it goes like this: If you are the narcotics defense lawyer and you don't have the facts on your side, you argue the law, and if you are the narcotics defense lawyer and you don't have the law on your side, you argue the facts, and if you have neither on your side, you attack the government. Of course, there is a fourth alternative left out. What do you do when you have all three of those on your side? You do what we are doing now.

"The government is in a sense on trial here because this case will in a sense set a precedent in the sense that you will be sending a message. How about monitoring informants. How about reporting phone calls. How about not creating crime. You know, let me go through this laundry list, undisputed facts in this case.

"The government choreographed all the conversations, the meetings. Before each meeting they had a meeting. They decided what subjects would be talked about, how they would be introduced, if they would be introduced, why they would be introduced. The government set up all the meetings, set up all the meetings. The government initiated all the talk about drugs. The government kept all the conversations vague and ambiguous. There is not a conversation that you heard in which we didn't hear about investors in financing. Why do you think that was done? It wasn't done to trick you.

"The government chose the drugs. Remember first they were going to choose heroin. They had a scheme to go out and get the heroin dealer and bring him in and put him together with John. Wonderful. Couldn't work it out because Mr. Hoffman would have been arrested in Thailand, or some bizarre theory, or would have seized the money. So they go out and get a cocaine scam. So the government chose the drugs, cocaine, and one of the witnesses told you, 'We didn't even care, cocaine, marijuana, pills, didn't make any difference as long as we got him doing something illegal.'

"They chose to supply it. They supplied the money. They supplied the alternatives. They established all the timing in this case. Mr. Perry referred to that as creative narcotics investigation.

"So what this case really comes down to is creative narcotics investigation, and it starts out like this: 'Gee, I

325

haven't seen John DeLorean in a long time, and the kids were such good friends, and here I am working full time for the government as an informant making all these drug cases, and I think I'll call John DeLorean and see how he is doing, my pal. My gosh, I met him—I knew him for nine days. We were real close in that nine days. Our kids rode bikes three, four days.'

" 'Hey, John, how are you doing? Look, do you want to do a dope deal?'

" 'Gee, it sounded preposterous,' Mr. Perry said. He was right. It is preposterous.

"Now, if it is at least reasonable that that first contact was preposterous, if as you go back there and you start trying to go through this case and you begin to analyze the facts, and you say, 'Well, you know what, I guess it's possible that he called them just for the kids,' but it is also possible he called them to try and set them up, and I remember Mr. Perry telling me, 'Look, that sounds preposterous.' Isn't it at least reasonable to believe it is preposterous, and if it is reasonable that you believe it is preposterous, that's it.

"For the rest of this case falls like a house of cards because then it's clear Hoffman went out there to deliver this man, and I didn't hear one witness get on the stand and say to you, 'I never told Scotti that,' because the witness couldn't say that."

For me, however, the most impressive aspect of the summation came when Howard said, "It [this case] is really about human beings. Like I said earlier, it's about the vulnerability that you and I have and these people have and John DeLorean has.

"It is about wanting to sit in this case as a juror, because it is interesting and fascinating. It is about wanting to gain a conviction for career enhancement, to say I did it. I guess it is probably about wanting to defend somebody like John DeLorean. I think the only person who doesn't want to be involved in this case is John DeLorean. . . .

"I suggest to you that the evidence proves beyond a reasonable doubt that John DeLorean is innocent, but I don't have to meet that burden. That's the government's burden. And I suggest at the very, very least, when you go back in that room and you say to yourselves, 'So what went on here; what were we doing here for four and a half months; what exactly did he do; what exactly did he do,' that it is reasonable to conclude the man's life, quote-unquote, was wanting to save his company and get money.

"It didn't involve doing a dope deal, because he'd have done it. It didn't involve posting worthless collateral, because you don't post worthless collateral if you want to invest. And it doesn't involve toasting to anything other than the war on drugs or crime.

"What happened here, ladies and gentlemen, is a result of ego. This man has no ego anymore.

"I'm going to tell you something. What happened here isn't right. Think about that. Because, if the message were going to be sent out that it's okay to do this, none of us has a chance."

It was almost over.

Judge Takasugi reviewed the charges against me and explained how the jury should weigh the facts presented in court when reaching their decision. Then they were adjourned to begin deliberations that would not only determine my future but also make an impact on the methods used by the government to make an arrest. In this instance, finding an innocent man guilty would also be handing the government agents a license to lie, falsify evidence, and railroad anyone in an effort to build their reputations.

I suppose I should have been nervous. Cristina was so nervous that she broke out in hives. Howard had trouble sleeping. By that time, the pressures of the trial had adversely affected the marriages of both Don and Mona, each of whom would emerge from this ordeal with those relationships destroyed. Everyone had put in endless hours preparing the case, pursuing evidence, living with the pressure that we were standing up against the representatives of one of the greatest countries on earth. And while we all knew we were in the right, for Howard, Don, Mona, and Cristina, the waiting was a period of endless tension. I can honestly say that I was the only one who was calm. I understood that the outcome of the trial was in the hands of the Lord. To have worried with that awareness would have been a sacrilege.

On Thursday, August 16, at twenty minutes past noon, the jury returned from their deliberation. After the usual preliminaries, the verdict was given:

THE COURT: "The Court is in receipt of Jury Note Number One dated this date, August 16, 1984, at ten-thirty-five, signed by the foreperson of the jury indicating that a unanimous verdict has been reached.

"Mr. Foreperson; is that correct?"

THE FOREPERSON: "That's correct, your Honor."

THE COURT: "Please present the written verdict to our bailiff. . . . Ms. Clerk, please read the verdict."

THE CLERK: "The verdict reads: 'United States of America versus John Z. DeLorean.

"'We, the jury in the above-entitled cause, find the defendant John Z. DeLorean not guilty as charged in Count One, not guilty as charged in Count Two, not guilty as charged in Count Three, not guilty as charged in Count Five, not guilty as charged in Count Six, not guilty as charged in Count Seven, not guilty as charged in Count Eight, and not guilty as charged in Count Nine of the indictment.'"

THE BAILIFF: "Quiet."

THE COURT: "Let's have a polling of the jurors."

DEFENDANT DELOREAN: "Praise the Lord."

And then it was *really* over. I hugged Cristina, my attorneys, and anyone else I could grab.

Praise the Lord indeed!

36

If this were a fairy tale, Cristina and I would have taken our children and ridden off into the sunset to live happily ever after. The British government would have admitted its mistakes and helped restore the company and the jobs that had been destroyed in West Belfast. In today's market DMC would be earning $100 million a year. But God's ways are not man's ways, and God's time is not our time. Almost as soon as the trial was over, a new ordeal began that has been a test of my commitment to Christ and a challenge to the faith I claimed in that prison cell.

About a month before the final verdict, Cristina seemed to grow very distant; she seemed resentful and withdrawn.

"Cristina," I finally said, "what's the matter? I get the idea you're going to leave me. If you're going to do that, please do it now. Don't let me go through this thing and then give me another kick in the head. I don't think I could stand it, and I don't think the kids could either. If you are going to leave, leave now. Let me get over my trauma all at once." As a gesture, I took off my wedding ring and laid it on the dresser.

In what appeared to be a meaningful display of affection and devotion, she put it back on my hand and said, "John, I'll never leave you. You aren't going to cheat me out of my moment of glory. I waited too long for this."

But the truth behind her words became evident shortly before the trial ended. Our home was in the East, but since the trial was in Los Angeles, we had moved in with Cristina's family for the duration. Then shortly before the trial ended, Cristina began looking for a house to lease. She never asked me to come along with her, and I couldn't understand this. We had always shared important decisions such as the choice of a home. Her actions made no sense to me, so I nervously said to her, "I get the idea that I am not going to live in this house with you."

"That's right," she said. "You're not moving in." She said she had been offered a job with ABC at a tremendous salary and that she was taking the children and leaving.

She implied that the stress of the trial had been too great and that she couldn't stand any more; the thought of another couple of years of government harassment and litigation facing me in Detroit was more than she could handle.

Then a few days later she told Kathryn and Zachary, "Daddy is not moving in with us because I am going to marry another man."

The words hurt me deeply. I could have understood if she was tired of the harassment, sick of the way in which her career had been damaged, and determined to lead her own life without the burden of my notoriety. What I could not accept was the fact that she had been living a lie for what was probably many months. She had comforted me during the trial; she had declared her faith in me; she had made love to me. Yet during those same months she had to have been having an affair with another man. I have never felt that

Cristina was a highly skilled actress, but in this instance she put on a stellar performance. In my private moments, I hurt; I wept; and I agonized over how foolish a man can become when he does not wish to face the truth. I began to put all the pieces together, all the little signals I had missed or ignored.

I recalled one of Cristina's actions during the trial that I felt, in retrospect, further showed her uncaring attitude and self-centeredness. At the time, it irked me.

The trial was rapidly coming to an end, and Don Re was presenting what I felt was a brilliantly reasoned summation argument detailing the reasons why the government's case had proved false. I was pleased with his words, pleased with the attention he was receiving from the jury. Cristina was sitting with Margaret Weitzman, Howard's wife, and as I glanced around the courtroom, I noticed that they were whispering rather animatedly. I assumed that they were pleased with Don as well.

As I turned my attention back to Don, there was a sudden commotion. To my horror, Cristina had collapsed in a faint.

Everything stopped. The court recessed, and Cristina was rushed to a back room, where she was placed on a couch. The door was shut so that we could have privacy, and I hurried to her side, terrified that the stress had at last proved too much for her.

"Cristina!" I said, reaching for her hand.

To my shock, she sat upright, laughing at me. "Don't say I can't act!"

In retrospect, I realize that this piece of attention-getting was not only childish, but ran the risk of affecting the outcome of the trial.

Shortly after the trial, Cristina filed for a divorce and for sole custody of the children. Once again I was betrayed. Sole custody meant that I would never spend time alone with Kathryn and Zachary. Zachary, the boy I had wanted so badly that I became a single parent and hired a nurse to ensure his presence by my side wherever I traveled, would be denied whatever nurturing I could give him. Kathryn, the daughter of my love for Cristina, would not be able to lighten my days with her laughter or share the troubles and joys she experienced as the passing years changed her from being my little girl into a young woman.

Cristina knew of my deep love for our children. She had met me when I was a bachelor who traveled everywhere with his son. The only possible reason for her seeking sole custody was to hurt me, to use the children as a bargaining chip while we worked out a property settlement.

I am only now adjusting to the loss of Cristina and its full meaning for me. But through this and the other hard lessons in my personal life, I believe God has taught me much about myself and my relationships. I have gained a sense of self-respect since coming to the Lord; I no longer dislike myself, no longer feel that I must prove my worth to be accepted. I can be myself, with my strengths and weaknesses. And I have learned that I want "real" relationships. Sex and glamor are hollow and fleeting. Through loss and betrayal, I have gained something that I hope Cristina will also one day come to understand.

I have several definite goals for the future. The first is to devote as much time to my children as they want and need. As I have said, at one point I feared that I would be denied their presence in my life. Then Zachary and Cristina argued, and according to my son, he was struck and told to get out of her house. Zachary has been with me ever since. I also regularly spend time with Kathryn. While this turn of events has eased the burden of separation from them, it has also increased their needs. Without answers, all I can do is talk with them, share my own lessons of growth and understanding, and try to help them with their own goals and dreams.

I have no big plans for my children, no direction in which I want them to travel. I do not expect them to become engineers or one day run their own car companies. Whatever their interests, whatever their abilities, that is what I want them to do. I just want them to be happy and well-adjusted.

While I am hoping to leave them enough money to buy the time they need to do whatever is right for their lives, I also want them to know that the only true wealth comes from being in touch with God's plan. As long as they look to the love of Christ for their own direction, whatever they choose to do will be blessed in a way much greater than all the riches of the world can buy. I praise the Lord that today both of my children have deep spiritual commitments.

Second, I know I will continue to be involved with automotive engineering in some capacity. I would delight in being able to resurrect the DeLorean car, and I have been talking with people who are supportive and share that dream. Above all, in this regard, I want to work to restore the interests of my shareholders, the people who believed in me. I know this will be done. Whatever I do will be only a part of my life, however, because the Lord has shown me that I must never put the pursuit of "things"—wealth, fame, a car that bears my name—ahead of His concerns.

And finally, I want to devote my life to the ministry I am currently developing. This involves the coordination of inner-city parishes with wealthier churches in surrounding areas. Through this program, families and individuals in need will have these needs made known to the Christian community at large. Then, through a nonprofit clearing-house, funds can be channeled, food provided, job counseling and training offered, and any other assistance made available.

My hope is that families who are able to provide personal or financial assistance, in any degree, will adopt an inner-city family in a relationship that will prove mutually rewarding. This may be anonymous or personal.

There are other programs around the country helping people, but I have found no one who is, as yet, coordinating a national effort to involve Christians everywhere. I am hoping that through the adopt-a-family concept Christians will be able to reach out to other Christians wherever there is need, uniting churches and their members in biblical ways.

For my own spiritual growth and nourishment, I have become a part of a church. Shortly after my conversion in October 1982, I became involved with Beth-Ariel, a deeply committed Gentile-Jewish fellowship in Christ. Louis Lapides was my pastor there, a wonderful teacher and a man I dearly love. I still attend Louis's Bible studies each Wednesday evening. This past spring I began attending Church on the Way in Van Nuys. This is a group of believers that does a lot of loving and hugging and praying for each other in small prayer groups, which has become especially meaningful to me, a man encased for so long in a shell that would not permit me to feel, love, or care to any deep measure. This is the exact opposite of my daily visits to St. Patrick's where I did not speak to or interact with anyone.

I actually feel badly for the other members of the Church on the Way on Sunday morning, because I always feel that Rev. Jack Hayford's message is directed right at me. But I suspect the others feel the same way themselves!

37

During my trial and since then, I have found great strength and confidence from my faith and from the prayers of thousands of Christians around the world. Prayer is a force capable of defeating any enemy. Ephesians 6:12 says, *"Our struggle is not against flesh and blood, but against the rulers, against the authorities, against the powers of this dark world and against the spiritual forces of evil in the heavenly realms."*

As I emerged from the emotional shell in which I lived for so many years, and as I went through my arrest and trial, I have been shocked at the number of people who have come forward with information to help me. Apparently, many Americans have been outraged by government abuses, especially members of minority groups who have historically been isolated from mainstream America and therefore

335

looked upon with skepticism when they complain about abuses of power. I am learning that my worst fears are true; the government's outrages are even greater than we suspected.

For example, when my case was being prepared, confidential defense strategy communications "found their way" into government hands. As far back as the early days with the first law firm I consulted, we found their lines were wire-tapped.

Since I have been absolved of wrongdoing, two former government agents have approached me about documents relating to the investigation of my case. They decided they wanted me to have them, after they learned that they were being abused by the government in their new work as security specialists in the private sector. The documents they showed us prove that details of our defense strategy were in government hands before their use in court. When this scenario was discussed with a representative of a national news magazine, he said, "That's not news. The FBI has been caught breaking and entering so many times no one cares." Thomas Jefferson, where are you?

After my unanimous acquittal on the jury's first ballot, I was accorded the rare privilege of meeting with the jurors in their deliberation chamber. Several of the women jurors were crying, and I had tears in my eyes as we hugged each other and talked of what had happened. A number of them said that through the verdict they hoped to send a message to the government that such misuse of power and outrageous conduct would not be tolerated by the American people.

Later one of the jurors, Nancy Anderson, an operating room nurse, was interviewed on Ted Koppel's "Niteline." She said that what the government had done to me could have been done to anyone, including herself and her husband.

The jury came to its conclusion without ever hearing my side of the case. Now that this book is written, I would like to have a reunion with them after they have read what I have to say. I would like to know if their perceptions of the case,

336

heard without my defense, paralleled what they would have thought had they known my side of it. Most important to me is the question of whether they understood that I truly had given Benedict Tisa my interest in the company and that any proceeds or profits the company might make in the future would have gone to him. The deal I made with the people I thought were organized criminals would have left me with nothing except the satisfaction of my name on a car and the knowledge that my employees still had their jobs.

My current problems with the British government and their alter ego, the DMC Creditor's Committee, are both complex and simple. There are thousands of documents to be reviewed and dozens of witnesses to be questioned. Yet I am certain that time and a costly trial will prove that the allegations are false, an expensive (and for me, traumatic) way for the British government to save face.

When the DeLorean Motor Company was in operation, we had strict procedures to follow to obtain the necessary funds from the British government. Every month we had to request the operating funds needed and detail the ways in which all of the previous month's capital had been spent. Our requests had to detail how the money would be used and who would be paid. These requests and statements of expenses were carefully checked by an accounting firm and the British government's oversight committee.

The present legal actions against me in Detroit sound strangely like the DEA case in Los Angeles, although the official misconduct may be even worse. For example, Shade, the British government's attorney, has falsely stated in affidavits that I was deliberately concealing company documents in my home. In truth, when I was arrested and the New York DMC office closed, the company controller and corporate secretary sorted out the files and sent what they thought were my personal files to my house. The corporate secretary later discovered that a small percentage of company documents were inadvertently sent to my farm without my knowledge. I saw none of them. The corporate secretary immediately informed the company's bankruptcy attorney,

Laurence Snider, who notified the creditor's committee attorney, Toll, and the British government's attorney, Shade. It was mutually agreed among them that the corporate secretary would go through the farm files and return to the company those that were theirs. Shade misrepresented this arrangement and said that the files were stolen and hidden by me. On the basis of his statement, they got a court order under which they ransacked my home and seized every piece of paper in the house including all of my attorney-client documents for the California case. They even took my Bible-study notebook.

I have since learned that by the time Howard had finished his cross-examination of Benedict Tisa, the British government was taking an action that would ensure DMC could not recover.

On July 12, 1985, Freddie Laker and his company won a $64 million settlement from the British government and their corporate "partners" as compensation for their destruction of his company. The parallels between the destruction of Laker's company and the British government's destruction of DeLorean Motor Cars with the assistance of corporate collaboration and the FBI are dramatic. Throughout their entire industrial development history, the British government *has never once failed to support new industrial development enterprise* no matter how much the enterprise lost. DMC was the only exception in two ways: It was profitable—DMC was the first major free-standing industrial development project the British had ever financed that made a profit in its first year in business. And DMC was the *only* such project they actively withdrew support from—and actively sought to destroy. We have recently learned that when it looked like DMC might come out of bankruptcy and rise from the ashes, the British government ordered the twelve million dollars' worth of body dies destroyed, dies essential for manufacturing the DeLorean motor car. Some of the dies were dumped into Galway Bay. Scuba divers have photographed the dies lying on the ocean floor. With this move, the British destroyed the value of the 8758 DMCs on the road in America.

The destruction of tooling of a car out of production less than ten years is against the law in most Western countries. When the British government instructed the firm holding the DMC body dies to destroy them, the company refused on the basis that such a malicious act violated their country's laws. Our understanding is that only after the British government supplied them with a letter freeing them from any legal liability did they finally comply.

Why is the British government doing this to me? I believe it is to cover up the fact that they alone are responsible for the company's failure and the losses to both the creditors and the shareholders. I personally borrowed every cent I could and put my family's assets up for sale to try to keep DMC alive when Britain reneged on their contract.

The GPD agreement had absolutely nothing to do with the failure of the company. The allegation that I misappropriated funds from DMC or the British government is hogwash. The much maligned GPD contract was not only publicly disclosed, but pre-approved before any payment was made by the Bank of England, the Minister of Industry, the Department of Commerce, and the Northern Ireland Development Agency, as well as their legal and financial staffs. In each case, a government attorney was present at the signing. Hardly a furtive atmosphere!

All funds were paid to GPD in accord with the public agreement. In fact, the entire matter was investigated by Scotland Yard, which found the charges to be invalid. In my files are letters from the Department of Commerce confirming this.

So why have the rumors persisted? Up to this point we have been prevented from presenting our defenses in the British government Creditor Committee case because of the overhanging U.S. government threat of a grand jury indictment in Detroit in the same matter. Everything has to be held back until the cases are brought to court or dropped, a fact that makes me suspicious of all the delays. There appears to be a deep conspiratorial arrangement between some members of the U.S. government and the British government's Creditors Committee. They appear to be illegally sharing information, and there is strong indication that the grand jury is being used to keep me from being able to defend myself in the U.K. Creditor's Committee action as well as attempting to force me into an unrealistic settlement. When all of the documents and facts are presented, I expect to be fully vindicated.

One reason I have been concerned about releasing too much information before any court hearings is because I am uneasy about the possible fabrication of counter "evidence." Recently published official reports have shown that the British government maintains a "forgery mill," which has fabricated such documents as official German Chancellery documents and false Argentine government letters to "prove" that Argentina was harboring Nazi war criminals. We have been concerned that if the British government should learn the details of our defense, they might possibly create documents in an attempt to circumvent our evidence. If they don't see what we have until we get into court, truth will carry the day.

38

As I move forward with my life, I am still adjusting to many changes in my family and friends, changes I could not have anticipated. For example, a recent incident showed me how fleeting the loyalty and caring of others can be.

I had arrived home late from a trip to New York, and Zachary's nanny, Jenny Moir, Zachary, and his English sheepdog, Bunky, had picked me up at the L.A. airport. It was too late to eat dinner at home so we decided to stop at the Hamburger Hamlet in Beverly Hills. When we pulled up in front, a man whom I had considered a close friend, with whom I had had lunch or dinner two or three times a week for the five years before my arrest, was standing, smoking a cigarette, in the doorway of Brussels' clothing store next door. I had not heard from him since my release on bail. We were parked within twenty feet of him, but since I had no

341

idea what his feelings were toward me, I decided to let him make the first move.

I conspicuously fumbled with the car door lock so that he would have time to approach me if he chose to do so. After a few seconds of this charade I started toward the restaurant, hoping, half-expecting, he would say hello as a friend. Instead, he ducked into the clothing store to avoid me.

I would like to say that his action did not hurt me. I would like to say that it is his problem, not mine. But the truth is that I was hurt, and the rejection was extremely painful.

Discoveries like this about people I counted my friends have in some ways probably been more hurtful than all the newspaper headlines in the world.

Tragically, many others have had to suffer for their involvement with my case. Among these was Judge Robert Takasugi who apparently incurred the enmity of the government by his rigid enforcement of my constitutional rights. After he was assigned to my case and granted the normal statutory discovery of evidence (sources within the Justice Department have told me that hundreds of documents were withheld from us), he, too, became a target. He has been subject to what I see as a deliberate "poisoning" of his reputation in the media, possibly by those few reporters who also do work for the government in exchange for money or special favors. I have also learned that he was the subject of an intensive IRS audit, a common retaliation technique.

Jerry Scotti, the courageous agent who abandoned his career to tell the truth during my trial, passed the California bar on May 31, 1985. He is planning to establish a law office with Anthony Brooklier in Beverly Hills. After passing his bar examination he was informed that he would not be admitted to the bar until an "investigation" was completed. Since this was not routine, I believe it was requested as a way of getting back at him for testifying at my trial. I believe the government was so upset with his truthful testimony that they may be determined to destroy him any way they can. I

342

am certain that the strength of character, integrity, and intelligence that he displayed on the witness stand will help him triumph over this and any other government "dirty tricks." I also predict that he will become a top defense lawyer. He has seen the best and worst of legal actions brought in the name of justice.

But the two people who were hurt the most were my children. And the horror of it is that I am helpless to change that. Fathers are supposed to be able to protect their children, but some things are just beyond our human power. Being a Christian does not magically make the world a perfect place in which to live; nor can it erase the past and its effect on the future. My children still suffer for both my troubles and my problems with their mother. My only hope is that they will grow into adulthood stronger and wiser for what they have experienced. But sadly, they have lost something they can never regain: that youthful innocence and joy we all want our children to experience as long as they can.

Not long ago Zachary and I were sitting at home. I was reading, and he was working on a puzzle. Zachary is always rather contemplative, but on this night he was quieter than usual. I wondered what was bothering him, but before I could ask, he looked at me and said, "Dad, why is so much coming down on me? I don't deserve it."

I didn't know how to answer him, so I just put my arm around his shoulders and squeezed him close to me.

Kathryn also has her private and unanswerable grief.

Not long ago the two of us went out alone for a special Sunday-evening father-daughter dinner together at Michael's in Santa Monica. I delighted in my chatty, amusing daughter. It was truly an enchanted evening.

Toward the end of dinner Kathryn left the table for a few minutes, and the diners next to us introduced themselves to me. They were Mrs. Meredith Wilson (wife of the composer of *The Music Man*) and well-known musician Nelson Riddle and his wife. Nelson Riddle explained that they had been watching me with my daughter.

"I never saw two people have a more wonderful and loving time," he said. "I have four daughters, and I envy you."

Somehow, I don't think he would have envied me the next evening when my daughter called me in tears.

Apparently Kathryn had been thinking all day about our fun evening together, about the fact that her parents now lived apart, that her mother had married another man, and that her young, secure world had been shattered.

"What's wrong, honey? Why are you crying?"

"Oh, Daddy, I had to talk to you. I'm so sad. I saw a commercial on TV that made me cry. It showed a daddy and his little girl holding hands, walking in the woods. The leaves were changing color, just like when you and I used to walk in the woods and pick flowers.

"It reminded me of when we were happy."

BIBLIOGRAPHY

Among the resources used in writing this book were:

Transcript of *United States of America, Plaintiff, v. John Z. DeLorean*, Defendant No. CR 82-910(B)-RMT Volumes 21A, 21B, 22, 23, 24, 25, 26, 27, 28, 29, 30, 31, 32, 33, 34, 35, 38, 39, 40, 41, 42, 43, 44, 45, 46, 47, 48, 49, 50, 51, 52, 53, 54, 55, 77, 78, 79, 80A, 80B, 80C, 81A, 81B, 81C, record of Thursday, August 16, 1984, containing the jury polling and verdict.

Letter to Tom Kimmerly, dated October 18, 1982.

Rolling Stone magazine interview, March 17, 1983.

DeLorean Motors Holding Company Preliminary Prospectus, November 25, 1981.

Letter to James Hoffman, July 9, 1982.

Memo to Tom Kimmerly concerning James Hoffman, July 16, 1982.

Letter to Howard Weitzman from Mary Thoman, August 23, 1983.

Letter to Howard Weitzman concerning Larry Flynt, dated November 14, 1983.

Background investigation memos concerning James Hoffman, prepared by Palladino & Sutherland. Memos dated January 18, 1983; January 12, 1983; December 29, 1982; December 22, 1982; December 15, 1982; December 16, 1982; December 11, 1982; December 12, 1982; December 13, 1982; December 9, 1982; December 5, 1982; December 6, 1982; December 7, 1982; December 1, 1982; December 27, 1982 (including extensive documents, listed as Appendix A, concerning *Fairchild v. Jet Marketing*, Hawaii State Court No. 56478 and same case but Hawaii District Federal Court No. 79-0119; January 17, 1983, including documents from *Horizon Cargo Transport, Inc., Plaintiff, v. Pacific International Airlines, James T. Hoffman individually and as President of Pacific International Airlines, Charles Hennigh individually, Mohr Enterprises, Jimsair Aviation Services, Wayne Stroud individually, Jim McGrew individually and as vice-president of Pacific International Airlines, Defendants,* Complaint; Summons 7800431, United States District Court, State of Hawaii; December 8, 1982, including documents from *Home Bank, a California Corporation, Plaintiff, v. Pacific International Airlines,* a Partnership composed of James T. Hoffman and Wayne Stroud; James T. Hoffman a.k.a. J. T. Hoffman a.k.a. J. Hoffman; Wayne Stroud a.k.a. W. Stroud; David A. Blumberg a.k.a. David Blumberg a.k.a. Dave Blumberg a.k.a. D. A. Blumberg a.k.a. D. Blumberg Doe Corporation; Roe Partnership and Does 1 through 10, inclusive, Defendants No. 027561 Complaint for damages; l. Fraud; 1. For Recovery of Monies Advanced on Negotiable Instruments; 3. Money Had and Received; 4. Declaratory Relief, in Superior Court of California, County of Los Angeles, January 24, 1983; January 22, 1983; January 21, 1983; January 19, 1983; January 16, 1983; January 13, 1983; and Ventura County, California, cases concerning James T. Hoffman (numerous documents all related to these cases).

Gerald W. Dahlinger, Plaintiff, v. Dahlinger Pontiac-Cadillac, Inc., a Kansas Corporation, and Roy Nesseth, Defendants, Case No. 78-C-2613, Eighteenth Judicial District, District Court, Sedgwick County, Kansas, Civil Department.

Settlement Agreement and Mutual General Release of April 19, 1982, between C. Richard Brown and DeLorean Motor Company and DeLorean Motor Cars of America.

Memorandum to Howard Weitzman and Don Re from DeLorean, dated October 25, 1983, concerning audiotape analysis.

John Z. DeLorean notes taken during trial, dated daily from the start (several hundred pages).

Chapter for The American Assembly book *Black Eco-*

nomic Development edited by William F. Haddad and G. Douglas Pugh.

Article in *Contemporary Christian Magazine*, October, 1984.

Memo from Marian Gibson, dated November 21, 1983, sent to John Rose, clerk, c/o Communications Office, Public Accounts Committee, House of Commons, London, England, regarding DeLorean Motor Cars Limited.

Attendance notes made by Robin Bailie, October 13, 1982, Re: DeLorean—Purchase From Receivers.

Note from Phil Meisinger to Sir Kenneth Cork, dated October 13, 1982.

Complaint for Damages for breach of written contracts; and for work, labor and services, Case No. 37 57 79, Superior Court of the State of California for the County of Orange, *C. Richard Brown, Plaintiff, v. DeLorean Motor Company, DeLorean Motor Cars of America and Does I through XX, inclusive, defendants.*

December 7, 1983, Marian Gibson memo to John Rose, clerk, c/o Communications Office, Public Accounts Committee, House of Commons, London, England, on subject: DeLorean Motor Cars Limited.

Affidavit of Marian F. Gibson, August 16, 1983, in regard to memorandum dated December 26, 1980, prepared by William F. Haddad, from various papers deposited in the House of Commons Library and in the Record Office of the House of Lords.

Letter from Marian F. Gibson to Lord Goodman, June 24, 1983, regarding allegations made by William Haddad, from various papers deposited in the House of Commons Library and in the Record Office of the House of Lords.

Letter from C. J. Pickrell, Investigative Associates, Inc., to Howard Weitzman, July 11, 1983, regarding General Motors Security investigation of John Z. DeLorean.

Ninety-eighth Congress, Second Session, Committee Print, Executive Summary of FBI Undercover Operations, subcommittee on Civil and Constitutional Rights of the Committee on the Judiciary, House of Representatives, Ninety-Eighth Congress, Second Session, April 1982.

Letter from John DeLorean to Jonathon Lubell, Cohn, Glickstein, Lurie, Ostrin & Lubell, dated August 30, 1983, notes on book *Grand Delusions*.

Letter to Jonathon Lubell dated August 15, 1983, concerning Strodes/Fallon book: *Dream Maker—The Rise and Fall of John Z. DeLorean*.

Letter entitled "Free John DeLorean."

Document entitled "The Termination of the DeLorean Motor Company."

C. R. Brown's file notes on background profile on William F. Haddad.

October 13, 1982 memo Re: DeLorean—Purchase from receivers.

Various memos and documents related to British government receivership.

Chronology of DeLorean audio and all video recordings, July 12, 1982 through July 31, 1982.

Letter dated February 9, 1983, from Craig Kennedy to Warren Ettinger, 700 South Flower St., Sixteenth Floor, Los Angeles, CA 90017, including long memo and testimony relative to Gerald Dahlinger Litigation in Kansas.

Letters from Marion Babson, dated 1984 and 1985.

Transcriptions of all audio- and videotapes made by the government during their investigation of John DeLorean. The majority of the tapes were made by James Hoffman.

Prenuptial agreement with Cristina Ferrare.

Documents related to divorce proceedings with Cristina Ferrare DeLorean.

Special assistance with this book project was provided by the Beverly Hillcrest Hotel, Beverly Hills, California, and by the United States Federal Marshall Service.

Special thanks to Dottie Zauner for transcribing over one hundred hours of interview tapes.

348

ABOUT THE ARTISTS

DAVID ROSE is best known as one of the small handful of contemporary American artists who draw directly in the field for the news media. He has covered some of the most famous trials and news events of the past decade for NBC, ABC, and Cable News Network. In addition to John DeLorean, his subjects have included the "Pentagon Papers" with Daniel Ellsberg, Patty Hearst, William and Emily Harris, Gary Gilmore, Claudine Longet, Roman Polanski, Manson-family member Leslie Van Houten, John Ehrlichman, Gordon Liddy, Wayne Williams, and the recent Soviet spy trials in Los Angeles. His illustrations of the DeLorean trial are used by permission of Cable News Network.

ELIZABETH WILLIAMS has been working extensively for TV networks for the last six years. From Los Angeles to New York, she has covered such major cases as the Hillside Strangler, the *NFL vs. Los Angeles Raiders*, the *Carol Burnett vs. National Enquirer* trial, the McMartin Pre-school child-abuse case, Joe Peppetone Drug case, the Grandma Mafia trial, and many others. Her TV clients include KABC-TV, KNBC-TV, NBC News, CNN, WCBS-TV, WABC-TV, and WNBC-TV. Not only does she illustrate for television, but her work has appeared in the *New York Times, Newsweek, Los Angeles Herald Examiner, Gameday* magazine, and she has just illustrated a cover brochure and poster for ABC Sports. Her illustrations of the DeLorean trial are used with her permission.